# Seven Wonders of the World

# SEVEN WONDERS

## OF

# THE WORLD

*by*

*Lowell Thomas*

**HANOVER HOUSE**
GARDEN CITY, N.Y.

# Contents

# Seven Wonders of the World

# Chapter I

THE SEVEN WONDERS of the Ancient World—what could sound more venerable? A travel-agency list of attractions for the tourist trade—what could sound less venerable? Yet they seem to have been pretty much the same thing.

The original list of the Seven Wonders was compiled in the Alexandrian period, when the city in Egypt founded by Alexander the Great was the center of Western civilization. It was the time between the cultural glory of Athens and the dominance of Rome.

This for the Greeks was an era of sophistication and of travel in their limited world, of which the eastern Mediterranean was the focus. In some ways it was a good deal like our own era. There was a vogue of sight-seeing. The tourist had already been invented.

Ship captains making a profit from the passenger trade told of the sights to see. Guidebooks were a feature of the time, just as they are for innocents abroad today, and the Seven Wonders seem to have been selected from the Hellenistic Baedekers. The earliest version of the list that we have was recorded by Antipater of Sidon, writing in the second century B.C., when Rome was master of the world.

Thus, according to the opinion of scholars, the venerable tradition of the Seven Wonders derives from a prototype of travel-agency business catering to the tourist trade, more than two thousand years ago.

The legend had an infectious quality which kept it alive and increased its fame down the centuries. The Middle Ages doted on the marvelous, also on the mystical number. The medievals speculated about the Seven Wonders, and added their own imaginings. In modern times archaeology has added scientific research by exploring the sites of those fabled phenomena of yore.

The ancient tourist business was likely enough to regale prospective customers with sights to be seen in Asia Minor, where there were sumptuous and ornate cities. In these the Greek of Athens or Corinth would find life much as at home, the temples, the beds, the cooking. The fabled cities on the coast of Asia Minor were, in fact, Greek.

In the early time, beginning around the eighth century B.C., the cities of Greece proper sent out colonies which established daughter cities far and wide—Syracuse in Sicily, the present Marseille in France, and places in North Africa and on the Black Sea. The Mediterranean world was dotted with centers of Greek civilization.

An ancient sight-seeing promoter would surely mention Halicarnassus, not the greatest but one of the most splendid cities in Asia Minor. There the visitor could gape at the lofty, gleaming magnificence of the Mausoleum.

For an account of this far-famed monument we of today can consult the Roman author Pliny, who wrote the *Natural History*. This is a prime source for information about the Seven Wonders. None were wonders of nature—all were man-made edifices and sculptures. But Pliny, compiling a sort of miscellaneous encyclopedia, had a naïve system of classification. Under the heading of minerals, as elements of nature, he'd put structures made of stone. Under the metal bronze, statues made of bronze. So his *Natural History* finds a place for the edifice of marble at Halicarnassus. He writes:

"The Mausoleum—such being the name of the tomb that was erected by his wife, Artemisia, in honor of Mausolus. This work came to be reckoned one of the SEVEN WONDERS OF THE WORLD."

Mausolus was a petty king who had an ambitious policy and

a devoted wife. When he died Artemisia held a contest of poets to celebrate his memory, and decreed for him a tomb so famous that we have the word "mausoleum" in our language today. Then she is said to have pined away of grief, and to have drunk the ashes of her husband in wine. Soon she followed him to the realm of the shades.

Pliny, after naming the artists who worked on the monument, writes: "Before this tomb was completed, Queen Artemisia died. They did not leave their work, however, until it was finished, considering that it was at once a memorial of their own fame and of the sculptor's art."

It was oblong in shape, 440 feet around, and 140 feet high, and consisted of a building on top of which were rows of columns; on these reposed a pyramid of twenty-four steps. At the summit stood the figures of Mausolus and Artemisia in a chariot. The whole structure was of Parian marble, gorgeous in coloring. Towering above Halicarnassus, the Mausoleum was visible far out to sea, fulfilling Artemisia's desire that the memory of her husband should dominate the city.

The Mausoleum stood until the Middle Ages, when Crusader knights used material from it to build a castle. Thereafter this wonder of the world remained a half-forgotten ruin. In the nineteenth century British archaeologists excavated the site and unearthed the statues of Mausolus and Artemisia that once stood at the top of the monument. They are now in the British Museum.

Three cities disputed for the honor of being the greatest in Asia (which in Roman parlance meant what we call Asia Minor). They were Pergamum, Smyrna, and Ephesus. The first was the capital of a Hellenized kingdom. Pergamum was rich and luxurious, had a politically important history, and remains today a town of local consequence, Turkish Bergama. The second was a Greek city of commercial pre-eminence, and after twenty centuries Smyrna is the metropolis of Asia Minor. Of the third nothing remains but what archaeologists dig up. Yet, in the ancient dispute between the three cities, Ephesus was undoubtedly the greatest in renown.

It was a Greek city whose importance was religious, dedicated to a goddess of Asiatic origin, identified with the Greek Artemis, the Roman Diana. The story tells how, in early times, Ephesus was threatened with a siege by Croesus, he of the fabulous wealth, who was King of Lydia in inner Asia Minor. The people saved their city by declaring it sacred to Artemis-Diana. Instead of besieging, Croesus sent golden gifts to the shrine of the goddess.

The wonder of the world at Ephesus was the successor to a previous great temple, which in 356 B.C. was destroyed by fire. This was the subject of one of the famous stories of antiquity. The mighty conflagration was the doing of an incendiary, who was apprehended and questioned. He was asked why he had set the great shrine on fire. He replied, to make his name immortal. He succeeded. His name was Herostratus, still on the historical record.

The temple was rebuilt, more magnificent than ever. To tell of it we can best revert to Pliny:

"The most wonderful monument of Graecian magnificence, and one that merits our genuine admiration, is the Temple of Diana at Ephesus, which took one hundred and twenty years in building, a work in which all Asia joined. The entire length of the temple is four hundred and twenty-five feet, and the breadth two hundred and twenty-five feet. The columns are one hundred and twenty-seven in number, and sixty feet in height, each of them presented by a different king."

Pliny then discusses a subject that puzzles people to this day—how ancient builders were able to raise and manipulate the giant masses of stone they used for construction. He explains that at Ephesus they made an inclined plane of sandbags up to the top of the lofty columns, then drew up the slope the ponderous slabs of stone that were to be laid on the columns. Brought to the top, the slabs rested on sandbags, which then were cut and the sand let out, so that the massive slabs sank gently onto the columns.

But the difficulty seemed insurmountable when they had to put into position the giant stone to span the spacious entrance of the temple. How that problem was solved is one of Pliny's delightful marvels. He always loved a good story.

"The architect," he writes, "was driven to such a state of anxiety and desperation as to contemplate suicide. Wearied and quite worn out by such thoughts as these, during the night, they say, he beheld in a dream the goddess in honour of whom the temple was being erected; who exhorted him to live on, for that she herself had placed the stone in its proper position. And such, in fact, next morning, was found to be the case, the stone apparently having come to the proper level by dint of its own weight."

For centuries people from near and far made pilgrimages to the Temple of Diana at Ephesus, and that traffic was the wealth of the city. The economic situation is indicated dramatically in the account of St. Paul's memorable two-year sojourn at Ephesus. His preaching of the Gospel stirred a riot among people whose pocketbooks were threatened, as related in the Acts of the Apostles:

"For a certain man named Demetrius, a silversmith, which made silver shrines for Diana, brought no small gain unto the craftsmen;

"Whom he called together with the workmen of like occupation, and said, Sirs, ye know that by this craft we have our wealth.

"Moreover ye see and hear, that not alone at Ephesus, but almost throughout all Asia, this Paul hath persuaded and turned away much people, saying that they be no gods, which are made with hands:

"So that not only this our craft is in danger to be set at nought; but also that the temple of the great goddess Diana should be despised, and her magnificence should be destroyed, whom all Asia and the world worshippeth.

"And when they heard these sayings, they were full of wrath, and cried out, saying, Great is Diana of the Ephesians."

The disturbance lasted long, as the New Testament narrative tells us: ". . . all with one voice about the space of two hours cried out, Great is Diana of the Ephesians."

The Apostle to the Gentiles made headway in the city of the goddess, and left converts there, as shown by his Letter to the Ephesians.

The Temple of Diana stood until the third century A.D., when the shrine was burned by the Goths in one of those barbarian raids that foreshadowed the later Germanic invasions that overthrew the Roman Empire. After that Ephesus and its cult of Diana never recovered their former glory. Christianity was conquering, and Ephesus was the site of two historic councils of the Church. In time the city was abandoned, probably because of epidemics of malaria. It was situated in a marshy valley, and was finally covered with mud from river floods.

Two of the Seven Ancient Wonders were monuments to sentiment: the Mausoleum, commemorating a wife's devotion; the Hanging Gardens, constructed by a king to please a favorite wife.

Nebuchadnezzar, King of Babylon, conqueror and master of empire, who destroyed the kingdom of Judah and carried the Hebrews of old into the Babylonian Captivity! The Old Testament rings with the terror of his name, and modern scholarship confirms the magnitude of his Chaldean dominion. He must have been an archsentimentalist as well. The story of the Hanging Gardens pictures him as the builder of the greatest prodigy every wrought for a woman.

Their marriage, according to one story that we read, was an affair of empire and the policies of conquest. It marked an important page in the history of the ancient world.

There were two Babylonian empires, earlier and later. The first dates back to remote times, about 2000 B.C., when Babylon established a hegemony over other city-states of Mesopotamia and dominated a realm extending to the Mediterranean. This was the Babylon of Hammurabi the Lawgiver.

The first Babylonian Empire fell, and power passed eventually to the Assyrians in the north, about 1300 B.C. Babylon became a subject city, revolted repeatedly, and finally was destroyed by its new masters. The Assyrian Empire was for centuries the terror of western Asia. Its capital, Nineveh. Its history, studded with the names of formidable kings, Shalmaneser, Sargon, Sennacherib, Assurbanipal. Then, about 600 B.C., Assyria went the way of all empires.

In the mountains of Persia the Medes had established a powerful monarchy. Their king was Cyaxares. The Medes were at enmity with Assyria. Babylon, rising from its desolation, and now a center of Chaldean power, revolted and put an army into the field. Cyaxares and the Babylonians joined forces, and Assyria was overthrown. Nineveh was destroyed, never to rise again.

A new Babylonian Empire took over the Assyrian dominion. Its king was the leader of the Babylonian revolt. His son and successor was Nebuchadnezzar, who built the Hanging Gardens for a beloved queen. Who was she? A daughter of the Median king Cyaxares, we read. The alliance that destroyed Assyria included a matrimonial alliance.

The story relates how, on the hot Mesopotamian plain, the Median princess longed for the summits, valleys, and forests of her native mountains. To please her, Nebuchadnezzar built, at Babylon, as much of a substitute as was possible. This was a structure of lofty terraces set with groves of trees, vegetation, and flowers. Doubtless there were fountains and singing birds in a sort of paradise. It was the nearest to the cool green highlands that could be created in the utterly flat and swelteringly hot land.

The term "Hanging Gardens" is a traditional misnomer, "hanging" a mistranslation of a Greek word, which could make later legend imagine gardens suspended from the sky. But from all accounts it was an enormous structure, terrace upon terrace, built of stone, which material was a wonder in itself. The Mesopotamian plain is without stone. Its prevailing building material down to the present day is brick. The stone for the Hanging Gardens was transported from distant mountain country, probably ferried down the river Tigris. At each terrace level deep loam was laid to support plants and trees, and tame animals of the forest were placed in the shady groves.

The second Babylonian Empire, for all its terrifying power,

had only a brief existence. The Old Testament relates that, in time, Nebuchadnezzar grew mad, and ate grass. Meanwhile the kingdom of the Medes, after the death of Cyaxares, was overthrown by Cyrus, the Persian, who embarked on a vast career of conquest. Not long after the death of Nebuchadnezzar the Persians besieged and took Babylon.

Thereafter the city declined, finally sank into ruin, and was covered by the encroaching desert. Herodotus, describing Babylon more than a hundred years after the Hanging Gardens were constructed, makes no mention of them. But they lingered in legend down the centuries as one of the Seven Wonders of the World.

Modern archaeologists, excavating the ruins of Babylon, have found at one place the remains of an extensive system for conducting water, which may have been used for the irrigation of the Hanging Gardens.

The only one of the Seven Wonders that stood in Greece proper was connected with athletics. This tells a good deal about the Hellenic regard for the human body, the ideal of physical as well as intellectual cultivation. The greatest religious effigy of ancient Greece was reared at the site of the Olympic games. The games included poetry contests and chariot races, but were primarily an athletic competition—foot races, the discus throw, hurling the javelin.

The home of the Hellenic gods was on Mount Olympus, in Thessaly, northern Greece. The Olympic games were held at Olympia, in southern Greece, the Peloponnesus. Probably there was some early connection between the mountain in the north and the city in the south. At any rate Zeus, the father of the gods on Mount Olympus, was the chief divinity at Olympia.

One legend says the Olympic games derived from a chariot race won by the hero Pelops, after whom the Peloponnesus was named. The prize he sought was the Princess Hippodameia, and that was a dangerous game. Her father, King Oenomaus, had been told in a prophecy that he would be slain by his son-in-law. So, naturally enough, Oenomaus took a dim view of the marriage of his daughter. He promised Hippodameia to any suitor who could carry her off in a chariot and not be caught by the king in his own chariot. The penalty for losing the race was death—the luckless suitor impaled by the royal spear. The trick of it was that, for his chariot, Oenomaus had winged steeds. The race, it seems, was fixed.

One suitor after another lost his life. But Pelops, entering the deadly competition, bribed the king's groom to tamper with the royal chariot, and in the ensuing race there was a chariot wreck, and Oenomaus was killed. Pelops, having won the race by trickery and brought about the king's death, married the princess, and became the king's posthumous son-in-law. Thereby the prophecy was fulfilled.

It was a memorable chariot race with a double fix; and, to commemorate it, Pelops founded the Olympic games. At least, so we gather from one legend. There are others, but this one, with romance and fraud, is particularly lively.

The Greeks based their calendar on the Olympic games, and reckoned time from the traditional date of the first one, much as we use the birth of Christ for our calendar. The date, 776 B.C., began the list of Olympic victors, which was kept for more than eleven centuries, and was a supreme roll of honor. The first winner of the athletic contest was Coroebus of Elis. The last was Varastad, an Armenian, in A.D. 393, at which time Christianity made an end to the Olympic games. Now, some fifteen hundred years later, they have been revived in very different form in this modern world.

The original games were held every four years in the summer, and the time was considered sacred. No matter what wars and feuds might be raging in Greece, anyone traveling to or from the celebration at Olympia was free from molestation. It was like a pilgrimage to a great religious festival, at which athletics were the principal part of the ritual. The games, in fact, constituted a sort of religious bond among the various Greek cities.

It is not surprising, therefore, that there was a great shrine of Zeus at Olympia. The original temple was one of the oldest in Greece, and its columns were made of wood. Later a new edifice was put up, one of the most famous buildings in the classical world, renowned above all for its imposing statue of Zeus, fashioned by Phidias, greatest of Greek sculptors.

The statue, made of gold and ivory, was forty feet high, and placed on a pedestal twelve feet high. It showed Zeus enthroned. The upper part of the seated figure was naked and of gleaming ivory. The eyes were flashing precious gems. The lower part was covered with a mantle sculptured of gold that fell in folds to the feet. The right hand held a symbol of victory. The left, a scepter surmounted by an eagle. Phidias worked on this masterpiece for five years, and it was universally reckoned as one of the Seven Wonders of the World.

The statue of Zeus remained at Olympia some seven hundred years. Its final fate is in doubt, but one account relates that, with the triumph of Christianity and the end of the Olympic games, it was taken to Constantinople, where it was destroyed in the great fire of A.D. 476.

Rhodes was famous for oratory and the Colossus. It had schools of rhetoric pre-eminent in the teaching of eloquence. The giant statue at the entrance of the harbor was rated as a wonder of the world. As one who has had a career of public speaking, I have a professional interest in this island devoted to the art of oratory.

Cicero tells us how in Rome different styles of eloquence were disputed by public speakers and their listeners in the forum. There were two extremes of the elaborate and the simple, called respectively the Asiatic and the Attic styles.

The former was flowery and flamboyant, ornate with purple passages, emotional with thunder and pathos. This was in the spectacular manner of Asia. Historian Albert Grenier describes the Asiatic style:

"More imagination than logic in invention, immoderate use of figures, effective phrases, and contrasts, vocal tricks of delivery which turned speaking into a kind of chant, and exuberant gesture—these were the characteristics of the Asiatic style."

The Attic manner, in contrast, exaggerated the classical tradition of Athens, with its reticence, its plain-spoken clearness, avoiding all extravagance of verbiage or manner. Cicero writes:

"They say that a man who speaks in a careless, unpolished manner, provided it is precise and free from unnecessary ornament, alone speaks in the 'Attic' way."

The style of Rhodes was in the middle. The island, off the coast of Asia Minor, was a sort of halfway station between Asia and Athens. The Rhodian teachers of rhetoric rejected the excessive luxuriance of the one and the dry austerity of the other, and taught a moderation of ornament and expression.

Cicero tells us how he began with the exceptionally violent Asiatic style. It must have been something to hear. "I made a whole speech . . . with all the force of my voice and my whole body." He says the powerful oratorical exertions were too much for his physical constitution, which was frail in youth. So he went to Rhodes, where he studied with Molon, most celebrated of the Rhodian professors.

"Molon did what he could to curb my redundance and the overflowing verbosity of my youthful unrestraint. . . . At the end of two years I came back a different man; my delivery was less violent and my style had, as it were, cooled down."

This was surely a necessary measure before Cicero could become the model of Roman orators.

The schools of rhetoric, no doubt, brought ample profits, but Rhodes was also a great commercial center and enjoyed the wealth derived from trade. This provided the means for splendor, and the Rhodians seem to have had a special fancy for large statues. Ancient accounts state that many lofty images of the gods stood in the city, but the greatest of all was the Colossus, dedicated to the sun god Helios.

This mighty bronze was, they say, erected with funds derived from a military success. A few decades after the death of Alexander, Rhodes was besieged by Demetrius, a Macedonian king, who beleaguered and assailed the powerfully fortified city for a long time but failed to capture it. Abandoning the siege, Demetrius left behind masses of equipment, engines of war. These the triumphant Rhodians sold, and used the money to rear the Colossus. Demetrius' siege machinery must have been an immense lot, because we are told that the cost of the giant of

[ 23 ]

bronze came to three hundred talents, anywhere from a million to several million dollars in our money. Other accounts relate that the statue was made of bronze taken from the engines of war left by Demetrius.

The Colossus standing at the entrance of the harbor was probably something over one hundred feet in height. Later legend loved to play with the marvels of the Colossus. The Middle Ages gave us the familiar story that it stood across the entrance of the harbor, and ships sailed in and out between the legs of the Colossus—a prodigy echoed in Shakespeare, whose Cassius says of Caesar:

> "Why, man, he doth bestride the narrow world
> Like a Colossus, and we petty men
> Walk under his huge legs and peep about
> To find ourselves dishonourable graves."

Pliny, some three centuries after the erection of the Colossus, describes it in terms sufficiently marvelous. Writing of great bronze statues in various places, he says:

"But that which is by far the most worthy of our admiration, is the colossal statue of the Sun, which stood formerly at Rhodes. This statue, fifty-six years after it was erected, was thrown down by an earthquake; but even as it lies, it excites our wonder and admiration. Few men can clasp the thumb in their arms, and its fingers are larger than most statues. Where the limbs are broken asunder, vast caverns are seen yawning in the interior."

The fallen giant lay for nearly a thousand years until, in the Middle Ages, the Saracens held the island of Rhodes. They sold the huge fragments to a Jewish merchant, and it required nine hundred camels to carry them away. The supposition is that the bronze was made into instruments of war, the source from which the Colossus had been derived in the first place.

Of the Seven Wonders of the Ancient World, six were of a monumental character, religious, funerary, aesthetic. Only one was of practical utility in workaday life. This was the Pharos, the lighthouse at Alexandria. Nothing is of a more useful nature, in the antique world or modern, than the tower with a beacon as an aid to navigation, and the Pharos was the king of lighthouses.

It was typical that this utilitarian masterpiece should have stood at Alexandria, where Greek science flourished—astronomy, mathematics, physics. Elsewhere classical culture was primarily artistic, literary, philosophical. Euclid with his geometry was a product of Alexandria and so was Archimedes, who astounded the ancient world as an inventor of practical gadgets. Alexandria excelled in industrial arts such as the chemistry of dyeing fabrics and coloring ceramics. Surely the proper place for the useful wonder of the world.

The city was founded by Alexander the Great when he conquered Egypt, and he picked the site with an eye for a harbor. This was near the western branch of the mouth of the Nile—a branch since silted up. Never was there a more successful selection. Alexandria soon became the greatest seaport of the ancient world, and still is Egypt's principal maritime gateway. A harbor is likely to need a lighthouse, and the entrance at Alexandria could be tricky for the galleys and merchantmen of antiquity.

The Pharos was built by Ptolemy Philadelphus, son and successor to Alexandria's general, Ptolemy, who made himself King of Egypt. Constructed of stone, it was no slender tower. The lighthouse was a massive edifice that rose 445 feet, higher than a thirty-six-story skyscraper. The architecture was striking, with levels of different geometrical form: the lower, rectangular; the second level, octagonal; the upper, circular—where a fire beacon, amplified by a mirror, flashed out to sea. At the top stood a huge stone figure facing the sea. Pliny gives us the following comment:

"There is another building, too, that is highly celebrated; the tower that was built by a king of Egypt, on the island of Pharos, at the entrance to the harbour of Alexandria. The object of it is, by the light of its fires at night, to give warning to ships of the neighbouring shoals, and to point out to them the entrance of the harbour. At the present day, there are similar fires lighted up in numerous places, Ostia and Ravenna, for example. The only danger is, that when these fires are thus kept burning without intermission, they may be mistaken for stars, the flames having very much that appearance at a distance."

Pliny's comment on the danger of mistaking a steady light for a star is the more interesting when we consider that beacons in later times were likely to be intermittent, blinking.

The Pharos figured prominently in one of the great dramatic stories of history—the romance of Cleopatra, her conquest of Caesar, which preceded her subsequent subjugation of Marc Antony. Caesar used the mighty lighthouse as a fortress when he tarried at Alexandria, beguiled by the charms of the Egyptian queen. The city rose against him. His force of Roman legionaries was small, and he was in grave peril. In his *Commentaries* he tells us (the John Warrington translation uses the first person pronoun, which Caesar did not):

"I immediately embarked some troops, and landed them on Pharos. The island of Pharos gives its name to a lighthouse, a miracle of size and engineering. Lying opposite Alexandria, it forms one side of the harbor, and earlier monarchs had connected it with the city by means of a narrow causeway. The channel [of the harbor] is so narrow that anyone controlling the Pharos may close the harbor to shipping from whatever quarter. This alarming prospect decided me . . . to land troops on the island; a move that ensured the safe arrival of our food and reinforcements, which had been ordered from the neighboring provinces."

Caesar stood siege in the Pharos, until reinforcements came, after which he occupied Alexandria, and continued his amour with Cleopatra.

The lighthouse stood for sixteen hundred years. When the Arabs invaded Egypt they tore down the upper part. Then, in the fourteenth century A.D., an earthquake demolished the remainder of what had been, in point of size, the greatest lighthouse of all times.

These were six of the Seven Wonders of the Ancient World. They have one thing in common. No trace of them remains, except what archaeologists have excavated. The only way they can be shown is in reconstructions made by scholars from ancient descriptions and archaeological investigation. You'll find them as illustrations in history and travel books, drawings, paintings.

Of the seventh, no drawing or painting is needed. One of the Seven Wonders of the Ancient World has survived, and is, indeed, a wonder of the modern world. Today streams of tourists proceed to the venerable site to gape and marvel, as did the sight-seers of two thousand years ago, who had been advised by guidebooks and the ancient equivalent of travel agencies: "You should not, under any circumstances, miss the Pyramids of Egypt."

That was the official list:

The Mausoleum at Halicarnassus.
The Temple of Diana at Ephesus.
The Hanging Gardens of Babylon.
The statue of Zeus at Olympia.
The Colossus of Rhodes.
The Pharos, the lighthouse at Alexandria.
The Pyramids of Egypt.

Sometimes there was a variant, such as the walls of Babylon, which giant fortification, in fact, had more historical clearness and certainty than the Hanging Gardens, though not so much lure for the imagination.

In subsequent ages there were efforts to bring the list down to date. In A.D. 550 St. Gregory of Tours revised it according to Christian principles. He struck off the Pyramids, the Olympian Zeus, and the Temple of Diana as being too pagan. For these he substituted Noah's Ark, the Temple of Solomon, and the theatre of Heracles. This last was strange, a place for shows and games. He preferred the walls of Babylon to the Hanging Gardens. So great a monument for love of a mortal woman was not according to the principles of a saintly cleric of the Dark Ages.

Gregory drew up a second list of wonders "created by the hand of God": the tides of the ocean, the growth of plants from seeds, the volcano Mount Etna, the rebirth of the phoenix, the cycle of the sun, and the cycle of the moon. These were wonders of nature, except for the phoenix, but that mythical creature rising from its ashes was accepted as a fact in the Middle Ages.

In our modern era the Seven Wonders idea has retained its charm, and various selections have been made. Often they got away completely from the original idea, which was limited to individual things, not generalities or classes of things.

In 1913, *Scientific American* magazine chose a list of seven from inventions of the day: the airplane and automobile, reinforced concrete, the X-ray machine, the phonograph, and motion pictures.

In 1937, *Current History* magazine asked such experts as Admiral Richard Byrd, explorer, Richard Curie, mining engineer, Carleton Beals, author, and Richard Halliburton, travel romanticist, for their selections. This time the New York subway made the grade!

Veteran globe trotter Burton Holmes, inventor of the word "travelogue," compiled a list in 1946 for *This Week* magazine, and included Los Alamos, home of the atomic bomb.

The American Society of Civil Engineers selected seven. One of their choices: the sewage system in Chicago.

Obviously, after some twenty-two centuries, people are still interested in picking Seven Wonders, and now a new way of doing it has come about, a most spectacular way of bringing the ancient list down to date.

# Chapter 2

Oɴ sᴇᴘᴛᴇᴍʙᴇʀ 30, 1952, a revolution in the art of motion pictures began. *This Is Cinerama* opened in a Broadway theatre. The change it initiated was as pervasive as the transition from silent pictures to sound, from black and white to color. Movie houses all over the nation made alterations, and the screen was never the same afterward.

Cinerama originated, years before, with Fred Waller, a veteran technician of film, whose engrossing thought it was to break motion pictures out of the confines of the narrow screen and fill the spectator's range of vision. The conventional motion picture was something like an illuminated postage stamp stuck on a black wall. You saw only what was in a limited square straight ahead, and the rest was darkness. Or, as someone said, you were looking at a scene through a keyhole.

Waller's idea was to break out of the constricted frame and include what the spectator sees out of the corner of the eye—peripheral vision. At the New York World's Fair, 1939, he presented a cyclorama of still pictures extending around the entire room. (Later, *Time* and *Life* used a modification of this, with still pictures on a wide curved screen.) Then he went on to motion pictures. In his experiments he hooked up eleven 16-millimeter cameras, and eleven films were thrown by eleven projectors to give motion pictures a great breadth and scope.

At this point the U. S. Air Force became interested, seeing

possibilities for a gunnery trainer, which would present targets in a simulation of air battle. The Air Force put up funds for research, and Fred Waller developed a gunnery trainer, using five cameras, films, and projectors.

So, during the Second World War, thousands of American airmen went to school at a motion picture show. In an Air Force version of a theatre, students sat at machine-gun mounts, facing a great concave screen. The pictures were scenes of sky and clouds, maneuvering planes, et cetera, and embraced just about all a gunner would see from his plane.

The students were, it seemed, in the midst of aerial combat, enemy aircraft, friendly aircraft, diving, whirling, zooming. A German Messerschmitt might appear to be coming at them, or a Japanese Zero. They aimed and fired their guns in simulated target practice, and became familiar with tactics they'd encounter in the war of the air across the Atlantic or out in the Pacific.

The Waller Gunnery Trainer is said to have saved thousands of American lives in the Second World War.

After the war Waller modified the gunnery trainer for motion picture show business. He simplified it, cutting down from five to three, using three cameras integrated in a unit, three films and three projectors, and a wide, curved screen encompassing enough to fill the range of vision of a theatre audience. Later, stereophonic sound was provided by Hazard Reeves, a top-ranking sound technician, whose laboratory developed a system with seven channels and seven sound tracks.

This was Cinerama. It was ready to go, and promptly got nowhere. Top motion picture executives came to see it, marveled, and shook their heads. Their business dealt with the movie houses of the nation, and Cinerama, with its three projectors and wide, curved screen, could not be adapted to myriads of neighborhood theatres. Therefore it had no place in the film industry. That was the orthodox view.

It was at this stage of the game that I first saw Cinerama. I was invited by "Buzz" Reeves to visit a former indoor tennis court near Oyster Bay, Long Island, which had been turned

*The flying camera crew, which made air shots: Bert Eason, assistant cameraman; Frank Schwelle, co-pilot and navigator; Harry Squire, cameraman in charge of photography; Paul Mantz, pilot for aerial photography; Jack Priestley, assistant cameraman; James Cortland Johnston, flight engineer.* Photo by James Cortland Johnston

*Your wonder seeker, as the quest for the SEVEN WONDERS OF THE WORLD is launched. At the right, a portrait of Lawrence of Arabia as he looked when he was leading the revolt in the desert.* Photo by Saul Cooper

*Mount Olympus, on whose broad summit the gods of the Greeks dwelt.*

The interior of the Dome of St. Peter's, designed by Michelangelo, a masterpiece of grandeur and decoration.

Photo by Edwin W. Sippel

Photo by Edwin W. Sippel

The vast throng gathered in the Piazza of St. Peter's to receive the blessing of the Pope.

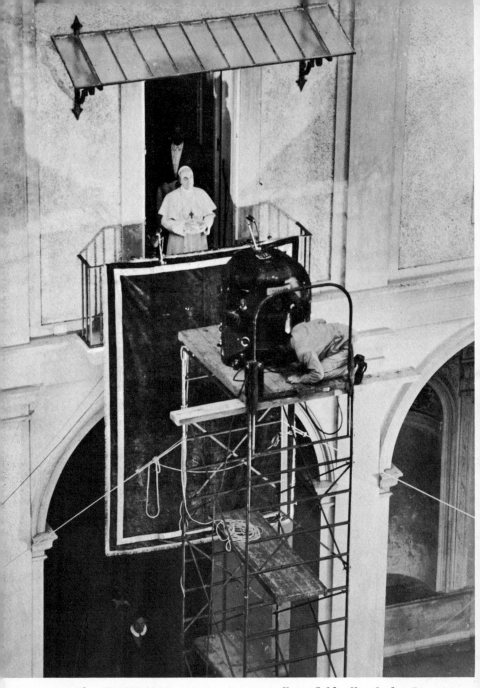

*The CINERAMA camera, from a tall scaffold, filmed the Pope at Castel Gandolfo.*

Photo by Edwin W. Sippel

*The Acropolis was the fortress of Athens, crowned by the Parthenon, sacred to the city's patron saint, the goddess Athena.*

*The Parthenon, although battered by time, still tells us that the Greeks were transcendent masters of architecture.*

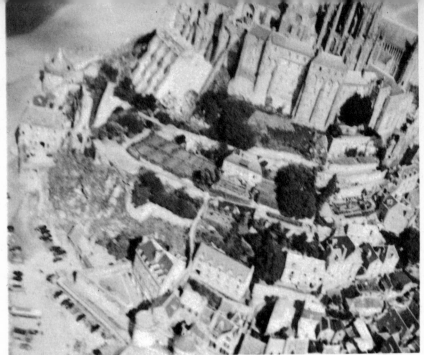

*Mont St. Michel, a fortress shrine on the coast of Normandy, built by the Normans of old.*

*The shell of the Colosseum stands as a durable relic of the days when Rome ruled the world.*

Photo by Edwin W. Sippel

From the air we look down into the saucer of the Colosseum, where gladiators once fought, where Christians were once thrown to the lions.

Only ruins remain in the Roman Forum, where decisions that shook the world once were made.

*Pope Pius XII bestows his blessing on the multitude.*

into a research film studio. I gazed, and was impressed. What I saw were no more than experimental shots. One, for example, was merely the scene of an automobile drive down a country road lined with trees in autumn colors. But they proved their point. My own feeling was that this was a magical medium for presenting the great sights of the earth.

I was not tied down to motion picture orthodoxy. I thought, forget the small movie houses. Put it in a Broadway theatre, along the lines of a regular Broadway show. I lined up a small group for financing, and a picture was made under the guidance of General Merian Cooper, a top Hollywood producer and an old friend of mine. "Coop" is a veteran who made motion picture history with successes such as that old fantasy of the grotesque, *King Kong*, and his earlier expedition films, *Grass* and *Chang*.

The Broadway opening of *This Is Cinerama* was a stunning success. The audience thrilled to the dizzy shock of the roller coaster, the eye-filling pageant of Venice, the breath-taking thrills of the flight into the Grand Canyon and Zion Canyon. The New York *Times*, the next morning, published its review on the front page. Never before had the *Times* reviewed a motion picture on page one.

*This Is Cinerama* ran on Broadway at theatrical prices for nearly two years and a half, breaking all records. It did the same in cities across the United States. Abroad the story was illustrated at the Damascus Fair and the Bangkok Fair, where crowds rioted to procure tickets, and a pretentious Soviet exhibit was eclipsed. That one picture grossed some thirty million dollars, breaking all records.

This occurred at a time when motion pictures were in a deep depression because of television, and here was a film jamming people into the theatre. Hollywood was startled, and the motion picture revolution was on. Hollywood imitated Cinerama as best Hollywood could. Wide-screen processes, some of which had been lying around for years, were revived. Movie houses everywhere installed wide screens. There was a temporary revival of 3-D. The motion picture industry tried to ride the tail end of the Cinerama bandwagon. The name was imitated. Far and wide a rush of words appeared ending in "rama."

In *This Is Cinerama* the idea was to present the familiar through a new medium. The hero was the novel technique. The subjects were such as were easily accessible in Europe—a troupe of dancers in Spain, a bagpipe march in Scotland, opera in Italy —and American vistas like Niagara Falls, an aqua-show in Florida, dazzling flying shots cross-country, the Grand Canyon. All were intentionally familiar.

Our financing was thin. Our group had subscribed to a small stock issue. We were working on a shoestring and couldn't afford any distant expeditions. We relied on the new magic eye, and that did it.

Nevertheless, my idea for Cinerama was to go to the far places and show the strange and exotic. After all, I couldn't escape my background, which was dominated by an enthusiasm for far places and exploration. So I had to think of the new magic eye in those terms.

The idea that suggested itself went back to that old legend of the Seven Wonders of the World, the list drawn up by the ancient Greeks, which has haunted the imagination of man for centuries and is still a byword. Why not bring it down to date? Now that we had Cinerama for revelation, why not seek out the Seven Wonders of the modern world? That would certainly include an abundance of the faraway and strange to see. I talked the matter over with Coop, and we decided on a Cinerama quest around the globe for wonders of the modern world.

The idea was to get a selection, as many as we could with as wide a variety as possible. Undoubtedly we'd miss some wonders that many people might name. But we'd see what we could get. It would be like a gamble—seven come eleven. Then let theatre audiences name their selection of the magic seven.

Meanwhile, the exhibition of *This Is Cinerama* had been taken over by a newly formed organization called Stanley-Warner, and they produced a second feature, *Cinerama Holiday,* after which another picture was needed. So it was that we decided to film the Seven Wonders, a round-the-world adventure of picking up where the Greeks of antiquity had left off.

# Chapter 3

THE TRANSATLANTIC air liner was gaining altitude as it left the coast. In the cabin every seat was occupied. It was midwinter, not the tourist season, but that middle-aged couple might be bound for sight-seeing in Europe. The sunburned chap might be an American oil man returning to a post at the Arabian oil fields. One passenger looked like a professor, another like a movie actress, while still another might be a diplomat. Some might be off on odd missions in Asia, Africa, or heaven knows where. None, probably, was on as odd a mission as I.

For the Cinerama *Seven Wonders,* I was to be both producer and narrator, and the plan was for me to appear on the scene from time to time and speak a few lines for camera and sound equipment at the location of some wonder or other. The filming had already begun abroad, and I was to check with the crews in the field on what they had been doing, and make further arrangements. I'd be traveling with them for some tens of thousands of miles and to some strange, remote places.

Our plan for the picture was to present the Seven Wonders of the Ancient World as a prologue. The six that have disappeared would be shown in paintings as deduced by scholars, paintings by Mario Larrinaga, a top-ranking artist. The Pyramids and the Sphinx would be disclosed by the Cinerama camera on the scene. I'd appear in this. Then on in quest of wonders of the modern world. This would take me on a trip around the globe.

The air liner was the Pan American clipper *Seven Seas*. Appropriate—Seven Wonders, *Seven Seas*. The pilot, as it happened, was a friend of mine. The last time I had seen Captain Charles Blair was on an interesting occasion. So after a while I went to the cockpit of the air liner and renewed acquaintance. The copilot was at the controls, and Charley Blair and I sat off to one side in the instrument-loaded space and had a chat.

I don't recall, but he might have asked me: "What's the trip this time, Lowell?"

I might have replied: "I'm flying around the globe, looking for the Seven Wonders of the World." Which would have sounded odd.

Actually I don't recall discussing my own journey in any detail with Charley Blair. I was more interested in questioning him about himself, although his itinerary was no mystery. Shannon, Ireland, was the first stop. Then London, then back to New York, after which he'd do the same thing all over again—on the ocean-shuttle job of a transatlantic pilot. But previously he had had an extraordinary career of adventurous flying—one exploit, in particular, a masterpiece of experimental daring. We chatted about that, and about things concerning him now. That, at the moment, was more to the point than the Seven Wonders of the World.

It was something for my radio program back home. I had got a leave of absence from General Motors, and Charles Collingwood of CBS was taking my place on the nightly news program. But I was to appear on it as often as possible, nearly every night in fact, with five or six minutes about that part of the world where I happened to be. Journeying to some of the remote parts of this planet, I'd do a reporting job, and pick up what features and bits of news I could.

So presently, in the air liner, I sat down with an oblong box and talked into a microphone connected with it. This was an electronic tape recorder, with which I could produce a sort of spoken diary, relating events and observations of the day. The recordings would be sent back to New York and played on the nightly programs. I had done this on previous trips.

Having made the recording, I packed and addressed it to my New York office. A day later it went back by that same plane, the *Seven Seas*, on its return trip. This was over the weekend. On Monday evening Charles Collingwood recited the news on my usual six forty-five spot, and then introduced the recording, which went as follows:

"Shortly after the *Seven Seas* took off from Idlewild, I discovered that her captain was an airman whom I had known for some time. In fact the last time we were together I happened to be toastmaster at the fiftieth anniversary banquet of the Explorers' Club, in New York, and although he was sitting out on the floor that night, not at the head table, I singled him out from more than a thousand rather distinguished men. I had him stand up so that all might see the only man who had ever flown solo across the North Pole, for that's what Captain Charles Blair did.

"It was in a P-51, a World War II fighter plane, with special gas tanks. He made this unique flight from near Comso Fjord in Norway to Fairbanks, in the heart of Alaska, in order to demonstrate his own new theory on the way to use celestial navigation—that is, to use it in remote regions where there are no radio aids.

"He's tall, handsome, gentle, and gay. He looks like a youngster and here's his record: more than twenty-two thousand hours in the air, more than four million miles in the air, and he has piloted planes across the Atlantic more than six hundred times.

"Now I've always been interested in what unusual people do when they're not doing what they usually do. As the captain of a transatlantic air liner, Charley Blair is in the air approximately two weeks out of every month, and what do you suppose he does the rest of the time, the other two weeks? I'll wager that you would never, never guess.

"He flies jets, the latest Sabre jets; he has over six hundred hours in them, and recently he checked out in the huge B-32, that's the six-engine superjet. He just likes to fly and especially fly jets. Since that solo flight he made across the North Pole, he has been a special consultant to the U. S. Government, and no wonder, and a consultant to the Strategic Air Force."

I ended the tape recording with a comforting reflection: "Except for the throbbing of the four motors driving this plane through the sky at three hundred miles an hour, there isn't a sound up here in the sky at this moment. The Atlantic Ocean is far, far below us. And I suppose that I am the only one on board who knows the record of the skipper of this clipper; but if the others did know I am sure it would make it much easier for them to sleep."

At London I changed planes and took an air liner flying south. Destination Egypt, Cairo, the Pyramids. In the cabin I noticed one of the passengers. He was tall and thin, and had a majestic beard. A character decidedly out of the usual, you knew at once.

I got to talking with him, and promptly fetched my tape recorder. I asked him if he minded being interviewed for my radio program in New York. He replied, "Not at all." Whereupon we talked alternately into the microphone, recording a dialogue that, in due time, went on the American air. Now I must ask you to exert your imagination and conjure up an accent both British and ultraprofessorial.

"I beg your pardon, sir," I began the recorded chat, "I hope you won't mind my asking who you are, where you are going, and why."

"Oh, I'm a scientist," he replied in that inimitable accent. "Mozley, Alan Mozley. Union College, upstate New York."

"Are you an American?" I inquired needlessly.

"Oh no, I'm English, with Canadian background."

"I see. And where are you going?"

"Oh, I'm going out to Africa. A hunting trip."

"Big game?"

"Yes, big game. Snails!"

"Snails! Why are you interested in the snails in Africa?"

"Well, d'you know, I think that snails are most interesting creatures. Well, you see, I often give talks in schools, in America, in England, perhaps in Africa, and I tell them snails are among the most important animals in Africa. Lions, rhinos, hippos, elephants, and so on—they're all right. You just have to keep out of their way. But snails are the most insidious creatures, the most dangerous animals in Africa. They carry disease."

"Oh, I see. That's the reason why you're going to study them."

"Yes. I've been to Africa many times in the past twenty years, and now I'm off for another look around."

"And what disease is it that the snail carries?"

"The disease is something called bilharziasis. Or, more simply, Bill Harris. The troops out in Egypt, in the last war, used to call it the Bill Harris. Actually an abbreviation or improvement upon bilharziasis, a disease carried by snails. No snails, no disease. What I'm concerned with is killing the snails."

"What sort of a disease is this?"

"Oh, not very spectacular. When people get this disease they just feel no good, lethargic, lacking in initiative."

"How large a part of the earth's surface is troubled by this illness that comes from snails?"

"Many of the warmer countries. As far as population is concerned, it applies to a large part of the human population of the world. And that makes it a serious thing, a really serious thing. So I'm on the job—one of the scientists on the job."

"Thank you very much, Professor!"

This interview made a few minutes' light material for the news program, but apparently Bill Harris is a more serious character than I had imagined. Upon my return home I found a letter from a professor at the School of Medicine, Tulane University, Louisiana:

Dear Mr. Thomas:

I am writing you particularly with reference to your recorded broadcast when you were flying to Cairo. I refer particularly to your interview with Mr. Alan Mozley, "the snail man." Although I have never met Mr. Mozley I have had considerable correspondence with him and have in my library two of his three monographs on snails in their relationship to blood-fluke infection (bilharziasis).

Mr. Mozley was entirely too modest in discussing this subject with you, and particularly the importance of certain snails in the transmission of serious, frequently fatal disease in man over wide areas of the earth. I have had intimate association with this disease since 1915.

By experience and present knowledge I am in a position to stress the importance of the disease, which is contracted by natives in infected areas when they bathe, swim, wash clothes, wade or in other ways come in contact with the stage of the parasite which emerges from the infected snails. After a short free-swimming period in fresh water the parasites become attached to human skin, invade the tissues and develop into destructive adults causing blood-fluke disease. At least 10% of the world's population, mostly in tropical and Oriental countries, is infected. Next to malaria, this infection is the most serious and most wide-spread of all present-day diseases in warm climates; and it is increasing in its extent as irrigation is being enlarged.

Forgive me for this long dissertation, but you as a globe-master of interesting information will probably not resent my communication.

> Most sincerely yours,
> Ernest Carroll Faust
> The William Vincent Professor of Tropical Diseases
> and Hygiene, and
> Head of the Division of Parasitology

That letter I found most interesting. Our adventures had taken us to remote places in the tropics, and we too might have got intimately acquainted with Bill Harris. He was one wonder we didn't want to find. Luckily, we didn't.

# Chapter 4

THE FIRST TIME I saw the Pyramids of Egypt was back in Lawrence of Arabia days, and the recollection still makes the shivers run down my spine. Few people have ever been introduced in such startling fashion to those geometrical monstrosities and the Sphinx.

I was on my way from Italy to Palestine to cover British General Allenby's campaign to conquer the Holy Land by driving out the Turks. Stopping off in Egypt, I wanted to see the most famous of Egyptian sights, and a Royal Air Force flier offered to fly me over and show them to me. We took off from a military flying field at ancient Heliopolis, and I soon wished I had chosen a more conventional way of sight-seeing—riding a camel, for example.

The pilot was a South African, descended on his mother's side from General Botha, South African leader, who fought the British in the Boer War. On his father's side he was Irish. His family name, Emmet—which went back to Robert Emmet, the Irish patriot hanged by the British. Curious ancestry for an R.A.F. pilot—maybe that was what made him so wild.

We were in a small fighter plane, style of World War I, a two-seater, single-engine Bristol. Major Emmet's way of showing me the Pyramids and the Sphinx was to dive down at them from high altitude, throwing his fighter plane into a tailspin, the tail whipping round and round as we plunged, with the

Pyramids and the Sphinx coming up at me. It looked as if we'd crash into the apex of the Pyramid of Cheops. But the plane leveled off and circled around for a more leisurely view. The impression I still retain is of the Pyramids and the Sphinx coming up at me.

I went on to Jerusalem and there, at Allenby's headquarters, met Lawrence of Arabia, and heard about his exploits, leading the revolt in the desert. I talked with him a bit, but soon he was on his way back to his headquarters—far to the south—in the desert, near the head of the Gulf of Akaba. After he had left, and I never expected to see him again, I was lucky enough to get permission from Allenby to join Lawrence in Arabia. But that meant a complicated journey. It would have taken a military expedition to go there by a direct route, through hostile country. I had to make a detour, back to Egypt, up the Nile to the Sudan, across to the Red Sea, by boat to Jedda, and finally north to the port of Akaba. There I was to meet Lawrence again, and go on getting his story.

While in Egypt, in Cairo, on this circuitous journey, I thought I might have another look at the Pyramids, in a less hare-brained way this time. British soldiers went on wartime sightseeing, and I joined a party of them. A lorry took us to Gizeh, where camels provided our locomotion. This time, in tourist style, I stood gazing as thousands of other visitors have done —much more sensible than seeing the Pyramids and the Sphinx from a diving plane doing a tailspin.

Now, years later, here I stood again, gazing and marveling as one always does. I had met the Cinerama film crew in Cairo, and here we were, with our new miracle of motion pictures, to get Cinerama shots of the only remaining survivor of the Seven Wonders of the Ancient World. They operated their camera and sound equipment, and I played my part and spoke my lines.

The Greeks of antiquity esteemed the Pyramids of Egypt as the greatest and oldest of the Seven Wonders. Writers down the ages, Greek, Roman, medieval, modern, never ceased to marvel. The massive monuments were surrounded by mystery, though now modern archaeology has laid bare many of their secrets, and is revealing more.

Egyptology is a fascinating branch of learning, and it would be interesting to refer to some of the latest books on the subject. They can be enlightening and instructive. But for entertainment we can best go back to the literature of nineteen hundred years ago. Our encyclopedic friend Pliny was impressed as much as anybody by those prodigies the Pharaohs reared, but the view he took was unfavorable.

"We must," he writes, "make some mention of the Pyramids of Egypt, idle and frivolous pieces of ostentation on the part of the monarchs of that country. Indeed, it is asserted by most persons, that the only motive for constructing them, was either a determination not to leave their treasures to their successors or to rivals that might be plotting to supplant them, or to prevent the lower classes from remaining unoccupied. There was great vanity displayed by these men in constructions of this description.

"The largest Pyramid is built of stone quarried in Arabia," Pliny goes on. "Three hundred and sixty thousand men, it is said, were employed upon it twenty years."

He continues with a list of writers, beginning with Herodotus, who described the Pyramids, and continues his sour opinion:

"These authors, however, are disagreed as to the persons by whom they were constructed, accident having, with very considerable justice, consigned to oblivion the names of those who erected such stupendous memorials of their vanity. Some of these writers inform us that fifteen hundred talents were expended upon radishes, garlic and onions alone."

Of the three pyramids at Gizeh, Pliny says the smallest of them, though gigantic enough, was considered the best-looking. This gives the Roman moralist an opportunity for a final touch of scorn.

"Such are the marvelous Pyramids; but the crowning marvel of all is, that the smallest, but most admired of them, was built by Rhodopis, a courtesan! This woman was one of the fellow-slaves of Aesopus the philosopher and fabulist, and the sharer

[ 41 ]

of his bed; but what is much more surprising is that a courtesan should have been enabled, by her vocation, to amass such enormous wealth."

In all this disapprobation, proper to a Roman philosopher, there is one shrewd touch—the supposition that the Pharaohs might have built the Pyramids "to prevent the lower classes from remaining unoccupied."

More recently, down in this modern era, it was thought the gigantic work was done inhumanly by vast armies of slaves under the lash. But the view now is that the labor force consisted of the peasant population in the off season, when the Nile flood was on and there was nothing to do while the fields were inundated.

Pliny, writing in the first century A.D., three thousand years after the Pyramids were built, is ignorant of their real purpose, which seems to have been forgotten. He thinks it nothing more than vanity and ostentation. Today he would be enlightened. The Pyramids, we now know, were tombs of Pharaohs of the Fourth Dynasty. Their purpose was to insure, in a gigantic way, the welfare of the king in the future life.

In another passage Pliny remarks that the Pyramids are surrounded by desert sand, with no buildings of any sort. This is true, of course, today. But archaeology shows that there had been elaborate buildings, extending to the neighboring Nile, shrines and other edifices of the cult of the royal deceased, served by priests in the interest of the Pharaoh's immortality. In a ritualistic way they served the royal mummy, in its magnificent sarcophagus, as the Pharaoh had been served in his life.

In his pyramid tomb he was surrounded by objects such as he had used in life, these being considered necessary for the future life. When our Cinerama expedition was at the Pyramids, archaeologists had just discovered the far-famed "solar boat" in an underground chamber near the Great Pyramid, a craft the Pharaoh would need for his celestial journey to the sun god. I got a glimpse of it in its subterranean receptacle—a typical Nile boat such as you see in ancient Egyptian drawings. Still there after five thousand years, though the mummy in the pyramid disappeared long ages ago—the pyramid tomb having been looted by grave robbers and its contents carried off as plunder.

In the religious belief behind all this was the Egyptians' idea of ka. It was thought that each man had a sort of shadow self, his ka, like his physical person, and this extended to his belongings, clothes, utensils. In death his body was preserved, mummified, and surrounded by needful possessions—all complicated, in a vague way, it seems, with the idea of ka.

This idea of ka, the shadow self, may seem strange and remote to us, but it shouldn't. After all, we are familiar with the belief in ghosts, which are still conjured up in spiritualism. A ghost often has the physical semblance of the deceased and may have the proper spectral clothing and astral objects—a shadow self, the shade of a person, both physical and spiritual, ka.

There is one point on which Roman Pliny would be disappointed, if his shade were to return to earth. He gloated over the fact that the kings who built such vast monuments to their vanity had been forgotten—not even their names remembered. That was true in his day, but not any more. Reading Egyptian history from the hieroglyphic inscriptions, the scholars of today could tell him that the Great Pyramid was built by Khufu, whom the Greeks called Cheops. The Second, by Khafra. As for the Third, the smallest, that would irk Pliny most of all. He rejoiced in the notion that it had been put up by the courtesan Rhodopis—that only her name was remembered. But now he would be told that the Third Pyramid at Gizeh was built by the Pharaoh Menkaura.

In his account Pliny gives attention to the Sphinx, and notes the mystery and silence which surrounded that giant, enigmatic effigy.

"In front of these pyramids is the Sphinx, a still more wondrous object of art, but one upon which silence has been observed, as it is looked upon as a divinity by the people of the neighbourhood. It was hewn from the solid rock; and from a feeling of veneration, the face of the monster is coloured red."

Today, no trace of red remains on the face of the Sphinx. The mystery and silence are less. Hieroglyphic inscriptions show that the Sphinx at Gizeh represented the sun god Harmachis, on guard in the vicinity of the pyramid tombs.

Five hundred years before Pliny's time Herodotus had written about the Pyramids, and in some respects he was better informed than the Roman encyclopedist half a millennium later. He knew the Great Pyramid was built by Cheops, to whom he gives an exceedingly bad reputation, and retails a bit of scandal:

"The wickedness of Cheops reached to such a pitch that, when he had spent all his treasures and wanted more, he sent his daughter to the stews, with orders to procure him a certain sum —how much I cannot say, for I was not told; she procured it, however, and at the same time, bent on leaving a monument which should perpetuate her own memory, she required each man who sought intercourse to make her a present of a stone towards the works which she contemplated."

With these stones, adds Herodotus, the Pharaoh's daughter built a Pyramid for herself.

Herodotus loved a good story, but he can't quite swallow the yarn about the third of the three Pyramids.

"Some of the Greeks call it the work of Rhodopis the courtesan, but they report falsely. It seems to me that these persons cannot have any real knowledge of who Rhodopis was; otherwise they would scarcely have ascribed to her a work on which uncounted treasures, so to speak, must have been expended. Rhodopis . . . was a Thracian by birth, and was the slave of Iadmon. . . . Aesop, the fable-writer, was one of her fellow-slaves.

"Rhodopis really arrived in Egypt under the conduct of Xantheus the Samian. She was brought there to exercise her trade, but was redeemed for a vast sum by Charaxus, a Mytilenaean . . . brother of Sappho the poetess. After thus obtaining her freedom, she remained in Egypt, and as she was very beautiful, amassed great wealth, for a courtesan; not, however, enough to enable her to erect such a work as this pyramid."

# Chapter 5

WHEN I MET the camera crew in Cairo, they had been on the filming job for weeks, traveling far and wide, making pictures of wonders. They really could travel. Hopping from continent to continent was a minor matter. They had their own special air transport, clipper *Cinerama,* an air liner assigned to us by Pan American World Airways, and fitted out for the Cinerama job.

They had gone out with a Hollywood director. We used top-flight directors from movieland for various phases of the filming. The first was Ted Tetzlaff, who had worked on the first part of the job, but he had fallen ill and gone home, and had been followed by Andrew Marton. Our chief Cinerama camerman was Harry Squire, a veteran of the camera who had begun with newsreel and adventured for years in the often exciting business of film. Harry is of the hard-boiled tradition of movie making, with a gravelly voice and untrammeled vocabulary.

They had been making pictures in Europe, where they had followed the trail of the classics. For this what better beginning than Mount Olympus, home of the gods of Greece? Seen from the air, the vista is one of a lofty, flattish summit, not very craggy, with billowing clouds hanging over that Homeric site. You might imagine the Olympian divinities: Jupiter with his thunderbolts, Apollo and his golden lyre, and Aphrodite, goddess of love, of whom old Homer sang. Then, from Mount Olympus, on past other classical sites.

"In Athens," Harry Squire reported, "I shot a lot of rocks."

That was no way to speak of the Parthenon, which was the glory of Athens when Athens was the glory of civilization. But, alas, there was only too much truth in Harry's descriptions. Of the Parthenon, masterpiece of classical architecture, only a skeleton is left. The columns with the architraves across their tops remain standing. It is a beautiful shell vividly suggestive of what the Parthenon once was. Around are fragments of fallen masonry and other ruins. Rocks, as Harry Squire said—relics of a cultural tragedy.

The Parthenon was constructed in the Athens of Pericles as a temple to the goddess Athena, called Parthenos, the virgin. After the triumph of Christianity it was turned into a church. When the Turks conquered Greece they made it into a mosque. During the long centuries it suffered from the hand of time and from human hands, but the masterpiece of architecture and sculpture, though roofless, was otherwise intact when the tragedy came in the year A.D. 1687.

The Turks were at war with the republic of Venice, which set out to expel them from Greece, and succeeded temporarily. The Venetian commander was an admiral, a sea hero in his day, Morosini, whose troops occupied Sparta and the Peloponnesus, and attacked the Turks in Athens.

The Acropolis, on which the Parthenon stood, was a rocky eminence which had been the citadel of Athens in the earliest days. The classical period had lavished its genius for architecture on it. The hilltop was the site of exquisite shrines, of which the temple to Athena was the principal gem. The Acropolis was a natural strong-point for defense, and the Turks used it as a fortress against the Venetians. They had a gunpowder magazine in the Parthenon.

The Venetians bombarded them. War has its barbarous vandalism, but it seems most unfitting of all for Venice to have bombarded the Acropolis—Venice itself a gem and home of the arts, which not long before had given to the world of painting Tintoretto, Veronese, Titian. The artillery of these days was primitive, but the guns could hurl bombshells. One of these struck

[ 46 ]

the Parthenon and touched off the powder magazine inside. The explosion rent the building, shattered the walls, and demolished the interior. What was left was standing columns with architraves and fallen masses of masonry and masterpieces of sculpture.

The story relates how Morosini, upon capturing Athens, was stricken with grief when he beheld the explosion-shattered wreckage of the Parthenon. Reared to venerate the arts of antiquity, he exclaimed: "O Athens, O nursery of the arts! to what hast thou come!"

The Venetian admiral tried to salvage something of the ruins, but that only made matters worse. Masterpieces of sculpture were further damaged by being mishandled in unskillful attempts to remove them.

The epilogue to the tragedy comes at the beginning of the nineteenth century. The British ambassador to Constantinople, Lord Elgin, made an arrangement with the sultan whereby he obtained the right to remove sculptured marble from the wreckage of the Parthenon. Much of this was taken to England, and is now one of the greatest treasures of the British Museum—the Elgin Marbles.

Clearly the Parthenon belonged on our modern list, ancient though it was. The Pyramids and the Sphinx remain wonders of the modern world. In our quest we'd film some of the magnificent ruins of times gone by, along with things ultramodern.

The question suggests itself—why was not the Parthenon included among the Seven Ancient Wonders? It stood in pristine glory on the Acropolis when the selection was made. The answer would seem to be—magnitude. If you scan the ancient list, you'll note that everything on it was huge, colossal—like the Colossus. Apparently the Greeks of the Alexandrian period preferred things bigger and better—sounds like us today. The proportions of the Parthenon were of classic moderation, in the Athenian spirit of harmony and restraint. Not big enough, maybe.

From Athens the trail led to Italy, where our air crew, flown and directed by Paul Mantz, filmed that architectural curiosity, the Leaning Tower of Pisa. One hundred and seventy-nine feet high, it's a gem of architecture that tilts over so far, you wonder how it stands up. Erected in the thirteenth century, it's the bell tower, the campanile, of the cathedral.

Italy is full of bell towers, cousins of the church steeple. In the Middle Ages, wanting to swing the bells high, the builders would put up a tower near the church. In northern Europe Gothic architecture evolved with its lofty, soaring style, and the towering spire became the belfry. Italy, for the most part, remained faithful to the campanile.

In Pisa the bell tower was built on an insecure foundation and began to lean at an early date. A century and a quarter ago it was fifteen and a half feet off perpendicular, now it is sixteen and a half feet. Modern engineering is employed to keep the Leaning Tower of Pisa from toppling over.

From the air we also got a masterpiece of Gothic—Mont St. Michel. Along the coast of Normandy, this Shrine of the Sea appears to soar out of the English Channel. On an island, a lofty mass of granite, the Normans of old built a monastery which was also a fortress.

It was typical of the warlike race that they should be devoted to St. Michael, the archangel with the fiery sword.

The Abbey of Mont St. Michel, a place of pilgrimage, a holy shrine, was at the same time a stronghold that stood many a siege. Today, with its lofty walls and slender spires, it seems to express the spirit of the Norman knight, dedicated to war and religion.

The ancient list of Seven Wonders immortalized architecture and sculpture, edifices and statues, all the works of man. But we planned to expand this. In a departure from tradition, we proposed to include natural as well as man-made wonders. What more proper, as a wonder of nature, than that most famous of all volcanoes? We got aerial pictures of the pageant of the Bay of Naples, passing the excavations of Pompeii and Herculaneum, and on to the summit of the historic fire-mountain.

At the beginning of the Christian Era, Vesuvius had been a sleeping volcano for centuries. At its foot flourished wealthy cities, Pompeii, Herculaneum, never dreaming the quiet mountain might be a stupendous bomb of nature. But in the year A.D. 79 came a series of earthquakes, and on August 24, Vesuvius exploded. The eruption overwhelmed the nearby towns with volcanic ash and lava, and Pompeii and Herculaneum became tragic names.

There was a Roman naval station near Cape Misenum, the northern tip of the Bay of Naples, and there the admiral of the fleet was Gaius Plinius Secundus, that same Pliny who wrote the *Natural History*. He was, throughout his career, a public official, able and conscientious. That he could, at the same time, be so voluminous and encyclopedic a writer was because of prodigious study and scholarly industry. His nephew, Pliny the Younger, relates an odd example of this. He says that, as a youth, he was reproved by his uncle for walking, the elder Pliny explaining that while riding one could also read.

When he learned of the volcanic eruption the author of the *Natural History,* with his insatiable curiosity, took a ship across the bay to investigate the extraordinary phenomenon. On this expedition he perished, as related by the younger Pliny in a famous letter to the historian Tacitus.

When he arrived at the shore near Herculaneum, showers of ashes were falling, and the fire-belching mountain was shrouded with smoke and volcanic fumes. Pliny surveyed the terrifying spectacle, landed with a party of companions, and made his way to the house of a friend nearby. There he spent the night. The eruption grew more violent, and in the morning they left the house, which seemed about to collapse from the shaking of the earth. The scene was a nightmare with clouds of falling ashes. The younger Pliny writes:

"It was now day everywhere else, but there a deeper darkness prevailed than in the most obscure night; relieved, however, by many torches and divers illuminations. They thought proper to go down upon the shore to observe from close at hand if they could possibly put out to sea, but they found the waves still ran extremely high and contrary.

"There my uncle having thrown himself down upon a disused

sail repeatedly called for, and drank, a draught of cold water; soon after, flames, and a strong smell of sulphur, which was the forerunner of them, dispersed the rest of the company in flight; him they only aroused. He raised himself up with the assistance of two of his slaves, but instantly fell; some unusually gross vapour, as I conjecture, having obstructed his breathing and blocked his windpipe, which was not only naturally weak and constricted, but chronically inflamed.

"When day dawned again (the third from that he last beheld) his body was found entire and uninjured, and still fully clothed as in life; its posture was that of a sleeping, rather than a dead man."

# Chapter 6

Our climax in Europe was in Rome, which was not surprising. Rome is the one city in the world that has had an imposing and continuous history, without a break, through the succession of ancient, medieval, Renaissance, and modern times. There are wonders left from the days of the Caesars, the Popes of the Middle Ages, the Renaissance artists, and, of course, Rome to-day is a modern metropolis. No wonder they call it—Eternal City.

It was a time, moreover, of especial splendor. The Roman Catholic Church was celebrating the Marian year, honoring the Virgin Mother of the Saviour, with superb ritual. A more propitious occasion could not have been selected for grandeur reminiscent of the days when the world knew how to be magnificent.

We began with that structure which symbolizes Rome in such a striking way—the Colosseum. It was built in the first century A.D. and, in a way, is a monument to the hatred inspired by Nero. One of the extravagances of the tyrant was to build a vast and sumptuous palace for himself in the heart of Rome—the Golden House, with spacious gardens. After his downfall and death the Golden House was torn down, as if to obliterate the memory of Nero, and on the site of its gardens the great amphitheatre was constructed by the emperors Vespasian and Titus. It is estimated to have seated forty to fifty thousand spectators.

There the gladiators fought. The savage sport of the arena was the rage throughout the Roman Empire, and the Colosseum became its principal center. The degree of bloodshed sometimes seems incredible. We read that in a prolonged triumph celebrated by the Emperor Trajan, which lasted for many days, five thousand pairs of gladiators fought.

They were prisoners of war, condemned criminals, slaves. Yet we hear of free citizens volunteering for the profession of fighting in the arena for the excitement of it and the glory. A champion gladiator was a popular hero hailed and feted more than a prize-ring champion of today.

In the Colosseum where Christian martyrs were thrown to the lions all was in accordance with a common mode of legal execution—that of a condemned criminal being thrown to the wild beasts in the arena. So, in the persecutions, the martyrdom of Christians was made a show for the crowd.

Tradition tells us that the bloody spectacles in the Colosseum came to an end in an episode of gladiators and a Christian martyr. Even after the Roman Empire became officially Christian the gladiatorial games continued. Then in the Colosseum one day, while the combats were being held, a Christian monk leaped into the arena, intervened between gladiators, and in the name of Christian morality forbade the savage spectacle. The enraged crowd set upon him and killed him, the last of the martyrs in the Colosseum. This brought about an imperial decree abolishing the spectacle of the gladiators.

The great amphitheatre remained, defying time and human destruction. In the Dark Ages the robber barons of Rome used the Colosseum as a quarry from which to obtain stone to build their palaces. Yet, in spite of this, much of the massive bulk of the structure still stands.

Nearby, the Roman Forum, with its arches and columns, reminds us that this for centuries was the political center of the classical world. The Forum was ornate with temples and triumphal arches. There stood the Senate House, where Cicero and Caesar debated in that august governing body, the Roman Senate. And the open space of the Forum was the meeting place of the Assembly of the people; where the mass of the citizens gathered to vote on the enactment of laws and to elect public officials, the consuls, praetors, and aediles.

As you stand in the Forum today, you may note one thing that tells volumes about a political problem that led to the end of the Roman Republic, the beginning of the Roman Empire. You may remark the size of the open space, about equal to a city block. But it was big enough for the Assembly of the people, the gathering of the citizens, legally the final authority, though the Senate assumed the administration. This was the government of the vast realm extending from Mesopotamia to the Atlantic, with a population of many millions and many great cities.

Rome began as a city-state, and the Forum was the market place. The political institutions were much like those of a municipality in our own time—the electorate which gathered in a body and voted, the town council which became the mighty Roman Senate, and the elected magistrates. This was proper for the government of the city but became obsolete when an empire was won.

It was as if our forty-eight states were governed by the municipal administration of New York City, and the local New York voters were the final political authority for the whole country. The Roman Republic was just that, in an exaggerated way. For the Assembly of the people became the Roman mob in the Forum, swayed by demagogues and political chicanery, and the Senate became a body of oligarchs. But the Roman Republic could never expand its republican institutions to meet the needs of an empire. The peoples of antiquity never devised representative government. So the republic, after prolonged strife, ended and was followed by one-man government, a species of monarchy, the Roman Empire.

These are your reflections when you gaze at the Forum today, and note the small space that contained the town voters, the Populus Romanus, who aspired to be the rulers of most of the then known world.

The stately wonder in Rome today is, of course, St. Peter's, with Michelangelo's majestic dome. But my plan was that we would not present this largest church in the world as mere architecture. The ceremonies of the Marian year were being concluded and would end in a blaze of glory with a papal procession and a blessing by Pope Pius XII for a vast throng in the square of St. Peter's. This could be a magnificent opportunity.

In New York I had approached Cardinal Spellman, asking his aid for the necessary permission at the Vatican to capture the ceremony for the vast Cinerama screen. He had given us every help, had communicated with the Vatican, and had provided us with introductions to the proper authorities at the papal court. Cardinal Spellman was indeed helpful, but I wonder if he ever guessed just how much we would ask for in Rome?

Cinerama equipment is bulky, and its requirements are exacting. It needs cumbersome installation, and is something to get in the way of orderly proceedings. Moreover, we intended to do an exhaustive job. We wouldn't just film a procession. In addition to the pageant in the open piazza, why not take Cinerama into the interior of St. Peter's, which had never before been lighted for films? For this the Cinerama camera would require an immense lot of lighting. But we wanted to get pictures of a papal procession inside the cathedral, as well as in the piazza outside. Further, we'd like to film the Pontiff in more intimate close-ups at Castel Gandolfo, the papal summer residence outside Rome. This might have seemed enough. But we even hoped to have a bit of light relief running through the majestic ceremonies.

British playwright William Lipscomb, an old friend of mine who had worked with Bernard Shaw, was helping us, and he devised a little story with comedy and pathos. A child has been ill, and his parents, a funny Giovanni and Maria, are thankful for his recovery, so they want to take him to the papal benediction. But they are delayed by comic misadventure, and the ceremony is over by the time they get there. Apparently, all they can do is offer a prayer at the high altar of the empty cathedral.

They do this, but then a prelate tells them that the Pope has gone to Castel Gandolfo, where he is to give a special blessing. If they hurry, they may be in time for that. They do hurry, and

[54]

nearly miss out again. But they just make it, and the little boy receives the blessing.

You might have thought it impossible to have the Roman Pontiff in a comic film story, but that was the idea.

The character of our proceedings was well stated by Bill Lipscomb in a report that he made later. Bill, the complete Londoner, has been in the United States a good deal—for some years a top film writer in Hollywood. But Bill is too delightfully British ever to become habituated completely to our American ways. He reported:

"When I first joined that strange collection of odd souls known as the Cinerama Unit in Rome, in November 1954, I thought they seemed the nicest bunch of thugs I had been mixed up with for a long time. When it was explained that the idea was to shoot the interior of St. Peter's with lights and a sound truck whilst the service was going on, I knew they were mad and what they expected was impossible. But I was delighted. Here were people in pursuit of the Holy Grail.

"When they explained they also wanted a close-up of the Pope himself, giving a blessing, I knew they were indeed mad. As my old mother used to say, 'What will they think of next?' Americans think up the nicest ideas even though they seem impossible in practice. The picture in my mind was that of His Holiness being confronted with a camera that weighed about two thirds of a ton, and his being asked to watch for the dickeybird. It sounded pleasantly fantastic.

"But it happened. Whilst I was saying it couldn't be done, the great event—the impossible—took place. The next thing I knew we had combed Italy for all the 'lights' in the country, installed them right *in* St. Peter's Church, arranged for generators and goodness knows what else, and there, with a full congregation of about fifty thousand people, was our strange band of technicians, lights, sound equipment, recording for the first time in history a service in St. Peter's—a chief ceremony of the Marian Year.

"There still remained that close-up of the Pope. I never thought they'd ever get that. But they did, and at his private residence at Gandolfo, on the hilltop. In the little square, a scaffold about twenty feet high was erected just opposite the little balcony on which the Pope comes to give a special blessing to the few who obtain permission. It must have been astonishing for the little crowd of about a hundred who had come for the blessing—astonishing to find a platform twenty feet high, with a dozen sweating American technicians led by the busiest cameraman in the world, Harry Squire.

"But if the crowd was astonished it was nothing to the amazement of the Pope himself. After all, he was coming out on his balcony to give a blessing as he had done a thousand times before. When he came out this time he found himself confronted with a monstrous camera, weighing about fifteen hundredweight, and looking something like a space ship. It was such a shock that he even hesitated over the blessing.

"Harry Squire, perfectionist as he is, could hardly ask a Pope for a retake! But, fortunately, the Pope himself is a perfectionist. He went back into his room and told his staff that he didn't think that was very satisfactory; could he do it again! And so he came out once more and performed the blessing of the crowd all over again—a magnificent austere figure indeed.

"I had been fiddling around with the story of the little family trying to get to St. Peter's for the blessing, and being delayed everywhere en route. Now the tale of the three little pilgrims could come to a happy ending.

"How Maynard Miller ever persuaded the Vatican authorities to agree to all this is his secret."

Maynard Malcolm Miller, a member of our Cinerama expedition, had previously been connected with the exploration of glaciers. Several years before this I had spent some time with a scientific expedition he had headed on a lofty glacier in Alaska. Mountain ice may sound cool, but no cooler than Maynard's diplomacy had to be in Rome.

Officials at the Vatican were the more cautious because Pope Pius was just recovering from a grave illness, which had had him at death's door. Later on the account was in the news of how, as he prayed, thinking his last moment had come, he had a vision of the Saviour. It seemed hardly the time to plague the Pontiff with our Cinerama requirements. But Maynard, armed with the recommendation from Cardinal Spellman, negotiated the arrangements.

The technical difficulties in all this were huge, particularly the lighting of the interior of St. Peter's for filming. Here's Maynard Miller's report:

"St. Peter's is the largest single room in the world. Upon inquiring about the possibility of filming inside the basilica, it seemed that permission would be next to impossible because it would require banks of lights and would break all precedent. But I was eventually successful in talking the authorities into it.

"The filming required the use of about seventy huge lights and a number of smaller ones. As I recall, we had to hire something like sixteen large generators to run enough power by cable into the church. The generators were set up on each side of the basilica (outside) and thousands of feet of cable strung through the burial vaults and along hidden passageways underneath the main part of St. Peter's in order to place the lights at strategic places. It was an almost impossible task to get enough light into this massive dark building to do the job. Then we had to build a series of ten- to twenty-foot scaffolds for each set of lights. To add to our burden, because of religious ceremonies constantly taking place, we could not work during these periods.

"About 11:30 P.M. Saturday night the local men in the basilica told me that we would have to leave by midnight as the basilica was to be closed. But we were nowhere near ready in our lighting. So again I had to talk them into allowing us to stay on, with the rest to be finished the following day.

"On the Sunday, while the devout were assembling, the lights continued to be put up. One Vatican official was so worried and upset that some one of his superiors would complain that he went away for the day and told me afterwards that he really believed he'd be arrested and placed in the Vatican jail. Every time the hammers started reverberating through the basilica, I really expected some cardinal would demand that the noises be stopped. Somehow sufficient lighting was put up by working right up to an hour before the ceremony began."

The pictures of the interior of St. Peter's turned out to be brilliant. Then, at Castel Gandolfo, they were equally impressive, thanks to the insouciance of Harry Squire, a cameraman not to be obfuscated by anything.

The Pope gave a blessing from a balcony, and the front of the balcony was enclosed by glass. This, for pictures made at close range, reflected glints of light into the camera lens—as Harry Squire discovered while making advance preparations for the filming. Never at a loss for courage, he asked that the glass front be removed from the balcony. The answer was that the glass was there to shield the Pontiff from the autumn drafts, he having been gravely ill and now convalescing. But Harry argued his camera point, and the glass was removed.

He also noted that at the back of the balcony there were glass doors which, when closed, reflected light that interfered with the pictures. It was the custom, when the Pope came out on the balcony to bless the crowd, to close the doors. Harry said they should remain open, and that was conceded. But he took no chances. Some one of the papal entourage might, out of habit, close the doors. He'd have somebody up there to make sure it didn't happen. He'd have two, in fact, one for each glass door, holding it open.

"You see," he told me, "I got these two characters. Tom Conroy, he's my assistant cameraman. Mike Mahoney is the snapper."

"What's a snapper?" I asked.

"Oh, he takes care of baggage and rustles things around. Me, I'm Episcopalian. But Conroy and Mahoney are Catholics. So I arranged for them to be up there back of the balcony. They met the Pope, and kissed his ring, and these two Irishmen will be grateful to me for the rest of their lives."

"So they were standing back of the balcony while the Pope gave the blessing?" I asked.

"Standing?" Harry snorted. "How could I have them standing? They'd be in the picture. They were lying on the floor, holding the doors open. When the Pope walked out on the balcony, there were Conroy and Mahoney on the floor."

I had to laugh at that, and Harry continued:

"In the picture you see the Pope, close up, bless the crowd. Then he goes back in, but he stops, as if he were saying, 'Should I give another blessing?' Actually he's talking to Conroy and Mahoney on the floor. He speaks good English, and he's asking should he do it over. They say yes. I'd have killed them if they didn't. So His Holiness comes out and does a repeat. You'll see it in the pictures."

Leave it to an old-time cameraman to be disconcerted by nothing, not even the august occasion of filming the Pontiff of the Church of Rome. Later I was told that the Pope had remarked: "Americans always want to be sure!" He was so pleased about it all that he gave Mal Miller silver medals for the camera crew.

St. Peter's represents the greatest architectural achievement of the Renaissance. The list of architects who presided over its creation during the course of a century is studded with great names—Bramante, Raphael, Michelangelo and Bernini, who designed the superb colonnade. The majestic edifice is a wonder of the world. And the way it was filmed, that, too, was something of a wonder.

# Chapter 7

Here in the southwest corner of the peninsula," says the *Cambridge Ancient History*, "was Arabia Felix par excellence, the El Dorado of the ancients, a happy land by contrast with the surrounding wastes and by reason of its precious products. From the third century B.C. the kingdom of Saba had been famous in the Mediterranean world as the richest and most powerful state in Arabia.

"Its prosperity was based on the cultivation of the soil and, above all, on the production and export of those aromatic substances—frankincense, myrrh, cinnamon and cassia—so highly prized by the ancient world for religious ceremonial and for the preparation of fragrant unguents, perfumes, spices and medicinal ointments. These articles, as well as gold, precious stones, pearls and other wares, were transported by the Sabaeans by land and sea to Egypt, Palestine and Syria. Greek writers have left glowing descriptions of the wealth and luxury of the Sabaeans."

The above is likely to astonish any present-day traveler who has been to southern Arabia, the Yemen, the Hadramaut. I, myself, have to gape at the description, when I recall what I saw of Arabia Felix, Happy Arabia, as it is now.

This remote region came next in our quest. The goal, some astonishing wonders in the Hadramaut. We flew from Heliopolis, near Cairo, in the big clipper *Cinerama*, on a long air journey down the Red Sea to Aden, the British bastion near the southwestern corner of the Arabian Peninsula. This provided an example of how, with a tape recorder, you can keep an oral diary, with each recording like a page out of a day-by-day journal. Pepys or Boswell might envy the mechanics of it.

"Last night we took off from the air field at Heliopolis bound for South Arabia, the part of Arabia that the Romans called Arabia Felix, Arabia the Blessed, the land of the Queen of Sheba, ancient land of frankincense and myrrh. At Heliopolis, I remembered that in the days of the Pharaohs here was located the University of Ahn (On), which Moses is said to have attended.

"Crossing the southern end of the Suez Canal, we flew over the Red Sea right about where the Israelites made that fabulous crossing on dry land, and then on past Mount Sinai, where Moses went up to the mountaintop and received the Ten Commandments from Jehovah.

"And then on through the night we flew through a sky full of stars, shining only as stars can shine over the Arabian desert. We were above, to me, rather familiar country now, a region full of memories, memories of the days when I was with Lawrence of Arabia. Skirting the Hejaz, the part of Arabia that includes the two most sacred and forbidden Moslem cities, Mecca and Medina, we swept on south, past the Yemen, a closed country, a country over which no airplanes are supposed to fly except those owned by the Yemen king, Imam Ahmed Seif el-Islam. Off to our right, only a few miles away, the African coast of Eritrea and French Somaliland. Below us the treacherous waters of the Strait of Bab el Mandeb.

"Rounding the cape that marks the southern end of the Red Sea, in a few minutes dead ahead we saw the brilliant lights of a new huge British oil refinery at Aden. No response to our radio calls. That seemed strange, Aden air field apparently closed for the night. And it's just one long narrow runway, down a peninsula that stretches out into an arm of the Arabian Sea. The lights around it were exceedingly dim, but we made it.

"One thousand three hundred miles non-stop from Cairo to a place which some regard as the end of the world."

If a professor of ancient history happens to read of this flight down the Red Sea, he might be inclined to sigh, "Alas, Aelius Gallus," recalling the Roman general who led a calamitous military march down the Arabian shore of the Red Sea in the days of Caesar Augustus. Aelius Gallus set out to conquer Arabia Felix, the kingdom of Saba, and what happened to his expedition is tragic to read. I looked up the story, and could only groan.

I have no doubt that Aelius Gallus was a competent commander of legions. That he was a man of education and intellect is clear. He was an intimate friend of the learned geographer Strabo, who got an account of the luckless adventure from him. I myself have never commanded a military force, least of all a Roman legion, but even I could correct the strategy of Aelius Gallus. To anyone who has traveled in Arabia it was a fine example of how not to wage a war. It was a classic of not knowing the country, the climate, the difficulties, the diseases.

His point of departure was Egypt, and one obvious plan of campaign would have been for the Roman general to take his army via the Nile to southern Egypt, which had harbors not too far from the coast of the Sabean kingdom, then across the narrow water for a landing. Instead, Aelius Gallus had his troops ferried across near Suez to a northern port about nine hundred miles north of the Sabean capital. This had the advantage of landing at a friendly harbor, while farther south the coast was hostile. But it meant a march of hundreds of miles across the blistering desert of the Hejaz before reaching the rich lands of Happy Arabia.

To make matters the more astounding, the campaign was undertaken in the summer. If you want to adventure at all in Arabia, winter is the time. The burning summer can beat you. The Roman army, mustered at the northern Red Sea port, was attacked by tropical diseases endemic in those parts and by scurvy because of a lack of vegetables. Soon they were in no condition for a campaign, and waited through the summer, while supplies were brought in and conditions improved. They waited, in fact, all through the winter. You'd suppose the idea

The interior of St. Peter's provides an appropriate setting for the brilliant pageantry of traditional Catholic ceremonies.

The Swiss Guards at Castel Gandolfo. Their uniform, designed by Michelangelo, is the most famous in the world.

Arabia—land of desolation, lush oases, sand, oil, and Cadillacs.

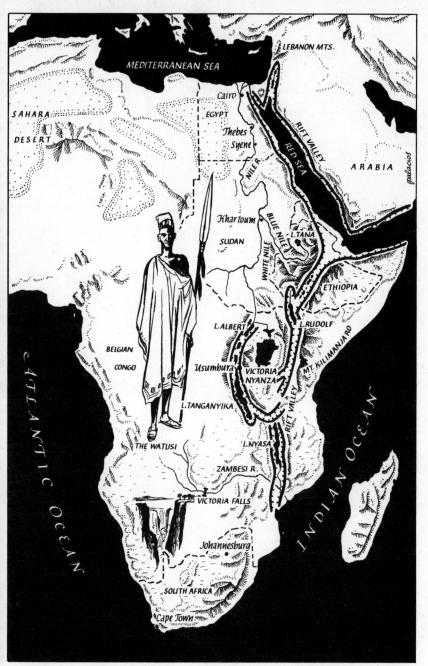

MEDITERRANEAN SEA

LEBANON MTS.

Cairo

EGYPT

SAHARA
DESERT

Thebes
Syene

NILE

RED SEA

RIFT VALLEY

ARABIA

palacios

Khartoum

SUDAN

WHITE NILE

BLUE NILE

L.TANA

ETHIOPIA

L.ALBERT

L.RUDOLF

BELGIAN

CONGO

Usumbura

VICTORIA
NYANZA

MT. KILIMANJARO

L.TANGANYIKA

RIFT VALLEY

THE WATUSI

L.NYASA

ZAMBESI R.

VICTORIA FALLS

Johannesburg

SOUTH AFRICA

Cape Town

ATLANTIC OCEAN

INDIAN OCEAN

Africa. The heavy black lines show the extent of the Rift Valley, a deep
depression formed in prehistoric times by a great convulsion which rup-
tured the earth's surface for about four thousand miles.

Young trainees at the elephant school in the Congo.

The African elephant herd, from which the natives capture baby elephants to train.

Photo by Edwin W. Sippel

*The burning desolation leading to the forbidding desert on the edge of the Rub al Kahli.*

Photo by Edwin W. Sippel

*Arabia is ringed by desolate mountains which enclose the blistering desert. Here and there on a summit we see a fortress village.*

Photo by Edwin W. Sippel

*A microphone records the conversation of Sherif Hussein as he talks with the author.*

*The skyscraper city of Shibam is in the middle of the sun-baked desert, but situated at an oasis as the vegetation indicates.*   Photo by Edwin W. Sippel

*The architecture is Islamic and would not look out of place in Syria or Egypt.*
Photos by Edwin W. Sippel

*The camel's padded feet are well suited to desert sand. In a skyscraper city of Hadramaut.*

*Unloading grain from boats that ply the Nile is still done according to primitive techniques.*

Photos by Edwin W. Sippel

*Another skyscraper city, Seiyum, and the Sultan's palace. The craggy mesa looks rather like those of our own American Southwest.*

was to be sure the march through the desert was made in summer.

They started out in the spring of 24 B.C., some ten thousand men, heavy infantry and auxiliaries. This sounds like a legion of six thousand, with cavalry, light troops, and others, like archers and slingers. For the legionaries, with their heavy armor, the march through the desert must have been doubly a nightmare.

Day after day they trudged across the sands. Water had to be carried on camelback. Progress was slow. Even at best a Roman legion proceeded with ponderous deliberation, and the plodding camels carrying the water were not rapid. Finally they came to the country of a people called the Aretas, tribes of the Hejaz, who proved friendly but could provide little food and little water. It took the army a month to cross the thirsty country of the Aretas. Then they made their way across a hostile desert for fifty days before they came to the border of the Sabean kingdom.

There they found a city called Negrama, which they captured. Days later they encountered a hostile force, which they defeated easily. The Arabs were no match for the power of the legion. Then they advanced on a city which the Roman records call Mariba, and besieged it. But they couldn't capture it. Attempts to storm the walls failed, and they couldn't take the time for regular Roman siege operations. Water failed, and after six days thirst forced them to give it up and retreat.

Some have supposed that this Mariba was the Sabean capital of Marib, some distance east of San'a, which is now the capital of the Yemen. But scholars point out that Marib was the place of the giant dam and reservoir on which much of the fertility of Sabean country was based. The Roman army would have found no lack of water there. Probably the town they failed to capture was some other place. From the story of thirst it would seem that they never did get into the happy part of Happy Arabia.

The Romans believed that, on this frightful march, they were betrayed by treacherous guides, but it may have been a mere case of trying to find a way through unknown country, through the bewildering desolation. In any case, they got out much faster than they came in. Aelius Gallus must have learned something of the topography. Strabo relates:

"He accomplished on his return journey the whole distance in sixty days in which, on his first journey, he had consumed six months." The historian adds that Aelius Gallus "arrived at Alexandria with as much as could be saved. The remainder of his army he lost, not by the enemy, but by disease, fatigue, famine and marches through bad roads; for only seven men perished in battle."

The peoples of antiquity regarded the expedition as a calamity, and the Romans never again sent a legionary army into the depths of the Arabian desert.

Probably the expedition had as much to do with trade as with outright conquest. The Sabeans, in addition to their traffic in frankincense and other spices, had a dominant position in the trade with India. Ships brought cargoes from India to South Arabian ports, where the merchandise was taken by camel caravan and transported along the land trail to Syria and Egypt, thence across the Mediterranean to Italy, Syria, Greece, and Gaul.

There was an all-water route from India to Egypt via the Red Sea, but that was beset by difficulties of navigation and piracy. The land route was preferred until the time of Augustus, when a great discovery in navigation was made. Greek sea captains of the Roman Empire learned to ride the monsoon.

The subcontinent of Hindustan is like a huge heating plant. In the summer India heats up, and masses of heated air rise. This creates an area of low pressure, and air is drawn in from the adjacent seas. Winds blow toward the land. In winter the subcontinent cools off, the process is reversed, and the wind blows from land to sea. That's the theory of the monsoon, though there are complications. In any case, on the western side of India a summer wind blows across the Arabian Sea to the coast of India. In the winter a wind blows away from India.

Thus it was possible to sail from the entrance of the Red Sea, for a voyage on the wind blowing toward India, and then return six months later on the wind blowing away from India. This system of navigation is said to have been practiced first by a Greek sea captain named Hippalus, and established the all-water trade route via the Red Sea.

The Sabeans held the eastern side of the narrow Red Sea entrance. This would provide good reason for attempting to establish control of Arabia Felix. After the failure of Aelius Gallus, the Romans, using naval power, safeguarded the sea route by holding strategic points along the coast, which enabled them to dominate the Red Sea and suppress piracy. They occupied positions on both the African and the Asiatic sides of the strait. On the Asiatic side they seized Aden, which they called Attana.

It was the establishment of the sea route that brought about the ruin of Happy Arabia. The profitable Indian trade lost, the Sabean kingdom declined in wealth and power and in time succumbed to the attacks of enemies. Then, in the course of centuries, most of Arabia Felix reverted to desert.

# Chapter 8

I STOPPED in Aden for several days and picked up bits of news for my radio program back home. There was no lack of bizarre things to relate, because this is, and long has been, a city where anything can happen, at one of the rowdiest corners on earth. What I had to report was not Arabian Nights enchantment:

"Aden, where I am tonight, is another of the world's boom cities. Aden has been an important trade center for some thousands of years. Although we don't know how long, we do know that the ships of the Pharaohs and of King Solomon came here. Now, however, may be the biggest boom in Aden's history.

"With the British pulling out of Egypt, this city, more than one thousand miles to the south of Suez, here at the southern end of the Red Sea, has become the chief British port in this part of the world. In fact the boom has been so swift that Aden almost overnight has jumped to the front as the third seaport in the British Commonwealth in tonnage of ships handled.

"Commissioner of Police John Vinson tells me that Aden has a daily floating population of over one hundred thousand, mostly men. They sleep on string beds, charpoys, which they rent. They just put 'em up anywhere in the streets at night, mostly in the section of Aden called The Crater, a desolate pocket surrounded by peaks that look like the mountains on the moon.

"You can surmise the crime and problems that arise with a

floating population of over a hundred thousand. For instance, Commissioner Vinson one night found himself in the midst of a pitched battle. One thousand five hundred Somalis were attacked by eight thousand local Arabs. An engineering firm of San Francisco had just finished building one of the world's largest and most modern refineries here for the British Petroleum Company. Somalis, who are natural technicians, had been brought in from Africa and given the choice jobs. The local Arabs naturally resented this and finally the whole thing exploded, eight thousand Arabs attacking one thousand five hundred Somalis, the fighting lasting all one night with more than four hundred casualties.

"And then the dope problem is one of the toughest. A drug called kat is flown in from Ethiopia. The people here chew the leaves. It gives them temporary courage or visions of bliss.

"Then there was a recent race riot. The police commissioner tells me some two hundred were killed before they broke it up.

"Local legend has it that this region was the original Garden of Eden—Aden, Eden. Here they point out the tomb of Cain, son of Adam and Eve, who committed the first murder when he killed his brother Abel. And since then the 'mark of Cain' seems to have been on this region, desolate and for most of the year a fiery furnace. Ever since Cain slew Abel the Aden corner of Araby has been a land of blood feuds."

Southwest Arabia is haunted by a famous name. In the harbor of Aden there's a station for dhows, known locally as the Queen of Sheba's Boat Yard. There you'll see, lying at anchor, or moving under sail, scores of seagoing Arabian craft, made of teakwood from the Malabar coast, the same sturdily constructed dhows that for ages have navigated—and still do—along the trade routes of the East. On the land side, leading into Aden, there is a canyon through the mountains, like a long corridor, which they call King Solomon's Gate. This the trains of camels have traversed for ages, along the caravan trail to the north.

To the north, in the Yemen, are the ruins of the ancient city of Marib, supposed to have been the Queen of Sheba's capital. Across the narrow water, in East Africa, the King of Ethiopia calls himself a descendant of the Queen of Sheba. The legend is that a son of that renowned lady crossed over to East Africa and founded the royal line of Ethiopia.

So what about this legended queen? Who was she? And what about her visit to King Solomon? Scholars have considerable doubt.

The Bible, telling of the wisdom of Solomon, says:

"And when the queen of Sheba heard of the fame of Solomon concerning the name of the Lord, she came to prove him with hard questions.

"And she came to Jerusalem with a very great train, with camels that bare spices, and very much gold, and precious stones. . . .

"And she gave the king an hundred and twenty talents of gold, and of spices very great store, and precious stones: there came no more such abundance of spices as these which the queen of Sheba gave to king Solomon."

Legend relates the biblical account of the kingdom of Saba, land of frankincense, and makes the Queen of Sheba a Sabean queen. But the dates seem difficult, and the question is raised— would the queen of a realm rich and powerful have paid so worshipful a visit to the distant king of a small Palestinian state? One supposition is that the Queen of Sheba may have belonged to some lesser principality not far to the south of Palestine, along the frankincense caravan route, and might plausibly make a pilgrimage to a Palestinian king. That later traditions magnified the story by attaching it to the kingdom of Saba, thereby enhancing the glory of Solomon.

Much of such legend comes from the Arabs, whose Islamic religion is derived largely from the Bible. They love to embroider on biblical themes and name places as biblical sites. However, those regions of Yemen and Hadramaut do seem haunted by the memory of the Queen of Sheba and King Solomon.

They are haunted likewise by no end of present troubles. My recorded travel diary says:

"Arriving here in Southwest Arabia, we seem to have run head-on into a small war. So far as I know, nothing about it has reached the outside world. The fighting for the most part is between the Mausatta and the Shahabi, in a wild region north of Aden, in the sultanate of Yafa, stirred up, so rumor has it, by the Yemenis, who say it is actually a part of Yemen.

"Yemen, a rich country of Southwest Arabia, is in fact a fabulous country and the rulers of the Yemen have as little as possible to do with the outside world. Travelers are seldom welcome there. It's almost as rarely visited by Westerners as Tibet. The story of how this fighting has come about seems complicated to us.

"Before World War I the Turks claimed nearly all of Arabia as part of the Ottoman Empire and then they lost it in that war. The British had a treaty with Turkey regarding a boundary between their Aden Protectorate and the Yemen, but the Yemenis refused to recognize that treaty. And then, in 1948, the British and the Yemenis got together and they made a deal to maintain a border status quo.

"Of course it had to be written in Arabic and the story is that the British at Aden were so eager to settle that they were not too careful when the agreement was put into Arabic. Result—the rulers of Yemen, Imam Ahmed and his brother, Al Hassem, the Prime Minister, now say that the status quo included not only the southern Yemen border but also all of the thirty or forty sultanates in the vast area of southern and southwestern Arabia over which the British claim to have a protectorate. So the Yemenis are blamed for stirring up the present border war, trying to make it tough for the British. Why? Because they don't think the British are going to be here forever. They see what has been happening to the British Empire, so the Yemen rulers propose to be ready to take over when and if they get a chance."

On the Red Sea coast of the Yemen there's a decrepit old town called Mokka. Another and more familiar spelling is Mocha. The ancient kingdom of Saba may have had its frankincense, but the more modern principality of Yemen has its coffee, and for many years Mocha was the world's chief coffee port. The aromatic bean is native to Ethiopia, where the

[ 69 ]

coffee tree grows wild. But the original home of coffee cultivation was the Yemen.

The history of the fragrant beverage is decidedly modern. Coffee is identified with the Arabs as tea is with the Chinese, but its use seems to have spread among them only since the founding of Islam. The Koran forbade coffee as an intoxicant, but that made little difference. We are told, in fact, that the consumption of coffee was fostered for religious reasons. Pious Moslem teachers drank it to keep awake during prolonged religious exercises.

In western Europe coffee came into vogue only in the seventeenth century. One story relates how an Austrian soldier, captured by the Turks in a siege of Vienna, observed coffee drinking among the Moslems, tried the stuff, learned to like it, and later introduced it in Vienna. In any case, Vienna has long been famous for its coffeehouses. In London and Paris coffeehouses were found toward the end of the seventeenth century, when they speedily became social institutions.

For centuries Yemen was the only source of coffee, but its primacy is a thing of the past. The cultivation of the plant was introduced into the East Indies, and Mocha was superseded by Java as a name for coffee. More recently Brazil became the chief source, and today most of our coffee comes from South America. But the coffee consumed so generally throughout Arabia still comes from Yemen, and the Mocha bean remains the principal export of the old kingdom of coffee.

In 1948, I had occasion to tell on the radio of savage doings in the kingdom of coffee. The aged Imam Yah-Yah was murdered, together with some of his many sons, in a conspiracy hatched by one of his officials, who seized the throne. The usurper was described as a coffee merchant, which seemed to add a characteristic touch. He should have made Mocha his capital.

But the Crown Prince Ahmed survived the massacre and rallied the Bedouin of the desert against the usurper. There was a flurry of fighting, and Ahmed won the desert war. The coffee merchant was decapitated, and so were many of his adherents. Heads fell wholesale in the traditional style of Yemen.

All this was involved with intrigue in the royal family, as is not uncommon where the harem system prevails with its many wives, concubines, and sons. Crown Prince Ahmed, having disposed of the coffee merchant, became the imam, but affairs remained uneasy in the kingdom of coffee. At Aden we heard of sinister court politics of brother against brother.

Shortly after my return home I had news from Yemen to relate on the radio—how a revolt had broken out, led by a royal prince, a brother of Imam Ahmed. The imam was besieged in a desert stronghold by his brother's adherents, but history repeated itself. That previous time Ahmed, as crown prince, had rallied the Bedouin against the coffee merchant. Now the crown prince, Ahmed's son, raised the tribes of the desert. The revolt failed, and again heads fell in Yemen, including that of the imam's rebellious brother.

Today the land of Yemen has long been known for having one of the most troubled, backward governments on earth. But recently the news came of the imam opening the country to American enterprise—Yemen was to be developed, in hopes of finding a wealth of oil.

# Chapter 9

THE MARIB DAM might have had a place on the ancient list of Seven Wonders had the Greeks of the third century B.C. known anything much about it. The Sabeans reared lofty shrines and their capital, the city of Marib, had its architectural glories, but their unique achievement as builders was the dam, which provided irrigation for immense fields in the garden land of Happy Arabia.

Until recently the Marib Dam was little more than a name and a legend surrounded by fantasies of the Arabs. The barrier and reservoir have an atmosphere of Arabian Nights enchantment. But now adventurous Western travelers have brought a good deal of the ancient Sabean kingdom to the light of knowledge, and the Marib Dam has become a reality for archaeologists to investigate.

Several years ago a party of American archaeologists headed by Wendell Phillips and Professor William F. Albright of Johns Hopkins made studies and excavations of ancient ruins in Yemen. Their work of scholarship was cut short by intrigue and violence, and they had to escape in peril of their lives. Nevertheless they were able to make discoveries, and much of their work was near the site of Marib and the fabled dam.

Wendell Phillips, in his book, *Qataban and Sheba*, describes the huge ruins of the temple to the moon god, a shrine of pre-Islamic days, where they found a wealth of inscriptions. They came upon six hundred ancient statues of alabaster, uncovered by the local Yemenis, who had destroyed many old edifices and used the stones for building forts of their own. But the most impressive sight of all was the ruin of the dam.

"Lying a few miles out from the old city," writes Phillips, "it is really a series of dams, sections of which are still standing. . . .

"We saw where whole sections of mountainside had been carved away alongside the dam to form spillways to irrigate the adjacent fields. The dam had served as the central control for the mass of waters pouring down from the mountains of Yemen, the spot from which it was distributed to create mile upon mile of green fields.

"Most amazing was the way the great stone walls had been put together. Huge boulders were so perfectly dressed that they fitted into each other like pieces in a jigsaw puzzle. We saw no trace of mortar of any kind, yet we looked at portions of the wall that were more than fifty feet high, standing as they had when Sheba's great artisans built them about 2,700 years ago.

"Other sections of the vast structure were missing, washed away no doubt by the great Sixth Century cloudburst."

That catastrophe lingered long in Arab legend. The Encyclopedia of Islam says: "There is hardly an historical event in pre-Islamic history that has become embellished with so much that is fanciful, and related in so many versions, as the bursting of the Marib dam."

The Koran relates: "The people of Sheba had beautiful gardens with good fruit. Then the people turned away from God, and to punish them, He burst the dam, turning the good gardens into gardens bearing bitter fruit."

Wendell Phillips passes along an old fable which has a fine flavor of the Arabian Nights. "King Amr was informed by a soothsayer that if he saw a mouse digging into the dam, that would be a sign from God that the huge structure was about to give way. The King then went to the dam and saw a mouse which moved, with its tiny feet, a great stone that could not be budged by fifty men. And the next day the dam burst."

The ruin of Happy Arabia has been ascribed to the bursting of the Marib Dam and Arab historians explain it in that way—the irrigation system was wrecked and gardens reverted to desert. But modern scholars regard the catastrophe as an effect as well as a cause, brought about by a long decline of wealth and civilization. Sabean prosperity was doomed by the change of the trade route at the beginning of the Christian Era, when the Indian trade shifted from the caravan trail to the sea route. During centuries of increasing improverishment the dam was neglected. There were, according to record, leaks and repairs in the earlier years of the Christian Era. Then maintenance was no longer kept up, and in time the Marib Dam went the way of neglected structures.

The ruins of the Marib Dam might have been a wonder for Cinerama to film, but that was impossible. The kingdom of Yemen was closed, a forbidden land. Even if we could have got in, it would have been dubious. The Wendell Phillips expedition, in their misadventure at Marib, had lost valuable equipment. Our Cinerama equipment was complex and costly and not easily replaceable.

The itinerary we had laid out took us to a place in the desert near the eastern border of Yemen. We had an invitation to visit a paramount sheik at the remote oasis of Wadi Beihan, who said he'd put on a show for us. There was no air field at Wadi Beihan capable of accommodating anything like a full-scale Pan American clipper. So we left the clipper *Cinerama* behind at Aden. The crew took a smaller plane to Wadi Beihan, while I went by a more circuitous route, thinking I'd make an aerial sight-seeing jaunt in this land where sights are so strange. This, I reckoned, would provide another entry for my radio travel diary. It did:

"I have just made a trip along what you could call the edge of the unknown, a flight across a country which has, for its eastern border, the sands of the Rub al Khali. That's the 'Empty Quarter.' Aside from Tibet, this journey was as far off the beaten path as I have ever been, or as I can ever hope to be without making a space voyage to some other planet.

"Two bronzed airmen were waiting for me at Aden airport, at dawn, ready to fly me into a region where they also had never been. Both ex-R.A.F fliers, one from New Zealand, the other from western Australia. After the take-off Robertson, the Australian, gave me his place in the cockpit so I would have a better view of the country over which we were to pass. Then for three hours we made our flight in their Dakota over a jumble of barren mountains and then out into the great Arabian desert.

"During the first hour we flew fairly low, five to eight thousand feet, so we could almost touch the jagged mountains of the Sultan of Zinzinbar, not Zanzibar, northwest of Aden. Then over a number of other sultanates, passing scores of mountain towns, fortresses, and villages, most of them perched on lofty peaks or knife-edge ridges.

"Evidently from the dawn of time these people have raided each other and waged endless wars. Every man carries a rifle and a curved sword. In the narrow valleys below their fortress homes, we could see the small fields where they raise grain and grow the wild fig, the tamarisk, and where troops of wild baboons raid the fields and then hurl insults as they flee to their distant cliffs.

"On the second hour of our flight we were over an even more forbidding region, farther inland, less rainfall, fewer villages, until we came out over a wide valley that extended to the horizon. This, we hoped, was the Wadi Beihan, ruled over by the Sherif Hussein, most important of the Arab rulers along the border between the Aden sultanates and the Yemen. The sherif had been advised by courier that we were going to descend upon him.

"My two desert pilots were uncertain about our destination, and we flew on north until we left the mountains and entered the desert, still not sure. Captain Adams, the New Zealander, took a wide swing to the west in search of a landmark that might coincide with something on his inaccurate map, the only map of this region just west of Yemen and south of Saudi Arabia. We flew for a half hour or so above the sand dunes that seemed to go on and on forever.

"With us in the plane was Bill Terry, veteran of several South Arabian expeditions. He pointed excitedly off to the left. There we saw the remains of a tremendous ancient dam. Terry said we were now over forbidden Yemen, that this was, in fact, the legendary Marib Dam, the bursting of which is described in the Koran. A moment later this was confirmed because Terry recognized a double series of columns rising out of the desert, also the outlines of a great circular wall below us.

"A couple of years ago an expedition, led by Wendell Phillips of California and Professor Albright of Johns Hopkins, excavated there for a short time and then they were forced to flee.

"Below us was Marib, said to have been the capital of the fabled Queen of Sheba, who may have ruled here some three thousand years ago. The great Marib Dam in those days was one of the wonders of this Eastern world, when this must have been a thickly populated region, not the desert it is now. There undoubtedly were large, rich cities then, with glorious temples of marble and alabaster, of which the one below us, dedicated to the moon god, may have been the most magnificant.

"The first Westerners ever to see this region were members of a Danish expedition led by Niebuhr, a German, in 1762. They all perished but Niebuhr. Two others, a Frenchman and an Austrian, penetrated here twice in disguise in 1870 and 1889. Then came St. John Philby, foremost Arabian explorer of our time. And in 1951 the Wendell Phillips expedition, which was caught right in the middle of a Yemen royal blood feud and forced to flee after abandoning a quantity of valuable equipment that may still be down there in that sand somewhere.

"After circling this lost kingdom of Saba, the half-excavated moon temple in the sands below us, and the remains of the Marib Dam, the greatest dam of antiquity, we skirted the edge of the Empty Quarter, the Rub al Khali. Then we went on with our search for the desert palace of the ruler of Wadi Beihan."

That was the account I recorded for the radio, and there's one correction to be made. Our pilots got lost on purpose. I asked them to. I wanted to fly into the forbidden realm of Yemen and over the great ruins. They were glad to oblige. Getting lost was an excuse for what amounted to a frontier violation. It would hardly do to state that on the American radio while we were in Arabia.

At Wadi Beihan we found an oasis with a village, a mud fort, and a rudimentary air strip. The British at Aden have introduced aviation conveniences far and wide across the desert; little is needed for flying fields to accommodate small planes. Often the desert itself does well enough.

The camera crew, having arrived ahead of me, were all set for picture making. Arrangements had been made by a young woman member of our expedition, Eileen Salama, who had been with the Wendell Phillips archaeological party at Marib a couple of years before. She is an Egyptian by birth, speaks Arabic as her mother tongue, and was invaluable. The camera crew told me that, when they landed from their plane at Wadi Beihan, they were startled by a fusillade of gunfire. It sounded like a hostile reception but was a tribal welcome. Arabs like to shoot guns on the slightest excuse.

Sherif Hussein turned out to be an impressive character, bearded and with rugged handsome features, as is likely to be the case with southern Arabians. The show he put on for us was spectacular—a camel stampede. But first I was introduced to a dozen or so subordinate sheiks, who had come in from their tribes on the surrounding desert. Sheik Hussein is an important potentate, and they paid their respects to him, each according to his rank. Some merely kissed his hand. Others kissed not only his hand but also the dagger which he wore on his hip. It looked odd.

The stampede began with a dash of horsemen shooting guns, the sort of fireworks that is part of any celebration. Then the rush of the camels was a sight to see, thousands of camels it seemed, charging straight at us, then veering off for a long procession. That was the wealth of Sherif Hussein.

All the while I was sitting with Sherif Hussein at the entrance of a handsome red tent. Inside the tent was the Cinerama camera, shooting over our shoulders. Cameraman Harry Squire tells me that he had his eye not only on the camel stampede but also on the mud fort across the way, on top of which vigilant guards were stationed with machine guns, to be sure we didn't start a war or something.

The Wadi Beihan is in broken, desert country. There are spaces of open sand varied with ridges and gullies. In the gullies you'll find a growth of brush and stunted trees. This vegetation, in dry ground, will hardly remind you of green forests back home.

In a world of magnificent oaks and elms, the lordly cypress and the giant sequoia, one of the least impressive of trees is a runt with branches that begin near the ground, with leaves that are small and bark that is gray. This scrub tree grows, among other sparse vegetation, in gullies of the desert country. Unimpressive, but it is the frankincense tree, the sap of which was ancient treasure, and is still a valuable commodity.

The method of production, which remains the same now as always, was to make an incision in the bark of the tree so that a greenish, sweet-smelling sap oozed out, forming a globule that hardened in the air. The globules were collected, and the cuts were deepened for a further oozing of sap. The hardened lumps were packed in sheepskins or goatskins. Such was the frankincense that made precious cargo along the caravan trail.

But this is prosy fact, and entertainment is to be found in the pages of Herodotus, father of history and lover of wonder. Telling of Arabian spices, he gives us the following:

"Arabia is the last of inhabited lands towards the south, and it is the only country which produces frankincense, myrrh, cassia, cinnamon, and ledanum. The frankincense they procure by means of the gum storax. For the trees which bear the frankincense are guarded by winged serpents, small in size, and of varied colours, whereof vast numbers hang about every tree. There is nothing but the smoke of the storax which will drive them from the trees. The winged serpents are nowhere seen except in Arabia, where they are all congregated together. This makes them appear so numerous.

"Such, then, is the way in which the Arabians obtain their frankincense; their manner of collecting the cassia [a kind of cinnamon] is the following: They cover all their body and their face with the hides of oxen and other skins, leaving only holes for the eyes, and thus protected go in search of the cassia, which grows in a lake of no great depth. All round the shores and in the lake itself there dwell a number of winged animals, much resembling bats, which screech horribly, and are very valiant. These creatures they must keep from their eyes all the while that they gather the cassia.

"Still more wonderful is the mode in which they collect the cinnamon. Where it grows, and what country produces it, they cannot tell. Great birds, they say, bring the sticks, and carry them up into the air to make their nests. These are fastened with a sort of mud to a sheer face of rock, where no foot of man is able to climb. So the Arabians, to get the cinnamon, use the following artifice. They cut all the oxen and asses and beasts of burden that die in their land into large pieces, which they carry with them into those regions and place near the nests: then they withdraw to a distance, and the old birds, swooping down, seize the pieces of meat and fly with them up to their nests: which, not being able to support the weight, break off and fall to the ground. Hereupon the Arabians return and collect the cinnamon.

"Ledanum [a fragrant unguent] is procured in a yet stranger fashion. Found in a most inodorous place, it is the sweetest scented of all substances. It is gathered from the beards of he-goats, where it is found sticking like gum, having come from the bushes on which they browse."

One can hardly blame Voltaire for saying of Herodotus: "Father of History? Father of Lies." But he no more than repeated stories told him, though he surely loved them to be marvelous. One supposition, nowadays, is that in antiquity fearsome tales were passed around by merchants to keep competitors away from places where they procured their wares. This might account for the terrifying character of Herodotus' winged serpents guarding the frankincense trees.

In ancient times frankincense burned in innumerable shrines. In Egypt it was used in the funerary ritual. The Book of

Nehemiah tells of a great chamber in the temple of Jerusalem where frankincense was stored, along with other spices. In the Gospels the three wise men from the East bring to the new-born Saviour gifts of frankincense and myrrh.

The medicinal use of frankincense was even more widespread. The great Arabian physician Avicenna prescribes it as a remedy for a whole series of maladies, from tumors to fevers. In China it is recommended as a cure for leprosy. Shakespeare has Othello say:

> Drop tears as fast as the Arabian trees
> Their medicinal gum.

Today, alas, medical science regards frankincense as having no curative properties whatever, though it is still used as medication far and wide in the Orient. The Hadramaut exports quantities of the fragrant stuff. One important market is the temples of India, where clouds of smoke rise from braziers burning frankincense from Arabia.

# Chapter 10

You'd hardly think of anything in this forbidding land to suggest the sky line of Manhattan. Most of us suppose America invented the skyscraper, and I once imagined the skyscraper era began not very many years ago, with the Flatiron Building in New York. Later, in Himalayan Tibet, I stood gazing and marveling at the lofty palace of the Dalai Lama in Lhasa, which rises story on story, reared upon and supported by a steep hill. Just as extraordinary in their way are the skyscraper cities of the Hadramaut. These were the bizarre wonder we had come to film in southern Arabia.

After the show put on for us by Sherif Hussein, the camera crew proceeded in their plane to the skyscraper cities, while I flew with the Australian and New Zealand pilots. Our destination was some hundreds of miles across the desert, and I reported to the radio program back home:

"We flew east and a little south of the only partially explored area where the British Protectorate of Aden and the little-known country of Yemen and the vast Rub al Khali desert come together. For an hour or so we were over completely uninhabited desert. Then slowly we became aware that we were above a waterless valley that was growing wider and deeper. This is the head of the Wadi Hadramaut.

"The valley resembles our Grand Canyon of the Colorado in Arizona, except that it is not so deep and the colors of the strata

[ 81 ]

in the walls not so brilliant. The color here in the Wadi Hadramaut is predominantly dark red.

"After flying for about an hour and a half from the eastern border of the Yemen, we came to what are known as the four principal cities of Hadramaut: Hauta, Shibam, Seiyun, Tarim. These are the skyscraper cities. The most striking of the four—Shibam.

"When it suddenly appears around a cliff that juts out into this great red valley, you simply can't believe your eyes. For here is a city made up of some six hundred of these skyscrapers, with streets between them like narrow canyons. The city is made up entirely of tall buildings. Most of them are dazzling white.

"The principal industries of the Wadi Hadramaut today are making yarn, weaving cloth, tanning hides, preparing indigo, and making the plaster that is used in the skyscrapers. But the chief export for centuries has been—young men. Around thirty per cent of their young men leave when they are in their teens.

"They go to the East Indies and Malaya, where they enter the world of commerce. Ninety-five per cent of the Arabs in the Straits Settlements and Indonesia are Hadramis. They seem to have a flair for commerce. After ten or fifteen years they return. Some of them bring hundreds of thousands of dollars. Then they build more skyscrapers.

"Today there's a new trend in the Hadramaut—as in our own skyscraper cities. For all the wealthy city dwellers now have villas in the country nearby, surrounded by palm trees. Every wealthy family has at least two homes. One in the skyscraper city, and one out in a date grove.

"The first European to write about this little-known part of southern Arabia was a German named Von Werder, who afterward went to America, in fact, to Texas. There the Texans refused to believe the tales he told about the skyscraper cities of southern Arabia. Whereupon in despair he committed suicide. Explorer Freya Stark wrote about him.

"A few British came here after World War I, including a remarkable Englishman named W. H. Ingrams. He became adviser to the Sultan of Mukalla and Shihr on the coast. Mukalla is a skyscraper seaport between Aden and where the Wadi Hadramaut enters the Indian Ocean.

"Until Ingrams started his work, when rich Hadramis returned home, they not only built tall buildings but they also got out their rifles. It wasn't until the years between 1934 and 1940 that Ingrams got them to stop these tribal wars.

"The Sultan of Mukalla didn't free his slaves until 1944. Inland, slavery still goes on.

"Four of us, our Australian and New Zealand pilots, Maynard Miller and I, landed on a stretch of desert midway between the cities of Seiyun and Tarim. First, we buzzed the Sultan's gay blue and white palace at Seiyun. Whereupon out came a car to pick us up. And what a car. It turned out to be an automobile that had been brought to this valley by camel caravan and then assembled, and it was the first one ever brought here. A 1929 Chevrolet. In spite of the beating it has taken, the like of which you can't imagine, it is still going strong.

"And, by the way, the first motion picture that was ever seen in the skyscraper city of Seiyun was shown the night that we were there. A documentary about Queen Elizabeth's recent voyage to Australia. It had been sent up by the British governor at Aden, nearly five hundred miles away.

"Hadramaut has a population divided into various classes. First the Saiyids, the aristocrats, at the top. They are descended from the Prophet's daughter Fatima and his cousin Ali. Then the sheiks, of whom there are many, some fairly well educated in a Moslem way. Next, the Euphatis, or Janizary troops. They were brought in long ago as mercenary fighting men but they stayed on and became a powerful group. Other classes are the tribesmen who live up and down the great valley; and the townsmen who are merchants and artisans and slaves.

"Finally, the Hucdon, who are like the untouchables of India and do the lowest menial jobs. They are said to be descended from invading armies of Abyssinians who came here during wars between the third and sixth centuries. They were captured and never had a chance to leave. And now they like it too well to leave. Musicians and dancers are at the bottom of this lowest class.

"We spent the night in the Palace of a Hundred Rooms. We had our dinner sitting on the floor, on Persian rugs, right in the middle of a vast hall. All sorts of strange dishes, topped off with pomegranates and dates. I felt like a caliph of old. That is, until I started to get up. And my knees creaked and I could hardly get off that floor."

Our Cinerama picture shows two of the skyscraper cities, Shibam and Seiyun, the tall buildings, the local life. Each is at an oasis, where there's underground water. The city waterworks is a well, where you'll see a group pulling a long rope at a run, which hauls a bucket of water out of the well. This they do all day long.

The tall buildings are made of mud bricks, and are an example of what you can do with that humble material. The style of architecture is Islamic. If you were to put a Hadramaut skyscraper in a town of Syria or Algeria, it wouldn't look at all out of place. Eight stories or so may not seem so lofty, but they seem taller because of the unexpectedness of finding any kind of structure at a remote spot in the desert and because they are clustered together, with narrow canyons between them, and all the buildings are tall.

The skyscraper idea derives from tribal conditions. A high building, it was explained, was valuable as a lookout for spying enemy raiders. So the habit grew of making houses high. This got to be the fashion, and you had to put up a tall dwelling to be in style. These skyscrapers, moreover, are warm in the mild winter and cool in the ferocious heat of summer.

Here in southern Arabia scholars seek the solution of an anthropological puzzle—the origin of the Arabs. The nomad tribes of the sands, with camels and black tents, are a picturesque challenge—how did they get there, and how did they get that way?

The Arabs themselves have a tradition that features two biblical names—Shem and Ishmael. The original Arabs, they hold, were descendants of Shem, Noah's son, from whom the term

"Semite" derives. Noah had three sons, Ham, Shem and Japheth, who peopled the world after the deluge. Genesis says: "These are the three sons of Noah: and of them was the whole world overspread." But the legend holds that the Arabian race also includes the descendants of Ishmael, son of Abraham and the concubine Hagar. Hence the term Ishmaelite, applied to the nomads of the desert. The tradition makes the Arabs primarily the sons of Shem, secondarily the sons of Ishmael.

But modern scholarship has its own ways of thinking—some quite ingenious. One striking conjecture is outlined by Lieutenant Colonel the Honorable A. Hamilton, the Master of Belhaven, an erudite British officer who traveled extensively in southern Arabia in the 1930s. For a clue to the puzzle he takes that fragrant substance of such long and sacred renown, incense.

He points out how, in earliest Egypt, incense was used in religious ritual. The *Book of the Dead* prescribes: "The chapter shall be recited over the divine chaplet which is placed upon the face of the deceased and thou shalt cast incense into the fires. . . ."

The Egyptians had to import incense from distant South Arabia, and the reasoning is that they would not have originally devised a religious form that would require material from so far away. "The inference to be considered therefore," writes the Master of Belhaven, "is that the early religion of the Nile valley at least took some of its primitive forms from South Arabia, the only home of incense."

He notes, moreover, that the earliest Egyptians were of identically the same physical type as is found among South Arabian tribes of today. Therefore he assumes they were of the same origin, descendants of people who came up from East Africa, one branch going across into southern Arabia, to become the Arabs; the other proceeding north along the valley of the Nile, to become the Egyptians.

Scholars take note of an Arabian proverb—that Yemen is the cradle and Iraq the grave of the Arab. Yemen is the southwestern point where migrants from Africa would enter, traversing the narrow strait, and the traditional saying might reflect a spread of people from Yemen to Iraq, across the desert. There are tribes in northern Arabia that clearly originated in the Yemen, and their northern migration can be traced. Far to the south there are many place names and traditions connected with tribes that are now in the north, in Iraq and in Syria.

R. H. Kiernan in his scholarly *The Unveiling of Arabia* suggests that the origin of the Bedouin may be found in population pressures in the ancient fertile lands of southern Arabia. There at an early date the agricultural people multiplied in numbers greater than the land could support, and the surplus was forced into the desert.

"So," he writes, "the emigrant movement set to the east and northeast. The last oases, springs and soil of Yemen were held bitterly, but the increasing pressure of fresh waves forced people clinging to the peasant life out into the wilderness, where in order to live, they adopted the nomadic life, raising flocks of sheep and herds of camel."

This presumes a transition from agriculture to desert, from farmer to herdsman, which began in a remote period, and continued for many centuries, and the desert was gradually populated with scattered tribes.

Beyond the desert were other fertile lands—Mesopotamia, Palestine, Syria—into which the nomads spread and founded great kingdoms like Babylon and Assyria. From farmer to nomad herdsman and back to farmer again.

# Chapter II

Back in geologic time, a million years ago, there was a convulsion of underlying rock, and the crust of the earth split open in East Africa and the western extremity of Asia. A fracture was formed along a line of four thousand miles, south to north. Highlands and lowlands were cleft, as if giant hands were cracking continents. The rupture of the subterranean strata occurred during thousands of years, and left a deep depression. This is the classic explanation of that geological prodigy, the Rift Valley, which extends for thousands of miles and across parts of two continents—all the way from South Africa to Syria.

The map of Africa, at a glance, gives graphic evidence of the Rift Valley in a series of long narrow lakes, which are strung along a line from south to north. Lake Nyasa, Lake Tanganyika, Lake Albert, Lake Rudolf are some of them. Broad and shallow Lake Victoria, by the way, is not a Rift Valley creation. The immensely long depression has branches, but the trend is north, as shown by the outlines of these lakes.

Africa is generally one vast plateau, like a flattened dome of continental rock, with the East African highland split longitudinally by the Rift Valley. The lakes fill the deeper cracks. Lake Tanganyika is the longest fresh-water lake in the world. Length, 450 miles. Width, 30 to 45 miles. Its water ripples at an altitude of 2536 feet, and its depth is 4708 feet, which puts the floor of the lake 2172 feet below sea level. It is the second deepest fresh-water lake in the world, second only to giant Lake Baikal in Siberia.

All the Rift Valley lakes have steep cliffs for banks, indicating creation by fracture, and are in jagged country that shows every sign of ancient turmoil of the rocks. All along the Rift Valley the geology gives evidence of a splitting open back in the dim days of time.

From the lake section the Rift Valley cuts northward through the highlands of Ethiopia to the southern end of the Red Sea, which body of water exhibits the typical signs—south to north, long, narrow, deep, more than 7000 feet deep, with steep craggy coasts. The Red Sea is part of the Rift Valley, which extends along the narrow, deep Gulf of Akaba and then across the Negev Desert to the Dead Sea, which again is long and narrow, south to north. And, of course, is the lowest body of water on earth. Its surface is 1300 feet below sea level. It is more than 1000 feet deep on the average. Its floor, 2300 feet below sea level.

The Rift Valley continues north along the valley of the Jordan to Syria, and there ends at the mountains of Lebanon, having spanned some fifty-five degrees of latitude—from 20 degrees south of the Equator, to 35 degrees north latitude.

Geologists speculate on the cause of this immense line of rifts, the series of faults and fractures that constitute the vast Rift Valley, a two-continent phenomenon. One supposition is that there was a collapse of the ancient continent off the east coast of Africa which had a splitting effect on the eastern side of Africa. In geological terms the formation of the Rift Valley was rather recent, continuing into the beginning of the Pleistocene Era, when the ice age was coming on in the Northern Hemisphere.

Along the Rift Valley in Africa there are abundant signs of volcanic activity. It's a volcano zone. When the continental cleavage occurred, subterranean fires were released. At the deeper cracks lava belched forth and fire mountains were formed. One can imagine a series of erupting volcanoes along the line of East Africa, phantasmal explosions, flaming craters, during the geological era when the underlying rocks were fractured. This volcanic activity lasted for ages, and lingers on to the present day.

Among hundreds of dead and sleeping volcanoes, there are live volcanoes. Among the peaks given the fabled name of the Mountains of the Moon you'll find many a fiery crater, burning with subterranean fires. These were a goal in our quest for wonders of nature.

The Cinerama job in tropical Africa had already begun before I went out to join the film makers in Egypt. After making pictures in Europe, they had flown down to East Africa and back again, shuttling between Europe and Africa in the clipper *Cinerama.*

We had, in addition to the regular crew for ground pictures, a unit for aerial photography. In *This Is Cinerama* the dizzy flying, like the whirl down Zion Canyon, had been done by Paul Mantz, a veteran of motion picture aviation, in a B-25 rigged especially for filming with our huge camera. Now Paul Mantz, with that same plane, was working on the *Seven Wonders*, making air shots to go with the ground pictures filmed by the regular crew, and getting thrillers on his own.

Sometimes you get your best results by accident. You fail to get what you expect, and come upon the marvelous unexpectedly. Paul Mantz, was assigned to get air shots of Kilimanjaro, Africa's loftiest mountain. That famous peak, with an ancient crater, is an example of the volcanic activity that accompanied the formation of the Rift Valley. Kilimanjaro is a mighty but extinct volcano. They failed to film it. Local weather conditions ruined their chances. But then, in flying around on the futile quest, they found a live volcano that looked as devilish as anything constructed by the fire god Vulcan.

In the wilderness of jumbled rock and summits stood a tall peak with a menacing crater, above which rose a column of yellow, poisonous-looking fumes. It was the very model of a sinister fire mountain, a wicked lord among volcanoes. It was a living survival of the flaming convulsions in the birth of the Rift Valley.

Now you can't challenge Paul like that. He flew around, and

picked his line of attack. With Gayne Rescher running the camera, he charged the crater. "We had the sun straight ahead," Rescher relates, "as we flew through the column of gas. We could smell the sulphury fumes." The sun was seen with a dim, ghostly effect through the mephitic vapor.

He flew over the crater, virtually down into it, banking to give the camera a long look. The caldron, half a mile or so across, was a deep basin scorched and tortured by fire, and on the floor were a superheated crust and areas of glowing fire. From the molten rock rose the cloud of sulphury gas. It was a scene for a pit of hell in Dante's Inferno. Paul was afraid the volcanic fumes would cut his motor for a forced landing in the crater, a truly infernal end.

Bill Lipscomb, who was with them in the Congo, reports:

"The effervescent Paul Mantz took off one morning to get a Cinerama shot of a volcano about which a Belgian official had told him. When they came back I thought the crew looked a little pale. Yes, they had photographed the volcano. Paul had flown round the rim twice and then said, 'Look out, boys, I'm going in,' and he had dived right into the center of it.

"'But,' I said, 'isn't it a live volcano?'

"They said it was—and that was why they needed beer very quickly.

"Apparently the volcanic fumes very nearly cut the engines. But the shot is in the picture all right."

Paul did the same sort of Cinerama stunt at still another crater, but with a different aesthetic effect. In some extinct East African volcanoes, the floor of the pit has dropped low, leaving a deep abyss. One Rift Valley mountain has a giant sunken crater filled with water, and there's a deep spacious lake at the mountaintop, a crater lake, a mirror lake of Africa, Ngorongoro.

With the plane swooping down on this, the Cinerama spectacle is one of incredible beauty. Blue sky and masses of brilliant clouds are reflected for a mirror picture in a dark frame of the volcanic rim of the crater. Like something from a never-never fairyland. But it has the somber mood of Africa. For Africa indeed is a continent most of which has its own dark feeling.

The regions neighboring the Rift Valley abound in freakish tricks of nature. At one place in Rhodesia a flat even plateau has cracked open, the rocks cleft apart, leaving a canyon more than 400 feet deep, as narrow as 80 feet, and 40 miles long. Above, across the plateau, flows the Zambesi River, and the deep, narrow chasm cuts straight across its path. The river, on the flat tableland, is at its widest, and plunges over the edge of the canyon. This is Victoria Falls.

At Niagara, the classic of waterfalls, the river goes over a cliff, down to an open area for the stream to continue its course. At Victoria Falls the Zambesi tumbles over one cliff and against another, down one canyon wall only to strike the opposite canyon wall. One hundred million gallons of water per minute cascade into the narrow gorge. There is no escape except down the long canyon, where immense masses of water boil along under great pressure. Because of the giant turbulence and pressure masses of spray arise, the telltale sign of Victoria Falls, and in brilliant African sunshine there's a fantasy of rainbows.

The scene, as shown by aerial photography in Cinerama, is unique. In the approach by plane you see flat country, the level plateau, on all sides. Uninteresting country, but in the distance there's a cloud of steam rising from the plain. As you fly nearer the view rapidly discloses masses of spray rising from a rift in the plateau. Then, suddenly, you see the Zambesi pouring into the gorge.

But here our irrepressible pilot sustained disappointment. Across the gorge is a bridge, one of the dizziest in the world. In New York Paul Mantz had performed a Cinerama stunt by flying under the bridges across the East River, all four of them, one after another. So at Victoria Falls he had ideas, as cameraman Gayne Rescher tells us:

"As soon as Paul sees a bridge, he wants to fly under it. There at Victoria Falls is a wonderful bridge. He thought he'd fly along the gorge, then on below the bridge. When you get under it, there is a ninety-degree turn. You have to fly very low and then make the sudden turn. He was determined to do it, but couldn't get permission. Everybody said no. The Rhodesian official in charge said they would put Mantz in jail. Paul was trying to find out what the fine would be—he would have been glad to pay the fine. But the official said he would lose his job. He was a fine fellow, and Mantz didn't want to hurt him. So, when he flew down the gorge, at the last minute he pulled out and went over the bridge. He claims he could have made it under. I wouldn't have done it."

Victoria Falls brings back the memory of its discoverer, Livingstone. It was in 1855 that Africa's most famous explorer first caught sight of the clouds of mist that signalize the mighty cataract of the Zambesi. This was during an early expedition in a long life of exploration. For thirty years David Livingstone was intrepid and indefatigable in the unveiling of the southern part of Africa, and he died in the wilderness, still pursuing that purpose.

Although a missionary, he devoted his life less to making converts than to exploration. There was no contradiction in that. Beginning missionary work among South African tribes, the young Scottish clergyman soon came to the conclusion that, for the spread of Christianity, he could best labor by making the country known for subsequent evangelical work, by preparing the way for other missionaries. Pursuing that object, he became one of the greatest of African explorers.

His name is forever linked with that of Stanley and with a characteristic phrase—"Dr. Livingstone, I presume?" This was in 1871, when Livingstone on one of his expeditions had vanished in the wilderness and was considered lost. He had left civilization five years previously. The story of how the American newspaper publisher, James Gordon Bennett, sent Stanley to find Livingstone is familiar. Henry M. Stanley was an Englishman of long experience in journalism in the United States. He made his way to the savage country around Lake Tanganyika, and for a climax uttered the famous salutation.

The phrase has become so well known it's worth while to look at the circumstances in which it was spoken. The stiff formal style of "Dr. Livingstone, I presume?" in the depth of darkest Africa, at the end of an epic of travel and peril, might be taken as the height of British imperturbability and understatement. But the mood was complicated. In his book, *How I Found Livingstone*, Stanley tells how, in a native village, he came upon a crowd, including Arabs, surrounding a travel-worn white man. He relates:

"My heart beats fast, but I must not let my face betray my emotions, lest it shall detract from the dignity of a white man appearing under such extraordinary circumstances.

"So I did that which I thought was most dignified. I pushed back the crowds, and, passing from the rear, walked down a living avenue of people, until I came in front of the semicircle of Arabs, in the front of which stood the white man with the grey beard. As I advanced slowly towards him I noticed he was pale, looked wearied, had a grey beard, wore a bluish cap with a faded gold band round it, had on a red-sleeved waistcoat, and a pair of grey tweed trousers. I would have run to him, only I was a coward in the presence of such a mob—would have embraced him, only, he being an Englishman, I did not know how he would receive me; so I did what cowardice and false pride suggested was the best thing—walked deliberately to him, took off my hat, and said:

" 'Dr. Livingstone, I presume?'

" 'Yes,' said he, with a kind smile, lifting his cap slightly.

"I replace my hat on my head, and he puts on his cap, and we both grasp hands, and I then say aloud:

" 'I thank God, Doctor, I have been permitted to see you.'

"He answered, 'I feel thankful that I am here to welcome you.'

"I turn to the Arabs, take off my hat to them in response to the saluting chorus of 'Yambos' I receive, and the Doctor introduces them to me by name."

So that was how Stanley met Livingstone.

In equatorial East Africa there are two branches of the Rift Valley with a rise of land between them, a spacious plateau. On the plateau is broad, shallow Lake Victoria Nyanza, which has no connection with Victoria Falls on the Zambesi hundreds of miles away. Nineteenth-century Englishmen liked to name things after their queen. Lake Victoria is the source of the Nile.

The river flows out of the northern end of Lake Victoria and cuts across to Lake Albert, which is appropriate, Albert having been prince consort to Victoria. British royalty was well served by British explorers. The Nile flows across the northern end of Lake Albert, and then runs north on its long journey to the Mediterranean. After several thousand miles the river of Victoria and Albert becomes the Nile of the Pharaohs.

The Rift Valley and the river system of the Nile are parallel to each other. They are neighbors and companion wonders. But their origins are different. The one was formed by cleavage, a cracking of continents. The other is of a river-valley character, in which the rock may be cut by ages of running water to form a trough, a valley. The valley of the Nile in Egypt, which has made so much history, is a creation of the river.

The hydrographic system of the Nile is a wondrous mechanism, a stupendous waterworks of nature which brings about the Nile flood and nourishes Egypt. The steady water supply, about the same month by month, is provided by the main stream rising at Lake Victoria Nyanza, the White Nile, so called because its water is colored by a milky silt. Its East African place of origin has a large even rainfall, and supplies water steadily. The annual flood is derived from the Blue Nile, which is the chief tributary of the great stream. The Blue Nile, so called for its clear blue waters, rises in Ethiopia, in Lake Tsana, where there's a heavy rainy season and the rest of the year is dry. Annually the Blue Nile is in flood, and pours its deluge into the White Nile, and there's a yearly inundation all along the line the rest of the way, and in Egypt the life-giving flood.

For many centuries the source of the Nile was one of the great mysteries. The ancient Egyptians knew their existence depended on the river but had no real idea where it began. They could trace its course to the south about as far as the juncture of the White and Blue Nile, present-day Khartoum in the Sudan, but from there on the course was unknown. Herodotus again gives us a characteristic account:

"With regard to the sources of the Nile, I have found no one among all those with whom I have conversed, whether Egyp-

The Sphinx guards the approach to the pyramid tombs of Pharaohs. The Greeks regarded the Pyramids of Egypt as the oldest and greatest of the Seven Wonders of the World, and your wonder seeker is inclined to agree with them. They are the only surviving ancient wonder.

The remaining six of the Seven Wonders of the Ancient World are depicted on the following three pages in paintings by Mario Larrinaga, based on reconstruction by scholars. They were photographed by Peter A. Juley & Son.

The Hanging Gardens of Babylon were a series of great terraces, with vegetation, erected to please a queen who, on the flat hot Mesopotamian plain, longed for the cool mountains of her native land. Across the river is the legended Tower of Babel.

The statue of Zeus at Olympia, site of the ancient Olympic games. The shrine was one of the greatest in Greece, the statue a masterpiece by Phidias, greatest of Greek sculptors.

The Colossus of Rhodes, a source of wonder down the centuries. Legend said that ships sailed between the legs of the giant bronze statue astride the harbor. All we know is that the Colossus was more than one hundred feet high.

The greatest lighthouse in all history. The Pharos at the entrance of the harbor at Alexandria was, in fact, a tall, massive skyscraper building of some four hundred and fifty feet high.

This is how the Temple of Diana at Ephesus must have looked at the time St. Paul preached in the city.

The most famous tomb of antiquity, the Mausoleum, which Queen Artemisia built at Halicarnassus for her husband, King Mausolus.

The columns of the Parthenon, with fragments of marble everywhere. The Acropolis once was crowded with temples, masterpieces of Hellenic architecture.

A flying shot over the Acropolis, where our camera plane speeds
above the ruins of Athenian glory. Straight ahead, the Parthenon,
as the plane banks.

Still slanting, as it has done for centuries, is the Leaning Tower of Pisa, which was built on a faulty foundation and soon began to tilt. Today, engineering has to support it or the Leaning Tower would fall over.

A superb air shot of St. Peter's, with the great Piazza and its covered colonnades. Alongside the world's largest church are the buildings of the Vatican. At the upper right, the Tiber.

The interior of St. Peter's was never before lighted for motion pictures, and the lighting was a huge task. For the first time you see St. Peter's like this, crowded with worshipers awaiting a papal procession.

Pope Pius XII on the balcony at Castel Gandolfo. Beside him is the sound equipment for recording the blessing. This is regarded as one of the finest portraits ever made of the Pontiff.

The Zambesi River pours into this long, narrow gorge. The impact of the water raises eternal clouds of spray with rainbows, increasing the grandeur of Victoria Falls.

Flying over the rim of the crater of a live volcano, a spectacular stunt of air photography in filming an African fire mountain.

At an elephant school in the Congo baby Jumbo takes a lesson. There used to be a legend that African elephants were too savage to tame. Hannibal used elephants like these when he crossed the Alps to attack Rome's mighty armies.

The Watusi in Africa are probably the tallest people in the world. The height of the bar can be judged by the seven-footer standing beside the hurdle. Watusi high jumpers use a stone for a foot prop in the running take-off. *Below* — the little girls join the warriors in a tribal dance.

Photos by Edwin W. Sippel

Photo by Edwin W. Sippel

Butera, the Nijinsky of the Watusi, is reckoned the greatest dancer
in Africa, so famous that his picture is on Belgian Congo bank notes.

Your wonder hunter visits a paramount sheik of the desert. Sherif Hussein is a lord of tribes that dwell in the black tents.

tians, Libyans, or Greeks, who professed to have any knowledge, except a single person. He was the scribe who kept the register of the sacred treasures of Athena in the city of Sais, and he seemed to me to be joking when he said that he knew them perfectly well. His story was as follows, 'Between Syene, a city of the Thebais, and Elephantine, there are two hills with sharp conical tops; the name of the one is Crophi, of the other, Mophi. Midway between them are the fountains of the Nile, fountains which it is impossible to fathom. Half the water runs northward into Egypt, half to the south towards Ethiopia.'"

Subsequent geographers of antiquity, like Ptolemy, made remarkably good guesses. From travelers' tales and rumor they deduced that the Nile originated in African lakes far to the south. Ptolemy's map shows two branches rising out of two lakes, which could represent the White Nile and the Blue Nile and the lakes Victoria and Tsana, although they are badly misplaced. The waters were supposed to be from melting mountain snows. Ptolemy knew of the great peaks of East Africa, which he called the Mountains of the Moon. But these vague understandings were bedeviled by a theory that the Nile began in the western Sahara, near the Atlantic, and then flowed underground to become Egypt's great river.

Ancient interest in the question was keen. Nero, who seems to have had a fancy for geography as well as tyranny, is reported to have sent two centurions to find the source of the Nile. They seem to have made their way far to the south until stopped by vast marshes along the upper course of the river. In the Middle Ages the source of the Nile was merely a favorite mystery.

In modern times the search for a solution of the mystery was one of the most prolonged efforts of exploration. One expedition after another added bits of knowledge with arduous and dangerous expeditions into darkest Africa. The truth was not disclosed until after the middle of the nineteenth century. The story, one of daring and peril with a drama of personalities, a clash of two characters, bitter quarrel and feud, the dispute between Burton and Speke.

Sir Richard Burton. The world of adventure, scholarship, and literature still rings with his name. He made the trip to Mecca, the classic exploit. Disguised as a Moslem, his fabulous knowledge of languages and the ways of Islam enabled him to make the pilgrimage to the forbidden city. Later his translation of the *Arabian Nights* established him as a paladin of the world of letters. But Burton's career was widely varied and included African exploration. He began by making a desperately hazardous journey into Ethiopia, to Harar. Then he turned to the supreme goal, the quest for the source of the Nile.

Captain John Hanning Speke was an officer of the British Indian Army who accompanied Burton into Ethiopia, though not to Harar. They encountered trouble in Ethiopia, which gave Speke a mistrust of Burton's judgment. They seem to have been antipathetic characters at heart, the clash of personalities that so often ends with a blaze of charge and countercharge. Nevertheless, in spite of Speke's misgivings about Burton's judgment, they went together on the search for the source of the Nile, with Speke as Burton's lieutenant.

In the background of their planning was the vague understanding that the origins of the river were to be found among mysterious East African lakes. They went in from the east coast, made a journey of difficulty and danger, and discovered Lake Tanganyika, the long, narrow south-to-north Rift Valley lake. This, decided Burton, was it. This surely was the source of the Nile. If his surmise had been correct, Burton would stand as the conqueror of the ancient riddle. Of course, it was not correct.

On the shore of Lake Tanganyika Burton was taken down with fever, and the expedition, with its party of natives, had to wait until he had recovered sufficiently to go on. In this interval Speke got Burton's permission to go exploring to the north. He made a journey onto a northern plateau and found Lake Victoria Nyanza, extending to the horizon. This, decided Speke, was the source of the Nile. It was no more than a hunch. He did no exploring to prove his point by going to the northern end of the lake to find a river there. But the hunch was correct.

Speke rejoined Burton and told him his theory. Burton rejected it. He was sure Lake Tanganyika was it, and he was the discoverer. He couldn't go on, was in no condition to, and they made their way back to the coast. They were in complete disagreement, but agreed not to argue about it. Burton claimed later that Speke pledged that he would not make any independent announcement of his discovery of Lake Victoria and of his contention that this was the source of the Nile.

On the coast Burton delayed. Speke went back to England and announced the solution of the riddle of the Nile. The news was received with enthusiasm. The Royal African Society decided that Speke should lead an expedition to Victoria Nyanza and trace the course of the Nile from the lake. This was the state of affairs when Burton returned to England and found Speke the lion of the hour. Burton announced his rejection of Speke's claim and argued his own contention that Lake Tanganyika, which he had discovered, was the source of the Nile.

Speke took his expedition to East Africa and made for the northern end of Lake Victoria. He had some lurid adventures, but found the river flowing out of the lake, traced it to Lake Albert, and far enough to the north to carry the conviction that it was the Nile. He returned to England and reported. But Burton stuck to his position. His view was that Speke's statements were hallucinatory. Speke had been accompanied by a companion, Grant, but that didn't matter. Burton said there was no Lake Victoria, no spacious body of water, only a lot of marshes. He wrote a book to prove that Speke had not discovered the source of the Nile. He was sure that he himself had.

Naturally this created a good deal of confusion, and the Royal African Society decided to have the two rivals present their contentions personally before a gathering of geographers and African explorers. It might have clarified matters, or possibly not. Speke was a diffident sort of character, no orator, and might have fared ill with the mighty Richard Burton. The meeting of the Royal African Society was held. Burton was there, ready for the clash, but Speke did not appear. Instead, the news came that, in hunting partridges that afternoon, he had accidentally shot and killed himself.

There have been mentions of a possibility of suicide, but that seems unlikely. Speke was right, as was to be demonstrated presently by Stanley. That explorer had won the headlines by his discovery of Dr. Livingstone, but his greatest work was now in settling the Burton-Speke controversy once and for all. Stanley went to East Africa and made a conclusive investigation. Lake Victoria was the source of the Nile.

The rights and wrongs as between Burton and Speke make a nice point in the ethics of exploration. When they were together Burton was the expedition leader and entitled to the credit for the results achieved. If he had accepted Speke's theory of the source of the Nile, how far would he have been entitled to the credit of the discovery, as expedition leader? What was the propriety of Speke's announcement back in England, anticipating his leader? Had he promised Burton to keep silent about it? After all, he had only a hunch to begin with, although it turned out to be correct. It would seem that Speke had acquired an unfair contempt for Burton's abilities as an explorer. Burton was, beyond any doubt, a titan in his field, but the fact remains that, in the controversy over the source of the Nile, Speke was correct and Burton was not.

# Chapter 12

AFRICA IS the continent where the animal kingdom is at its largest. Africa has the largest number and variety of great beasts. In Asia there are the tiger, the elephant, the rhinoceros. But Africa has the lion, leopard, elephant, rhinoceros, hippopotamus, giraffe, not counting myriads of antelope. It's the continent of the big game. The wonders of animate nature had a place on our list, and the Cinerama camera caught scenes of herds of galloping hippos, clouds of pink flamingos, riverbanks slithering with crocodiles. But the interest focused on a school for elephants.

There was an old theory that the African elephant, unlike the Indian species, could not be tamed, that it was too intractable, too savage in temperament. How incorrect that was could be seen at the elephant school in the Belgian Congo, where the proceedings began with the capture of a baby elephant from a wild herd and continued with the education of the pupil. The tribesmen use trained elephants to shunt off the wild ones. You see them isolate the calf from its mother, and drive it off, while the old bull of the herd trumpets in protest. A place outside the village is the school. Tethered to stakes, the pupil is made to kneel and rise at command, and given bananas and other rewards for good performance. The baby elephant trumpets with resentment but takes the bananas with its trunk. The day of class work ends with a procession of elephants, the natives riding them singing a song. In the distance is the old bull of the herd, trumpeting.

This education for African pachyderms brings to mind the most remarkable affair of elephants in all annals—the story of Hannibal's elephants. In his astounding march to strike at Rome, the Carthaginian hero's army included a squadron of war elephants, and one historical question has been, Where did he get them? The consensus of historians today is that they were African elephants.

In India war elephants were an old story. Alexander encountered them when he invaded Hindustan, and his successors brought elephants from Asia to their wars in Europe. This was most famous in the case of Pyrrhus, whose name still survives in the term "Pyrrhic victory." This King of Epirus, in northern Greece, brought an army with elephants to Italy during a war with Rome. In the first battle the Roman legions were unable to face the charge of the monsters, and sustained a military disaster. But, with experience, the Romans learned how to deal with elephants—meeting them with a shower of javelins. A wounded war elephant was likely to go berserk, a danger to its own army. Pyrrhus won another battle, much less decisive. Success against the Romans cost him such heavy losses that he exclaimed: "Another such victory and we are undone." The Pyrrhic victory.

The Carthaginians, in northern Africa, trained African elephants, if the historians are correct, and used them extensively in war. So it was that, when Hannibal set out to conquer Rome, his army was supported by a squadron of elephants. These apparently carried castles on their backs from which archers shot arrows, but seem to have been most formidable for the terror they inspired and for the crushing power of the elephant charge, trampling down a hostile line. The war elephants were the tanks of antiquity.

The Carthaginians held large possessions in Spain, and Hannibal's march began in Spain, then across the Pyrenees and across Gaul. Polybius, historian of the wars between Rome and Carthage, tells us that he arrived at the river Rhone with thirty-seven elephants. In crossing the Rhone, Hannibal had a fight with native tribes on his hands. Then, having won the battle, he had a problem in getting the elephants across the broad stream. How he did it is one of the famous stories of ancient history.

Great rafts were prepared to ferry them across, but the elephants shied away from the water and could not be made to go aboard the rafts. The dilemma was solved by covering the rafts with earth and by constructing a runway covered with earth. The elephants took it for dry land and, led by docile females, marched onto the earth-covered runway and rafts. Then the rafts were cast off and proceeded across the river.

When the elephants saw themselves on water, they were terrified, but they had no means of escape, with water on all sides. It must have been a furor—a panic of elephants on rafts. Some were pushed into the river but were able to wade ashore by keeping the ends of their trunks above water and breathing thereby. The others were ferried safely across, and the war elephants went on to a far more arduous ordeal.

Hannibal's crossing of the Alps was one of the great exploits of history, matched only by Napoleon's crossing of the Alps two thousand years later. In each case it was the conquest of a lofty alpine pass. Napoleon did it in May, Hannibal in November. He was a month late in reaching the Alps, and it was winter. In each case the problem was the alpine snows, and Hannibal made the crossing with elephants. It seems like a nightmare to think of the great beasts from Africa among the glaciers and snow—choked ravines of the Alps in winter.

Yet Hannibal got his elephants through. That page of history tells of terrifying scenes as his army traversed icy trails overhanging alpine passes. Men, baggage, and animals plunged over cliffs. No mention is made of elephants lost that way, but it can be imagined—the ponderous beasts hurtling down icy precipices. Some may have perished from cold. Polybius tells us that it was all the worse for the elephants because of a lack of forage at the frosty altitude.

But most of the thirty-seven came through, apparently. They

were, actually, of decisive importance in the crossing of the Alps. All through the march through the mountains Hannibal's army was subject to attack by the alpine tribes, which assailed the long-drawn-out line with sudden charges and with ambuscades. But, we are told, they never molested a section of the line where elephants were. The mountaineers had never seen one before, and were terrified by the strange monsters.

The elephants made a prominent appearance in Hannibal's first great victory over the Romans. Having got his army down onto the rich plains of Italy, he now had to face the power of the legions. The clash came at the Trebbia River, where the battle was won by Hannibal's superior strategy. The Roman historian Livy gives us a glimpse of the great Carthaginian commander in action. Livy writes:

"The elephants had now come up against the center of the Roman line. Yet, in spite of all the dangers that surrounded them, the ranks stood firm and immovable for some time, even, contrary to all expectations, against the elephants. Some skirmishers, who had been placed so that they could attack these animals, flung darts at them, drove them off, and rushed after them, stabbing them under their tails, where the skin is soft and easily penetrated. Maddened with pain and terror, they were beginning to rush wildly on their own men, when Hannibal ordered them driven away to the left wing, against the auxiliary Gauls on the Roman right. There they instantly produced unmistakable panic and flight, and the Romans had fresh cause for alarm when they saw their auxiliaries routed."

The Romans, having had previous experience with elephants in the days of Pyrrhus, could deal with them, but their allies, the tribal Gauls, knowing nothing of elephants, were panicked by the monsters. This aided Hannibal's strategy of encircling the legions, which strategy included outflanking movements and an ambuscade. Then, after the Roman ranks were broken, the elephants rushed in and trampled the enemy, playing their part in the final Roman disaster.

Yet, after this triumph, Hannibal's war elephants soon vanished. The campaign was in December. Italy is renowned for a mild climate, but in northern Italy the winter cold can be intense. We read that presently all the elephants had perished in the frigid weather, except eight. Then Hannibal, to break into central Italy, essayed a passage of the Apennines, mountains that are less than the Alps. But they are forbidding in midwinter, and the army was driven back by an icy storm. In this seven elephants were lost, leaving only one.

In the spring the move into central Italy was accomplished. The line of march led across a great marsh, difficult of passage. Hannibal, stricken with illness, rode on the sole remaining elephant. It would be interesting to know what, in the end, happened to that one. But history is silent, and that closes the story of Hannibal's war elephants. They were not of decisive importance. Without elephants Hannibal went on to win still greater victories, though he failed to conquer Rome.

Africa, among its wonders, includes the tallest people in the world. It used to be said that the champions for lofty stature in the human race were the Patagonians of South America. But those Indian giants of the southern Argentine are almost extinct, and that in effect entitles the Watusi of East Africa to be called the tallest. They are found at the eastern border of the Belgian Congo near the greatest of the Rift Valley lakes, Tanganyika, and are an anthropological wonder.

Arrangements for filming the Watusi were made with their king, who has the right royal style of Charles Mutara III Rudahigwa. His lineage is impressive, scion of a dynasty that goes back eighteen generations. His subjects know him familiarly as the Mwami. John Gunther, in his *Inside Africa*, tells of a visit he made to the Mwami, "about forty, very sober in character, even somber, lean, handsome and six feet nine."

Gunther was entertained at the Mwami's palace, a building in the European style, with leopard skins on the floor. Rooms were decorated with Watusi spears, some shaped like broad harpoons. Then there was an exercise machine, used by the Mwami, which might have come from a New York sporting goods store. "Everywhere, in this part of Africa," writes John Gunther, "yesterday kisses tomorrow."

Bill Lipscomb dealt with the Mwami for Cinerama, and gives his impressions in the Land of the Tall People:

"One has preconceived notions of places. To me, the Congo suggested Livingstone and miles of bearers carrying things on their heads. All wrong. Usumbura is a smart town of new buildings, four-lane roads, good cafés and restaurants where you can eat as well as one can in Brussels. The Belgian banks are marbled halls, and instead of natives carrying burdens on their heads they carry them inside their heads and work adding-machines. Even the post office is a beautiful pillared hall with politeness and attention thrown in.

"However, my business is with the King of the Watusi warriors, the Tall Men of Africa. So the King graciously receives me. He drives up in his sports Studebaker, gets out, he is nearly seven feet, he is dressed in perfect English tweeds. He speaks in perfect French. Who's embarrassed? I am, with my fourth-grade French.

"'Our dances,' he tells me, 'are traditional—like your square dances, or even your Maypole dances; but they do not reflect our life to-day. We are modern; all Africa is going modern.'

"And, charming though he was, he had the look that all Africans have at the back of their eyes—the question, 'When are you Europeans going to get the hell out of here and leave us to manage our own affairs?'"

The Mwami appeared in our Cinerama picture garbed in the traditional costume of the Watusi, with royal robe and tribal ornaments, a truly regal figure. His Belgian adviser, beside him, in Western clothes looks runtish and commonplace.

The Watusi of the Ruanda country are an aristocracy. The majority of the local people are Bantus of ordinary stature, peasants who cultivate the land. The Watusi are indolent and lordly. Their principal amusements, it seems, are high jumping and dancing.

They put on an exhibition of jumping for Cinerama, and its amazing to see the excessively tall athletes go over the bar at more than seven feet. I thought, offhand, they might be high-jump champions of the world in terms of Western competition, but then I noticed that they used an aid in vaulting. Running to the bar, they'd place one foot on a take-off stone before vaulting, which wouldn't be according to Western rules. But the seven-footers looked as if they'd make top-notch basketball material.

The great feature in the traditional life of the Watusi is the dance. With the Mwami presiding in full tribal regalia, they put on a spectacular show for the Cinerama camera. They are magnificently costumed, and wear flowing headdresses made of monkey tails. Around their ankles they tie strings of bells, for a jangling musical rhythm, along with the beat of the African drums. The riot is wild but disciplined, with a tremendous amount of leaping and violent shaking of heads and monkey tails. The star was Butera, called the greatest dancer in Africa.

John Gunther, who also saw this Nijinsky of the tribe perform, says: "The leading dancer, by name Butera, seven feet five inches tall, weighs something like three hundred pounds; he is so celebrated as a dancer and high jumper, and so typical of the old Watusi, that his portrait appears on the local bank notes."

The dancer on the bank notes or, as Gunther says: "Yesterday kisses tomorrow."

The Watusi are coal black but not negroid. They are of a Hamitic race and seem to have come down from the north. The cause of their excessive stature is not clear. Anthropologists are not sure, but Bill Lipscomb got an explanation. Bill got it from the Mwami.

"He told us the royal 'joke.' It's his one joke and it is told with due dignity. The reason why all the Watusi are so tall? Because, when you are very young, your father boots you in the behind every morning to make you jump. So you jump and grow tall! It's a very little joke but it's the King's own and therefore very laughable."

Africa has a city with a wonder name—Timbuktu. Time was when there were three famous forbidden cities—Mecca, Lhasa, Timbuktu. Mecca still remains closed to non-Moslems. Only a handful of Western travelers have been there. Lhasa in Tibet was for many centuries a difficult, usually impossible goal for travelers. The trip that my son Lowell Junior and I made to the city of the Dalai Lama was a high spot in the lives of both of us, the more so as Tibet and Lhasa are now behind the Bamboo Curtain. Today Timbuktu is open to any traveler hardy enough to make the trip into the wilderness of the southern Sahara, and Cinerama took advantage of that.

Lowell Junior went there in advance and made arrangements for filming at Timbuktu, at the time when we first projected the *Seven Wonders*. He flew to a flying field the French have on the coast, where the Sahara meets the Atlantic Ocean. Then the trip to the city was made by automobile across the desert. He found a town sadly decayed since the days when Timbuktu was the fabled metropolis of a powerful empire of the southern Sahara. The city is situated on the Niger, where the river makes a great northern bend up into the desert. The site is the key point of a great caravan route. The ups and downs from grandeur to misery in the old history of Timbuktu depended on the shifts of power and brigandage and the security of the caravan route.

With an especial interest Lowell Junior noted the Tuaregs, legended of old as the veiled warriors of the Sahara. The tradition of Islam is to veil the women, but with the Tuaregs it's the other way around. The men wear veils, their faces never seen in public. Their reputation of old was as sinister as possible. Dubois, in *Timbuctoo the Mysterious*, writes:

"Theft was their natural industry—a branch of education, in fact—and they augmented the meagerness of their herds by extorting ransoms from some of their neighbors and completely despoiling others. Travellers and merchants were their principal victims, but when these failed they robbed and killed each other, for their tribes were divided by the most bitter and persistent hatreds."

Today, under French rule, the Tuaregs have been tamed. They live a tribal life out in the desert, and some occasionally come to town at Timbuktu, where the population is Negro. Lowell Junior saw them there, still the veiled tribesmen. Over their heads they wear hoods of blue. He tells how he could see their eyes through holes in the hoods, and chin and mouth when they raised their veils to eat. The color of the skin is the brownish complexion of the Berbers. Why the Tuaregs are veiled seems an impenetrable mystery of ancient custom, the origin of which has been forgotten.

The importance of Timbuktu lies in that simple necessary commodity—salt. In the lands to the south there is no salt, which is as precious as gold to the tribes down toward the Gold Coast. Deep in the Sahara, in the heart of the desert, are salt mines, whose product is transported by long caravans. Timbuktu, on the Niger, is the way station controlling the camel trail. That was the source of its wealth in its day of glory and mystery. Salt still remains the dominating element in the economy of the southern Sahara, and seemingly endless caravans wend their way south from Timbuktu, laden with treasures of salt.

The history of that homely white sodium chloride has its points of interest. In a publication got out by the Arabian American Oil Company, which gives odd bits of information, I find the following:

"Nobody knows when man first discovered salt. The earliest evidence comes from caves in Belgium, where men used salt at least five thousand years ago. Not long afterward Phoenician galleys plied their cargoes of salt to Mediterranean ports, and the salt of Palmyra reckoned heavily in the flourishing ancient trade between the ports of Syria and the Persian Gulf. In our own time the impetus to build the Erie Canal came from the need to get the salt of Syracuse [New York] to market.

"One of the oldest roads in Italy, still an important street, was built to carry salt from Ostia, at the mouth of the Tiber River, to Rome. The Latin word for salt was sal, and the road became known as the Via Salaria. Soldiers guarding the road were given as wages a salarium, a portion of the valuable salt. This is the origin of our word 'salary' and our expression 'not worth his salt.'

"Salt has been as important in the religions of the world as in its commerce. Because of the impressive enduring quality of salt

[ 107 ]

and its power to guard against decay, the white crystals became a symbol of eternity and immortality. The Egyptians used salt in embalming their kings and in sacrifices to their gods. The Greeks and Romans seasoned their sacrificial cakes with salt. The Roman Catholic Church still uses salt in baptism, a practice that began in the fourth century.

"The sanctity of salt in religion partly explains why salt has been used to confirm an oath or compact or to establish friendship in the most diverse countries of recorded history. An Arab 'swears by his salt.' Partaking of a man's salt creates a sacred bond—thus the Arab phrase, 'There is salt between us,' to express deep loyalty. Salt has penetrated, too, into the folklore of many lands. In England a girl can retrieve the wandering heart of a lover by throwing a pinch of salt into the fire on three Friday nights in a row. In the United States many Americans can recall being told as children that they could catch a bird by throwing salt on its tail. This gentle joke may be a vestige from the days when it was believed, quite seriously, that salt thrown on a flying witch would make her motionless."

# Chapter 13

"CHRISTMAS GREETINGS from the Persian Gulf." That was the way I began my next recording for Charles Collingwood and the radio audience back home. I had flown from the Hadramaut of southern Arabia to a fabulous place along the East Arabian coast.

"Greetings from the island of Umm A'Sabaan," the recording continued. "The name means 'Mother of Sea Shells,' which is appropriate. The island is a mass of coral rising out of the sea, but is covered with a layer of shells. These are pearling waters, the oldest in the world, where most of the real pearls come from.

"The island is owned by Max Weston Thornburg and his wife Leila. Max is an authority on the economics of the Middle East, an American oil man who pioneered in the vast affairs of Arabian oil. The principality here is Bahrein, an archipelago in a gulf. The Sultan of Bahrein, father of the present sultan, presented Umm A'Sabaan to the Thornburgs seventeen years ago. It's all a story of flowing gold.

"The British had their big oil fields in Iran and Iraq, and these islands of the Persian Gulf were, and still are in a sense, a part of the far-flung British Empire. But they hadn't suspected that there was another oil field here at Bahrein.

"A New Zealander, Major Frank Holmes, got the original concession. He sold it to Andrew Mellon of Pittsburgh. When Mellon became Secretary of the Treasury in Washington he wanted to divest himself of all international holdings, so he sold out to Standard of California, and they made a fifty-fifty deal with the Texas Company.

"The geological work was all done by Fred Davies, in 1930. Then Ed Skinner struck oil on Bahrein Island, in '32. The third step came in 1936, when Max Thornburg from California came out and built a great refinery. In 1940, Max extended the concession to all of Bahrein, the entire archipelago.

"The oil field brought undreamed-of wealth to the sheik. So naturally he and Max became warm friends—and out of that friendship came the presentation of the island.

"It was flat, utterly barren, uninhabited, without a drop of fresh water. So you can't help wondering whether Sheik Hamed thought that the Thornburgs would ever even put up a hut. But modern engineering has its genii who perform miracles equal to any performed by genii who came to carry out the wishes of Aladdin when he rubbed that magic lamp.

"An artesian well was drilled right through the top layer of sea shells and on through the coral and the limestone, down to a depth of 260 feet, and out came a geyser of cool, clear, sweet water that brought the ruler of Bahrein and all his sheiks over in a hurry to behold the wonder.

"Since then, in the past sixteen years, the island has been transformed from a blazing, treeless desert in the roaring-hot Persian Gulf to a veritable Garden of Eden—without the serpent. There are no serpents on the island; in fact, few insects.

"Gardens now cover about a third of the mile-long island. The trees that dominate the scene are tall coconut palms, shorter date palms of ten varieties, and fruit trees, such as banana and pomegranate, and especially tall oleanders.

"Running the length of the oasis is an avenue right through a long green tunnel. This runs north and south. East and west are more such green avenues leading to the homes of the number one boy, Mohammed, a Persian; the cook, who is from Goa; the head boatman, a black Arab; and the gardeners, who are from El Hasa.

"The many Europeans and Americans, oil personnel, Navy

and Air Force people, representatives of Britain, the civil aviation crowd, sheiks and others who live on the main island, with its 120,000 people, come to Umm A'Sabaan to swim in the sea or the Thornburgs' swimming pool and enjoy the cool breezes here.

"Lowell Junior and his wife, just in from Central Asia, from an expedition to the Himalayas, the Karakorams, flew here in their own plane. When they saw Umm A'Sabaan they figured that there was still enough room on the south end of the island for an air strip. So they rounded up all the manpower they could find on the island—and soon their plane was flying back and forth to the capital, Manama, on the main island, several times a day.

"The rest of the time the plane is parked at the far end of that main avenue of oleanders, in contrast to the dhows that sail by, manned by the sons of Sindbad."

That was quite a paradise at which to spend Christmas, a paradise with old memories of the pearl fisheries and present marvels of oil.

In the King James version of the Old Testament there is mention of "slime." Genesis speaks of "slime" as occurring in Mesopotamia and of "slime" pits. It is clear that the "slime" was petroleum.

In the Latin Vulgate, the translation of the Bible made by St. Jerome in the fourth century A.D., the word "slime" is given as "bitumen." This was the term used by the Romans, "petroleum" not coming into vogue until a later date. The classical writers make frequent mention of "bitumen," and give ample evidence that petroleum was well known in antiquity and that there were abundant signs of the great oil fields in the Middle East. Herodotus notes the presence of oil in Mesopotamia.

But was petroleum of any great consequence in antiquity? The answer might seem to be—no. It was used for unguents and in medicines of those days, minor purposes. It was not employed systematically for light and heat in the ancient world: the chemistry of kerosene, gasoline, and other petroleum fuels was undreamed of. Yet that Mid-Eastern oil of early days played a dominant part in history. Without it the course of civilization might have been very different. It was the principal ingredient of Greek Fire.

For centuries Greek Fire was a thing of mystery and terror in war, the prime weapon of the Byzantine Empire. It was employed destructively against ships, streams of liquid flame setting them ablaze. From the walls of Constantinople Greek Fire beat off naval attacks and gave the victory to the Byzantines in battles between warships at sea. Byzantium, with its cultural heritage for subsequent Western civilization, could hardly have survived without it.

The development of Greek Fire is attributed to a Greek architect, Kallinikos, who came to Constantinople from Syria about A.D. 650 and gave the Byzantines the formula. Its essential ingredients were petroleum and quicklime. When the mixture was exposed to moisture, it burst into flame by spontaneous combustion. The quicklime, in contact with water, generated heat enough to ignite the petroleum. Sulphur increased the burning potency of the stuff.

The liquid mixture was propelled through a tube by a powerful pump and hurled in a stream. Water from a hose was applied as the stream left the tube, and the liquid took fire as it shot through the air. It was sometimes called wet fire or sea fire. Striking a wooden ship, it would set it ablaze, the liquid fire clinging to the wood and burning stubbornly. Today this old idea has been revived in another form, the flame throwers and the napalm of modern warfare.

The appearance of Greek Fire came at a touchy moment for the Byzantines. The great sweep of Arab conquest launched by Mohammed was in full career. The Christians lost Syria, Palestine, Egypt; the Moslems made Constantinople their goal, sending fleets against the imperial city.

In 677 a Moslem armada sailed into the Sea of Marmora, near Constantinople. There was a naval battle. The Byzantine galleys closed with hostile warships and discharged streams of Greek Fire. Arab ships were set ablaze, and the Byzantines won an overwhelming victory. Forty years later the Arabs besieged

Constantinople, but again Greek Fire was decisive, and they failed to take the city.

The most remarkable Greek Fire story tells of a naval battle of fifteen ships against a thousand ships. This occurred in a war between the Byzantines and the Russians who, in the early Middle Ages, established a powerful state north of the Black Sea. They made raids across the water against Constantinople, and one of their princes, Igor by name, launched a huge expedition. Robert Forbes, in a treatise on the use of oil in ancient times, relates the following:

"When Igor's Russian fleet, consisting of no less than 1000 small ships, threatened Byzantium, many were burned, and the remainder driven back by a Byzantine squadron of a mere fifteen vessels. A frank and ingenious admission of defeat was made by the Russian fleet on its return home, A.D. 941. The report of the commander stated that: 'The Greeks have a fire resembling the lightning of heaven—and, when they threw it at us, they burned us. For this reason, we could not overcome them.'"

Gibbon, in the *Decline and Fall of the Roman Empire,* calls Greek Fire the "Palladium of the Byzantine state."

The Greeks kept the formula a secret for a long time, safeguarding it with stringent precautions. It was an early-day version of a military secret guarded by security. But, in time, the knowledge got out. Still we don't hear much about Greek Fire in western Europe.

In 1139 the Second Lateran Council of the Church met in Rome. Among its decisions was a decree prohibiting the use in warfare of Greek Fire, together with some other devices, on the ground that it was inhuman. The Church decision was observed in feudal Europe, a thing to shame this modern atomic civilization of ours.

Greek Fire, in time, passed out of mind with the coming of gunpowder.

Today the "slime" reported in Genesis, the greasy stuff oozing out of the ground or appearing on the water of lakes or streams, as described by various ancient writers, is a dominant factor in the modern world. It is producing strange results, as I reported when we were filming in the explosive Middle East.

"The atomic era may be just around the corner, but if the world's flow of oil suddenly stopped, well, can you imagine what would happen to our present civilization?

"Bahrein, where I am, is the focal center of this Middle East realm of oil. All around us are the installations of the Bahrein oil field. To the west, we can see the low desert coast of Arabia. At night the Aramco flares at Dhahran are visible. Headquarters of the enormous Arabian oil field, owned by American companies and the government of Saudi Arabia, this is the largest of all the oil fields of the world. To the north of us, at the head of the gulf, is Kuwait, another vast oil empire. In fact there now seems to be a question as to who is the richest man in the world, the King of Saudi Arabia or the Sheik of Kuwait.

"Adjoining Kuwait is Iraq, with more immense oil fields, and across the gulf to the east of us is Persia, Iran. Everybody knows about Persian oil, especially the huge Abadan refinery, and the major role it has played in recent world affairs critical for us.

"To the south of us the crescent-shaped coast of Oman curves around the bottom of the Persian Gulf, almost transforming it into a lake. Here, presumably, beneath the sands of Oman and Muscat, there is more oil.

"So Bahrein is the center of an area that is pouring out more oil than all of the rest of the world put together. And strange as it may seem, only a few people outside of this area know the name of the capital city of Bahrein and the name of its ruler.

"The capital is Manama, from which I am giving you this report. Its absolute ruler is a Persian Gulf prince whose lineage goes back to the days when the caliphs ruled in Baghdad. He says all the way back to Adam and Eve. His name: Sheik Suleiman ben Hamid el Kalifah.

"His own family is of Arabian origin, pure Arab, he tells us. But his subjects come from almost every land in the East. For this has been a crossroads of the world for thousands of years. So Bahreinis hail from many lands in Asia, as well as from the

East and from Central Africa. Here also are a sprinkling of Europeans and a colony of American oil people.

"Planes fly from the Persian Gulf to the United States almost daily. ARAMCO, alone, has two a week to New York. Then there are BOAC, KLM, TWA, and various feeder lines from a dozen countries. Recently I flew in with U. S. Air Force General Lee Grover, who at one time was chief of staff to George Kenney in the South Pacific. Grover told me that he and his airmen operate a great military air network now, the hub of which is Muharraq, a suburb of Manama, capital of Bahrein.

"So much for the background, now for news of what is happening here. An echo of what's happening all over this part of the world; happening to a couple of hundred million people. And since we Americans are trying to play the sort of role that we have assumed—or had forced upon us—in this post-World War era, we ought to know more about this explosive area. Alas, it is all too apparent—obvious here on the spot—that we are playing our role clumsily—not wisely.

"Ten days before we started on this flight around the world, a news story came from Bahrein, telling about a general strike in these islands of the Persian Gulf. It sounded like a popular revolt against Sheik Suleiman, the Prince of Pearls and Oil. Then we heard no more about it, so I wondered what had happened. I've just discovered how complex it is—as all things are out here.

"Since the period between 1930 and 1940, when American engineers Fred Davies, Ed Skinner, Max Thornburg, and others opened up this first American Middle East oil field, almost endless millions of dollars of liquid gold have flowed from beneath these sands and these layers of coral. Can you imagine what all that wealth has done to the Arab ruling clans that have pocketed a lot of those millions!

"True, some of it has been wisely spent. Sir Charles Belgrave, adviser to Sheik Suleiman ben Hamid el Kalifah, has seen to it that one third of the income from Bahrein oil has gone into roads, sanitation, schools, hospitals, modern public buildings, and so on. Even so, wealth in astronomical figures has gone into the pockets of the local aristocracy, with results that you can guess. Corruption, accompanied by injustice, is said to have been the order of the day.

"So agitators have been at work. But, in a realm where the ruler can say, 'Off with your head,' not many of the abler and more sober citizens have wanted to speak up. However, a secret committee of one hundred was organized, including many important people, and there was some sort of mysterious check made person to person, among key people. A fairly wide canvass, I understand. Whereupon they announced that they had held an election, and that certain of their number were chosen, by the people, as a committee.

"This group of eight then asked the ruler for an audience to present grievances. He refused. After a number of requests, the committee threatened a general strike, all business to come to a standstill in these islands.

"Sheik Suleiman and his satellites thought, oh, this is merely an empty threat. But the strike was called. And there was the news I had over my press wires before I left New York. Followed by—silence. No more word.

"Now I find what happened was this: The sheik quickly found that he was in real trouble. So he appointed his own group to meet with the committee of eight. For everything at Bahrein had come to a full stop. Since then there have been repeated sessions behind closed doors, with no definite word of the outcome. But it's easy to predict approximately what is going to happen.

"The rumor coming from the meetings is that as a minimum Sheik Suleiman ben Hamid will no longer be able to rule in the arbitrary way that had been so successful for a thousand years. Henceforth he'll have to report to his people, tell them the things that he has done for them and why. He has in fact done much, a benign ruler, in many ways. But from now on he will have to tell his people what he hopes to do for them in the future.

"Of more immediate importance, he will announce a reorganization of the law courts.

[ 116 ]

"Hitherto their courts of justice have been run by lesser members of the royal family. To this one objection is religious. The two great divisions in the Moslem world are the Sunnis and the Shiahs. The ruler here and all his relatives are Sunnis. But the people, most of them, are Shiahs. Henceforth, it's a safe prediction, some of the courts will be presided over by Shiah magistrates. In the past there have been none.

"Just another illustration of how all of the Middle East is in a ferment. Because of oil alone, we are deeply interested and deeply involved."

As I look over the script of that news report, I realize it might be too much to expect the American radio audience to be aware of subtleties of Mohammedan theology. Who are the Sunnis and Shiahs? The answer takes us to a fascinating page of history, and can be simplified in broad lines.

From its beginning Islam, like all religions, showed a tendency to split into sects, and Sunni and Shiah represent the first and the basic religious division. The cleavage goes back to the days immediately following the Prophet Mohammed.

In the history of Christianity the earliest dissensions were doctrinal, and concerned chiefly with the nature of Christ, with subtleties of the dogma of the Trinity. In Islam the dispute concerned the succession to authority. Who should the leader be? Who should take Mohammed's place? The question was less one of theology than of government and dynasty.

Mohammed, when he died, named no successor. He had no son, only a daughter, Fatima, married to his young cousin Ali. There were some who thought that Ali should be the successor, the caliph. He represented the claim of family inheritance. The choice was made by the leaders among the followers of the Prophet, his old companions. They passed over Ali, and named Abu Bekr, the aged father-in-law of Mohammed, distinguished for ability and wisdom. This ignoring of the claims of the Prophet's son-in-law laid the seeds of dissension and marked the beginning of the split between Sunni and Shiah. The Sunnis accept the official successors. The Shiahs hold to the inheritance of Ali.

Upon the death of the aged Abu Bekr the question came up again, and this time the choice fell on Omar, who had been one of Mohammed's chief companions. Ali's claim was rejected again. Omar was one of the greatest of caliphs, and for ten years presided over the conquering sweep of Islam. When he died, the story was repeated—Ali was passed over again. The faction opposing him prevailed, and Othman became caliph. He was a kinsman of the Prophet and a disappointment. His reign was weak and corrupt.

These arrangements for the succession, with Ali's claim ignored three times, brought about a feeling more and more that injustice was done. Ali's partisans increased in numbers and bitterness. The division was hardening, and subsequent events made it catastrophic.

Caliph Othman was assassinated, and then at long last Ali was chosen. But a kinsman of Othman was military governor of Syria, and he revolted. Ali brought an army against him, and a battle was fought. It was indecisive, and Ali agreed to a compromise. This weakness of the caliph enraged some of his own followers, and Ali was murdered. He seems to have been an ineffectual figure destined to calamity, but he left a large body of devoted adherents.

Ali and Fatima had two sons, Hasan and Husein, grandsons of Mohammed, who succeeded to Ali's claim and inherited the rights of descendants of the Prophet. Hasan, the elder, was acknowledged as caliph, but this involved him in war with the governor of Syria, who had the military power. He was not of the sterner stuff, and soon went into retirement, resigning the perilous eminence of the caliph.

But there was no reconciling the partisans of Ali. They invited his younger son Husein to make a bid for the succession, and this led to the final catastrophe. Husein and a band of followers marched into Iraq, and there were defeated and massacred. The slaying of Husein, grandson of Mohammed, became the supreme martyrdom for the faction of Ali, and to this day is bewailed by the Shiah sect with liturgies of lamentation.

The dynasty at Damascus assumed the caliphate, and this

was accepted by the Moslem world in general. It was the official succession, acknowledged by the Sunnis. They represent orthodox Islam.

The Shiahs continued as a sect, giving their fealty to a line of descendants of Mohammed and Ali, the twelve imams. The twelfth imam vanished in the Middle Ages, but he, they believe, will return as the Mahdi. The Shiahs, who split into sects of their own, were scattered everywhere in Islam as dissidents, rising to dominance at one place or another from time to time. Today they prevail in Iran and Yemen, where theirs is the dominant religion. The Shiah is the more elaborate branch of Islam, with saints and shrines and mystical practices.

# Chapter 14

In the middle of the eighteenth century Mohammed Ibn Abdul Wahab made his appearance as a religious reformer on the Arabian scene. For years he had traveled and studied, seeking the true light of the Koran. At Damascus and at Basra he had sought knowledge, and had made the pilgrimage to Mecca. Now, in middle life, he was convinced that Islam had fallen into corruption and had abandoned the way of the Prophet. Islam had always had a strain of extreme puritanism, and Ibn Abdul Wahab was one of the most austere. An extreme Sunni conservative, he preached a return to primitive simplicities. He denounced elaborations of doctrine and religious practices, and all the ways of luxury and frivolity. He founded the Wahabi sect.

After his travels, he returned to his home town of Ayaina in the Nejd, the great desert of Central Arabia, and taught his doctrine of zealous faith and the austere life. He soon discovered the soundness of the old saying about a prophet not being without honor save in his own country. The local ruler considered him a nuisance, and Ibn Abdul Wahab found it expedient to depart. He took refuge at the court of a desert sheik, where he preached and was accepted. His experience was not unlike that of Mohammed, who was rejected by his native Mecca and accepted at Medina.

His host, Mohammed Ibn Saud, was a petty but ambitious

potentate of eighteenth-century Arabia, who found the teaching of Ibn Abdul Wahab not only good doctrine but also excellent politics. The Bedouin of the desert were always susceptible to an appeal to fanaticism. The Wahabi doctrine was preached among them and they rallied to it. In time Ibn Abdul Wahab departed to the gardens of paradise, and Mohammed Ibn Saud was left at the head of the Wahabis. With an army of tribal zealots he was off on a career of conquest.

During the ensuing years the Wahabi movement conquered nearly all of Arabia. Under the dynasty of Saud the puritan host carried war to the borders of Oman and Yemen, and captured the holy cities of Mecca and Medina, where they ravaged the sites of pilgrim veneration not deemed orthodox according to the austere simplicities of Wahabi doctrine. This was at the beginning of the nineteenth century, and it seemed as if Saudi kings were destined to rule over a United Arabia.

A vague sovereignty over Arabia was claimed by Turkey, which held the fringes of the desert, and the sultan at Constantinople could not look with equanimity on the formation of an Arabian empire. But the sultan of the day was in no position to interfere. He had his troubles elsewhere, especially in Egypt, where his governor, Mohammed Ali, was setting up as an independent potentate. In time Mohammed Ali established an Egyptian dynasty which, with vicissitudes, lasted until our own day with King Farouk, recently overthrown.

The sultan, confronted by the Wahabis in Arabia and his refractory vassal in Egypt, adopted a subtle policy. He commissioned Mohammed Ali in Egypt to break the Wahabi power in Arabia. Mohammed Ali obliged. An Egyptian army invaded Arabia and began a war against the Wahabis which ended finally in the collapse of the puritan empire. The Saudi king was sent to Constantinople, where he was beheaded.

For years after that Central Arabia was in turmoil. The Wahabi movement persisted as a fanatical religious sect. In time a prince of the lineage of Saud established a minor principality with its capital at the desert town of Riyadh, under the nominal sovereignty of Egypt. The Wahabi power was rising again, and by the middle of the nineteenth century it seemed to be on its way to dominating Arabia again. But it foundered in a maze of feuds and intrigues in the dynasty of Saud. Two brothers fought for the sovereignty of the Wahabis, and this brought anarchy.

It likewise brought opportunity to a rival principality in the north, the Shammar, which had a ruthless, able ruler, Mohammed Ibn Rashid. He overthrew the Wahabis, captured Riyadh, and drove the members of the dynasty of Saud into exile. Ibn Rashid, during the remainder of a long life, ruled most of Arabia with energy and efficiency. In the later years of the nineteenth century the Wahabis were a mere sect of desert puritans. The descendants of the House of Saud were scattered exiles, but fate had strange tricks to play.

Among the exiles was a youth who grew to manhood watching the course of events in his family's former realm. His name: Abdul Aziz Ibn Saud. He was much interested by the tidings he heard. The potent Ibn Rashid died, and affairs in his family were falling into confusion. Discontent was rife in the Wahabi country. Ibn Saud was twenty, a young giant. With a band of companions, he made his way secretly to Riyadh, the old Wahabi capital, which was held by an alien garrison. By night they scaled the city wall, and fell upon the defenders by surprise. Ibn Saud killed the governor with his own hand, and summoned the Wahabis to rise. In a brief time he was master of Riyadh and the surrounding country.

This began a long series of desert marches and battles. Once again the Wahabi puritans were in the ascendant. Ibn Saud, with enemies to face on all sides, conducted years of warfare, varying from raids by camel riders to military engagements. He won control of Central Arabia and was hailed as the greatest warrior of the desert. This threat of a new Arabian empire brought about the intervention of Turkey, but Ibn Saud fought Turkish forces to a standstill.

Such was the situation when the First World War broke out, and Turkey was in it on the side of the Germans. Ibn Saud seemed a likely ally for the British, and an emissary, Captain W. H. I. Shakespear, was sent. He joined Ibn Saud, but presently was killed in a desert battle. In any case, British policy veered away from the potentate of Central Arabia.

At Mecca was Sherif Husein, who had large dynastic claims of primacy among the Arabs of the Hejaz. He negotiated with the British for an Arab revolt against the Turks, and an agreement was made. This brought into the picture Lawrence of Arabia, as British agent in the insurrection of Arab tribes. Lawrence joined Husein's son Feisal at the head of a Bedouin army, and was the effective leader of the Revolt of the Desert, which aided in the defeat of the Turks and made Lawrence immortal.

In Central Arabia Ibn Saud waited. Presently Husein proclaimed himself King of Arabia. A conflict was inevitable, and it came shortly after the end of World War I. Ibn Saud won a complete victory, invaded the Hejaz, and took the holy cities of Mecca and Medina, which he annexed to his kingdom. This made him the lord of all Arabia except for the extreme south and some isolated corners.

A master organizer, assisted by another British political officer, Captain St. John Philby, he consolidated his kingdom along Wahabi lines—a puritanical regime of the desert. As the head of the Wahabi sect, he was orthodox, rigorous, though Wahabi puritanism never did extend to the matter of wives. Ibn Saud was an enthusiastic polygamist and was reputed to have had a hundred wives.

Then occurred one of the fine ironies of recent history. The great oil strikes of the Middle East were made, and the greatest of all was in Saudi Arabia, the realm of the puritanical Wahabi. American oil men negotiated concessions with Ibn Saud, and soon wealth was pouring forth from under the sands along the Persian Gulf. For ages the deserts of Central Arabia have been just about the most poverty-stricken lands in the world. Now they produce one of the greatest outpourings of wealth ever known.

The result is a fantasy, a singular wonder of the world. Ibn Saud died at a great age and was succeeded by his son, named Saud. I visited the court of King Saud, and here is a recorded account.

"I called on American Consul General John Kerrigan at Dhahran, who told me that I should first pay my respects to the local Arab governor. So we drove ten miles to the governor's headquarters.

"Squatting or standing outside were maybe a hundred men of the desert, all armed to the teeth, many with strong faces and flashing eyes. They looked us over rather coldly; no smiles of greeting. Inside we went along a corridor lined with guards, some with rifles, others with scimitars and side arms, and were ushered into a room about the size of the average small hotel ballroom. It was high-ceilinged, rather dim, with oriental rugs on the floor, low, overstuffed, heavy chairs and divans all the way round the wall, maybe half of them occupied by more bearded sheiks.

"At one end, only one person—the largest man in the room, huge. He rose as we entered. We strode across and I was introduced to the Emir Saud ben Djului, the most powerful man in this part of Arabia, Governor of Alhassa, which contains most of the oil. Face like a full moon, only dark, and with a massive black beard.

"For the first time since I landed in Saudi Arabia, I saw an Arab smile. He greeted us warmly, asked for our health, about our long journey, and motioned for a slave to bring coffee. This was served to us in tiny cups—and magician John Mulholland couldn't have gone through the ceremony with greater dexterity.

"This giant black, with tribal slashes on his cheek, a pistol on his hip and a rifle across his back, whipped the spiced coffee out of a long, delicately curving spout in a two-foot stream, hitting the little cup right on the button. He was holding it over my lap at the time and looking me in the eye without a flicker of expression. I thought surely it would go all over me—but not a drop! You drink it bottoms up.

"A young sheik interpreted for us. He remained on one knee at the feet of the emir throughout the audience. The conversation for the most part was just jovial banter. Emir Djului evidently likes to kid his guests. He certainly did me.

[ 124 ]

"He asked about Lowell Junior, who was engaged, as I told him, on a project in Asia and Africa, and flying his plane. When I informed him that I had only one son, he said he would like to supply me with another wife for my stay, no matter how brief that might be. True desert hospitality. When I told him that my wife was just across the gulf, on the Thornburg island of Umm A'Sabaan, he laughed and said: 'Well, that's far enough away.' The emir himself has many, many wives and children by the dozen.

"Consul Kerrigan told me that our host is one of the strong men of modern Arabia, his father a companion-in-arms of the late King Ibn Saud. He was with Ibn Saud on that historic night when they went over the wall and captured Riyadh, the city that is now the Saudi capital. Consul Kerrigan added that Djului is the right arm of the present monarch of the sands, King Saud.

"Suitable respects having been paid to the governor, the next thing was a trip to Riyadh. With the possible exception of Lhasa, the Dalai Lama's city in Tibet, and San'a, the lofty mountain capital of the Imam of Yemen, I suppose this is the least-known capital in the world. When last I was in this part of the Middle East only two Europeans that I knew of had been to this walled city in the middle of the Arabian Peninsula.

"The first was Captain W. H. I. Shakespear, who accompanied the giant young Bedouin warrior Ibn Saud on one of his desert campaigns, and was killed. The other, his British successor, the foremost of all Arabian explorers, St. John Philby, who turned Mohammedan and stayed here.

"But this old planet has been undergoing violent changes. With perhaps the most violent of all right here. And now you can fly to Riyadh, the capital of Saudi Arabia—*if* you can get a Saudi visa, and *if* the king personally will permit you to leave Jidda, his seaport on the Red Sea, or Dhahran, his oil port on the Persian Gulf.

"My arrival at Bahrein luckily coincided with the return to Riyadh of King Saud from a hunting trip in the desert. He gave the necessary royal nod, and up I flew from Dhahran, in a plane manned by two young Americans.

"The pilot said they were not allowed to fly over Riyadh, and he landed me on a desert strip east of the city, where I was met by an Arab military officer on King Saud's staff, and by his personal secretary, Sheik Abdullah Bulkhair, who apparently is to be my constant companion.

"The first thing that impressed me about the Saudi capital was the number of autos, and the modern metaled road from the air strip into the city. Mostly American cars, and many of them of the more expensive type. I was told that the most profitable Cadillac agency in the world is here. Because it's the car the king prefers. He and his father, the late King Ibn Saud, bought fleets of them for their many wives. The present ruler and all of his forty-odd brothers and all the members of their families have them.

"One of the first buildings I saw, after my arrival, was the royal school, attended only by the sons of the present king. He has twenty-five sons. The eldest, the Emir Fahid, is twenty-seven years old. And each of the twenty-five sons has his own Cadillac, a driver, and a personal servant who goes to school with him to stand by to pour tea whenever his youthful royal master feels he needs a spot of tea. Each son before going to school has breakfast with his particular mother.

"Later, when I met King Saud, he asked me how many sons I had. When I replied that I had one, but wished I had twenty-five, Prince Fahid, who was with us, spoke, and in perfect English said that one was enough! He said it with feeling.

"Prince Fahid, by the way, is not the crown prince. The next in line for the throne is Saud's brother, Prince Feisal, who is well known in the West.

"When the mighty Abdul Aziz Ibn Saud, was gathered to his fathers a year and a half ago there were rumors coming out of Central Arabia to the effect that Saud, his eldest son, might not succeed to the throne. That it might go straightway to his cosmopolite brother Feisal. But what differences there may have been were composed. Saud became king, and fairly recently it

Another view of the elephant school.

*You can see why the Greeks gave them the name of hippopotamus, mean-ing "river horse."*

Photo by Edwin W. Sippel

*The tribe assembles for the dance.*    Photo by Edwin W. Sippel

*The Watusi, the Tall People, make a great point of retaining their traditional tribal dances, though life is becoming modern in the Belgian Congo.*

Photo by Edwin W. Sippel

The entrance to Jerusalem by St. Stephen's Gate, which honors the memory of the first Christian martyr.

Photo by Edwin W. Sippel

The Church of the Holy Sepulchre, with scaffolding that indicates how the walls of the venerable shrine are often in need of repairs.

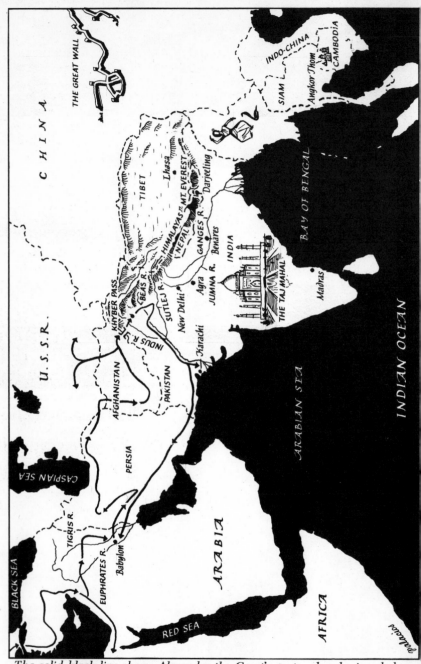

*The solid black line shows Alexander the Great's route when he invaded India in 327 B.C. Soon after crossing the Indus he turned back.*

The CINERAMA crew and camera film the dances of the Watusi warriors, in the presence of the Mwami and his Belgian adviser. Photo by Edwin W. Sippel

Butera is a cheerful genius, as well he might be, considering his African fame as a dancer. Photo by Edwin W. Sippel

*The Mwami, king of the Watusi, dwarfs his Belgian adviser, who is of normal stature.*

Photo by Edwin W. Sippel

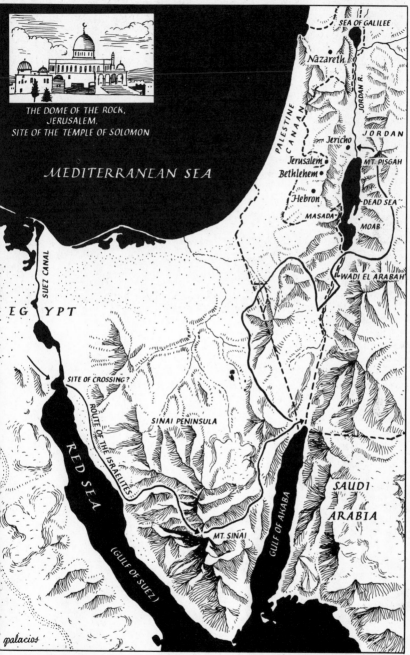

THE DOME OF THE ROCK,
JERUSALEM,
SITE OF THE TEMPLE OF SOLOMON

MEDITERRANEAN SEA

SEA OF GALILEE

Nazareth

PALESTINE CANAAN

JORDAN R.

JORDAN

Jericho

Jerusalem

MT. PISGAH

Bethlehem

DEAD SEA

Hebron

MOAB

MASADA

WADI EL ARABAH

SUEZ CANAL

EGYPT

SITE OF CROSSING?

ROUTE OF THE ISRAELITES

SINAI PENINSULA

RED SEA

(GULF OF SUEZ)

GULF OF AKABA

SAUDI

ARABIA

MT. SINAI

palacios

The Holy Land. Scholars differ on the actual site of the Israelites' crossing
of the Red Sea. The map shows a likely spot.

*The Via Dolorosa in Jerusalem.*

*King Saud, sovereign of the desert and oil fields, whose income is reputed to be a million dollars a day. Here he is seen with some of his numerous sons.*

was announced that Feisal would be next in line, and in the meantime would be prime minister.

"It's great to be the king out here. The output of the Arabian oil fields this past year was nearly a million barrels a day. And of this King Saud's share is fifty per cent. With the current price of oil at two and a half dollars a barrel, his income is over a million dollars each day!

"The night after my arrival at Riyadh, I was lodged in the king's guest house, next to the room Dr. Frank Stinchfield occupied when President Truman had him mysteriously flown over in the White House plane, the *Independence,* about two years ago.

"Our top oil people were afraid the mighty Ibn Saud was about to depart for the Moslem paradise, and they and our State Department people wanted to postpone that departure as long as possible. So one of our top surgeons was rushed here on a secret mission.

"His reward for being away from his practice for a month was one camel saddle. It would be natural for the king to figure all this was at the behest of our President. Which it was. Otherwise he, a most generous king, would have given the great surgeon at least a couple of Cadillacs—plus a Buick for the lady in his harem.

"My room is thirty by thirty by twenty-five feet high. Oriental rugs, twin beds, and nearby a palatial reception room three times larger, with ornate Italian heavily gilded chairs around the wall, and many glittering chandeliers. A giant Sudanese brought me coffee; and now I sat wondering what was going to happen next.

"On the following day Sheik Abdullah Bulkhair had to be with the king part of the time, and I was taken in tow by a young American who has been in Saudi Arabia for ten years. When I met him he was acting as a sort of wazir of finances in connection with the king's personal life and personal possessions, including the royal rugs, furniture, and so on, in the many royal palaces. A unique job if there ever was one.

"I was having breakfast alone in a great banquet hall—enjoying my morning repast of goat's cheese, olives, and pomegranates from the king's garden at Naseriah Palace. Sitting at the end of a long table, with maybe a hundred empty chairs, waited on by two tall black Somalis.

"Al Foster, gaunt and soft-spoken, dropped in unannounced. In a voice just above a whisper he said he had come to greet me. This unexpected call from this young man, who said he was born and raised in Portland, Oregon, was a shock, for I hadn't heard a word about him.

"I asked Al about the chairs, where they had come from. In this land of Araby you usually sit on rugs and cushions. He turned up one of the chairs, glanced at a symbol on the bottom, in Arabic, said he had written it, and that the chairs were made in Italy. He added that once a year one of his duties was to take an invoice of the furnishings in all the palaces, to see what needed replacing—also what had been moved from one palace to another, at the whim of one of the king's wives.

"Later in the day Al took me a few miles outside the city to the largest oasis I visited, and we went through the most attractive of the palaces I saw in Central Arabia. When he was still crown prince, Saud built Bedeeiah Palace for himself. One day the aged Abdul Aziz Ibn Saud said to his son: 'Take me out and show me what you have been doing at Bedeeiah.' When he saw, he liked it so much that he said: 'Fine! I'll move out here at once.' Which he did.

"Whereupon the crown prince had his men rush to Bedeeiah, take away all of the spick and span new furniture and replace it with some of his father's more beaten-up things from other palaces. He knew that the desert Bedu who were always around the king would demolish his ornate newly imported possessions in a hurry.

"At Bedeeiah Palace Al pointed out sloping ramps between rooms, and between different elevations in the gardens. Ibn Saud suffered from arthritis during his later years, and though a giant, finally his legs wouldn't bear him.

"President Roosevelt, when they met aboard the presidential warship, after Yalta, gave him a wheel chair—the spare he had along. The report was that from then on the king always sat in it, usually propelling himself. But I learned here that it was not the presidential chair at all. That hadn't been big enough. So Ibn Saud had had it copied in a larger size. The ramps at Bedeeiah Palace were constructed for that chair.

"Al Foster told me he thought one of the reasons he himself had stayed on so long was that the present king likes to play pool, has six pool tables in his main palace, and will get Al out of bed late at night for a fast game of 'rotation' or 'fifteen ball.' Or to play skee ball, an American modified bowling game that he likes and at which he is a whiz. Young Foster also said his stay at Riyadh might have lengthened because he plays jazz on the piano in a way that delights the monarch who rules the land of Araby.

"Anyhow Al likes life in Riyadh, enjoys driving about in the car King Saud presented to him, and doesn't want to hurry back to the city of roses on the banks of the Willamette in the shadow of Mount Hood. He prefers the excitement and romance that go with life at the strangest court on earth, in the walled capital of Riyadh."

# Chapter 15

On the following morning young Sheik Abdullah Bulkhair called for me. I was to have dinner at the palace that evening, but in the meantime, it seemed, I was to be given a glimpse of the king in advance. The sheik bowed me into his eight-passenger limousine and we drove to the main square in the heart of the city of Riyadh.

"Dozens of others, most of them bearded sheiks in their flowing robes, were stepping out of their big cars as we drove up to the old palace, inside the ancient city walls, where the Arabian king conducts most of his affairs of state. A few minutes later, the sound of sirens in the distance. Then two jeeps, four men in uniform in each, one of them the commander-in-chief of the army. In each jeep a machine gun mounted on a tripod, ready for action.

"Then the king, alone, in his limousine. I was told no one ever sits beside the king. Then came six more jeeps, also with bristling machine guns. As His Majesty Ibn Saud stepped out a great shout went up: '*Allah homma towel omr jala la telmalek* [God save the king]!' Or something of the sort, said Sheik Abdullah.

"During the day His Majesty would deal with the routine problems that a desert potentate must handle—internal matters, differences between sheik and sheik. For his brother Prince Feisal handles foreign affairs, when he is not far out in the desert shooting oryx and gazelle as he was at the time.

"Meanwhile, after a glimpse of desert royalty, I was taken for a tour of Riyadh, a city that not many outsiders have seen. Even the Americans who have developed and hold the key posts in the largest of all oil fields, and are supplying the wealth that is transforming Arabia—most of them are never given a chance to visit the king's capital, far up on the central plateau.

"A courier overtook us with a copy of the morning paper, the only daily printed in the country. Published in the holy city of Mecca, it had just been flown up in one of the king's planes— from a city from which all but Moslems are still absolutely excluded. The newspaper was printed in Arabic of course. But in the middle of the first page were pictures of President Eisenhower, British Foreign Secretary Eden, and Secretary of State John Foster Dulles.

"My companion read the headlines to me in English with an American accent. For the king's 'man Friday,' like so many of the top men in the Near and Middle East, is a graduate of the American University at Beirut, the number one educational institution in this part of the world.

"The sheik next drove me to the Riyadh date market, then through the narrow and winding streets of the old city to a famous gate. There he jumped out and pointed to a piece of metal embedded in a massive door. The tip of a spear, and above it a great splash of blood, which has been there for fifty-two years.

"It was a grim reminder of how, in 1902, the late Ibn Saud, then an exile, scaled the wall one night with a few companions, entering the city of his forefathers, which was then in the hands of blood enemies. They hid until morning, and then, when the governor emerged through a small opening in the great door, Ibn Saud impaled him with his spear. The tip of it is still there, and now a place visited daily by pilgrims.

"The story tells how the giant young warrior sang out to the people: 'Here is your governor. Come and see him! It is I, Ibn Saud, who speak to you. I, who have returned to take what rightfully belongs to you and to me!' That began his rise to the mastery of Arabia—thirty-eight years before American oil geologists came here and found that under this desert were subterranean lakes of oil.

"Then for a five-hour drive Sheik Abdullah Bulkhair proceeded to show me what magic has been wrought by the wealth that has spouted from hundreds of Arabian-American wells. He took me to a building of which he seemed to be proudest of all, a brand-new hospital, where he had the director, a Syrian, Dr. Shewiki, show us the reception rooms, offices, operating and X-ray rooms, laboratory, up-to-date wards, and modern kitchen.

"He showed me block after block of new government administration buildings, new palaces built by the many Saudi princes, mansions of other rich Arabs, a modern hotel only recently opened, and where I was told you could get a room, with meals, for around thirty-five dollars a day. Living costs are jumping in Arabia, as in many other countries.

"We visited the power plant where the electricity for the city is now generated. If you want electric lights you must first get a chit signed by the king, and then you don't have to pay for it. You can also have a telephone. But only if the king wants you to have one.

"The sheik pointed out areas where subdivisions of modernistic houses are to be built. He even took me into one such home —his own. And introduced me to his beautiful young wife; a most unusual privilege in this Eastern land. For in Riyadh the women are still heavily veiled, and even then you seldom see them. The sheik's bride spoke excellent English, and was charming. She, too, was from Syria, and educated in Egypt.

"Finally my guide took me proudly to the Riyadh railway station. For the king has built one short stretch of standard-gauge track across the desert to Dhahran, with American air-conditioned cars for those who travel first class. A train was standing on a siding, and under it, seeking shade from the desert sun, a flock of goats.

"It was about an hour before sunset that Sheik Abdullah Bulkhair drove me through the old walled city, and then along the new four-lane parkway that leads to Naseriah Palace and gardens. This, I was told, is now the best stretch of road in the country—three or four miles of it. It is in perfect shape, in contrast to other short stretches of metaled highway, like the one to the airport, which is full of holes almost like shell craters.

"A couple of miles beyond Riyadh we passed through a large double stone and stucco four-lane gate, festooned with many colored lights. In a country where electricity is one of the new blessings with which Allah has rewarded the faithful, through his genii, those American oil engineers at Dhahran, they now string lights in all directions.

"Leaving the car at an inner gate, we walked through the king's garden, where great roses, as large as I have ever seen, were in bloom among the palm trees. Passing perhaps a hundred guards, high officials and male relatives of the king, I was escorted straightway to a small audience chamber, where I sat on the king's right and chatted with him for a while—with Sheik Abdullah, the interpreter, down on one knee before his sovereign.

"We talked about the things I had seen during the day, and drank coffee until the voice of a muezzin rang out from a nearby minaret. A reminder that the sun had set. The king led me to the terrace, and there for fifteen minutes he led his advisers, sons, and others in prayer, while I strolled in his garden.

"Sheik Abdullah came for me, asked me to walk beside the king, and we went into a brilliantly lighted banquet hall, some fifty by one hundred feet, the walls all a continuous mirror. The table was U-shaped and large enough to accommodate several hundred.

"The king sat alone at the head, with his top adviser, the elderly Sheik Jamal Husseini, a few feet below on his left, perhaps twelve feet away, and with me on his right in relatively the same position. Then along the table on both sides of the hall sat his advisers, guests, and twenty-five sons. Hanging behind him, a green flag, with its Saudi insignia of a palm tree and crossed scimitars in gold.

"The table seemed spread for a banquet. But I was told the king always dined like this when in Riyadh. Serving us were tall blacks, striking-looking men, all in white, including white turbans and white gloves. When the soup was brought on my royal host explained that he was on a diet. But then he proceeded to enjoy the many-course meal as much as I did. No wonder. For, like his father before him, he is a large man.

"Sheik Abdullah Bulkhair stood to one side, between us, throughout the dinner, and I did my best to keep up a running conversation, for King Saud himself is not a talkative man. Sheik Jamal Husseini, who speaks fluent English, occasionally took part in the conversation, which was mainly about Saud's forty-day trip to America, during the war, when I had first met him.

"He said he had seen so much, and had moved so fast from city to city, that some of his impressions were all mixed up. But he added that two sights stood out above all the others: the Empire State Building and the Hoover Dam. He said he was particularly interested in the latter, because he has hopes of building dams like it.

"Then he spoke of a suggestion made some years ago by former President Herbert Hoover when he flew over the Middle East. Mr. Hoover at that time said he thought it ought to be possible to divert the waters of those two great Mesopotamian rivers, the Tigris and the Euphrates, and make a paradise out of great areas of the desert. King Saud says he intends to do something about this—if the government of Iraq will co-operate.

"As course followed course I marveled at the food. Aside from a few exotic touches it was a meal such as you would get in the finest American hotel, plus an American 'home cooking' touch. Instead of wines we had a series of non-alcoholic drinks, starting with grape juice and ending with camel's milk.

"When a large glass of milk was put before me, I must have looked puzzled, for Sheik Jamal Husseini said: 'Don't worry, it's pasteurized!' He explained that it was cow's milk from the royal dairy, on a nearby oasis. I remarked that I was wondering whether it could be camel's milk. Whereupon the king said something to a servant and a moment later the cow's milk was whisked away and in its place appeared my wish, a tall cool glass of camel's milk—also pasteurized! So, even though I had just topped off the banquet with a large wedge of typical American coconut cake and ice cream, I now added an Arabian flourish —dates and camel's milk!

"The finding of oil, and the presence of American geologists and engineers, of course means that new words and phrases are finding their way into Arabia. If you ask an Arab, 'What is this?' he'll tell you it's a Stillson wrench. The king was dining with some of our top oil people one night at Dhahran, when the usual American dessert was brought on. Through an interpreter one of the ladies asked the king what they called it in his language. 'Ice cream,' he replied, adding: 'What do you call it in America?'

"Long years ago I discovered that you should not mention a tangible wish to an oriental monarch unless you are prepared to have him do something about it. At this dinner I had another example of how kings like to humor the whims of a guest. For one course we had a delicious bird. He told me it was a bustard he had shot on the desert hunting trip from which he had just returned.

"I said I didn't believe I had ever seen a bustard. Half an hour later when we stepped out on the terrace, lo and behold, up came one of the king's men with a live bustard in his arms! A bird somewhat like a wild turkey. The bearded group—most Saudi Arabians seem to go in for the traditional beard of the desert sheik—gathered in a circle. Their robes closed it completely, and King Saud had the bustard released in our midst, so I could study it.

"While we stood chatting on the terrace up came two servants, not blacks, but Arabs. One sprinkled rose water on King Saud's hands; then on mine. The other held a brazier of glowing coals, so we could dry them. That, I had been told, would be a sign that the party was over, and that His Majesty was about to retire to the harem.

"Puzzled over how such a dinner could be served here in the heart of Arabia, I asked if I might visit the royal kitchens. In response I was taken to the kitchens. As I walked in a man jumped up, embraced me, and said: 'I know you!' and added: 'My name's Bill Gross. I'm from Brooklyn!' A crack American chef. On his visit, when he was crown prince, the king had hired one of our top-flight cooks. My visit had included many shocks, of which this was the climax.

"Several hours later, laden with presents, robes, and a gold watch with His Arabian Majesty's picture on the face, I left for the Persian Gulf. In the middle of an Arabian night, returning from an adventure right out of the *Arabian Nights*."

The one feature of royal Arabian life which excites the most curiosity is the royal harem. Male guests are never invited to the quarters of wives and concubines, but Western women sometimes are. After my return home I noticed a report on the United Press wire about the visit of American Air Force General William H. Turner and his wife to the palace at Riyadh. The dispatch stated:

"Mrs. Turner was introduced to the king and then was taken to the harem to meet his three wives.

"One of the wives wore a diamond the size of a small ash tray on a gold chain, she said. Another had a ring almost as large as a golf ball.

"All wore Parisian evening gowns, bracelets, necklaces and watches encrusted with diamonds.

"The Arabs have a fascination for watches, Mrs. Turner said, but they tell time by the sun.

"Mrs. Turner said she walked through a 'fantastic' garden into the wives' living quarters which were furnished in French furniture of pale pink brocade, rugs from Persia and occasional neon lights.

"She said the Arabs bring back foreign gadgets from their travels and neon lights apparently appeal to them.

"Mrs. Turner said she was joined in the chat by Mrs. Harold E. Talbott, wife of the former U. S. Air Secretary.

"Their husbands were chatting with the king in the main palace in the meantime, she said.

" 'Both Mrs. Talbott and I felt lucky to get our husbands out without any additional wives,' Mrs. Turner said. The king jokingly offered them two each."

All this gives a picture of the state of affairs in the realm of the Wahabi, the puritans of the desert whose austere sect was founded by Mohammed Ibn Abdul Wahab back in the eighteenth century.

Yet things remain exceedingly puritan in some ways. While at Riyadh I made arrangements for the Cinerama crew to film that fantastic technological wonder, Arabian oil, including King Saud at his court. The king entertained all eighteen at luncheon in that same dining hall surrounded by mirrors. For drinks they got camel's milk, and what struck them particularly in Saudi Arabia was prohibition.

Even in the American oil city of Dhahran—this is a dry era. The law of the Koran forbidding alcoholic beverages is strictly enforced, and the American oil man has reverted to the old life of prohibition time in the U.S.A. The Pan American navigator of our clipper *Cinerama*, Ed Sippel, told me afterward how they marveled at home brew and homemade hooch in the American residences at Dhahran. A guest congratulates his host on the quality of the whiskey he has just made. Ed Sippel says it was horrible stuff, reminiscent of the Eighteenth Amendment.

My own story in Arabia included the fulfillment of an ambition I had cherished for years—a look at the Rub al Khali, the Empty Quarter. The first to cross it was my old friend the British explorer Bertram Thomas, who did it by camel caravan twenty years ago, from Muscat. A year later his rival St. John Philby explored another part. Now the Rub al Khali is being opened by the ceaseless quest for oil. Planes fly over occasionally, and I, too, made the trip in our clipper *Cinerama*. Here's the radio report I gave on that unusual flight:

"We flew over a hard, flat region like our own great American desert. Then came the sand dunes. And after that we saw sand dunes of more varieties than I ever dreamed there could be. The first were short in length, giving the desert the appearance of a choppy sea. Only vast, silent and motionless. Then for another thirty or forty miles the dunes were longer. Which must mean that the prevailing winds, the deeper you get into the Empty Quarter, blow with greater constancy.

"I was particularly fascinated about a third of the way across when we looked down on one great section of the desert where the dunes were not shaped as we think of them at all. Here they were round islands of sand—each a hill, coming to a peak in the center, with the sides fluted, as though designed by a cosmic pastry chef. Obviously caused by circular winds. In no other desert in the world had I seen anything like this. And these curiously peaked dunes all seemed to be about the same size— a hundred feet or so in diameter. In height, maybe fifty feet.

"In the heart of the Rub al Khali we crossed over a wide stretch where the sand dunes were high and long, like the great waves you find in the middle of an ocean. The resemblance between this uncharted, little-known desert and the sea is so startling that it's no wonder the Arabian camel, the dromedary, is called 'the ship of the desert.' The shape of these great dunes made it clear that here the prevailing winds are from north to south, and blow steadily.

"Sometimes we were looking out over lakes of salt. But never a sign of moisture, except for some stretches where we saw a low scrub growth; evidently a form of plant life that provides nourishment for that rare, highly prized antelope, the oryx.

"However, so fast are things changing in this present day that within no time at all now the Rub al Khali will be as well known as our own desert regions in Nevada, California, Utah, Arizona, and New Mexico. Because Aramco, the Arabian American Oil Company, working with King Saud, plans to prospect for oil all over the Rub al Khali.

"One outfit, with an air-conditioned motor caravan using huge sand tires, already has penetrated to the heart of the Empty Quarter. There at a depth of two thousand feet, under that previously waterless desert, they have found fresh water. This may mean that within a few years there'll be an oasis, with palm trees, and so on, right in the center of this hitherto mysterious region of silence and death. Why, you may even be flying there to spend a vacation. Could be. Until a few years ago it was just like the Rub al Khali out where Palm Springs and Indio now are in southern California! Lowell Junior, this week—tonight— in his own small plane—is somewhere in this desert.

"Oil geologists believe that the rock structure is just right for the object of their search. They haven't found it yet. But they think they will come up with another ocean of oil under the Empty Quarter. If so, King Saud's income may jump from a million dollars a day to two or three times that.

"Our plane crossed, and recrossed, this little-known region five times, for a total of more than three thousand miles above the Rub al Khali. And that, I believe, should entitle our Pan American clipper skipper to be known henceforth as Captain Page Rub al Khali Smith. And the same for his colleague and copilot John Bateman, navigator Ed Sippel, and purser Pat Hogan."

# Chapter 16

IN PALESTINE, nearly everywhere there's a site and a name hallowed in the Bible. Passing from one to another, you can have a pageant of places to recall the tragedies and the glories from Genesis to Revelations. So we planned to take the Cinerama camera on a trip to trace the Wonder Story of the World.

But there were difficulties. Palestine is tense and disturbed these days with the feud between Israel and the Arabs, and the apprehension of war is everywhere. The border between Israel and the Moslem countries cuts right down the line of the sacred sites. Some are on one side, some on the other, with crossing forbidden much of the time. Permission to film at any place had to be procured, and sometimes was refused because of military security. This made it complicated for the ground crew. I had briefed Paul Mantz on a zigzag series of air shots along the line of the biblical epic. But an airplane straying from one side of the border to the other might get shot down. The anti-aircraft batteries of Israel and the Arabs were many, and we hoped to fly low for our Cinerama panorama of the sacred places.

The result of the political difficulties meant some disappointments. Much that I had wanted to picture in the Holy Land was missing. We had generalized air shots and not enough ground shots. The deficiency would have to be made up by the narrative.

Later we cut the pictures in story form, in two sequences, Old

Testament and New, one beginning with Exodus and showing a sequence of places in the progress of the children of Israel; the other beginning at Bethlehem and going on to places in the Gospel narrative.

Years ago, in World War I days, I had developed a formula for storytelling in combination with film, and now I had a unique opportunity along the same line. In Cinerama, the nature of the medium is such that scenes should run long, as compared with the fast cutting and short scenes of ordinary film. Fast cutting would seem choppy in Cinerama. Long scenes give space for a storytelling technique. As a crowning grace, we were able to work into the text abundant quotations from the King James version. Scene after scene the words from the Bible itself could give the narrative. In large part the Bible could tell the story.

This would need music, music virtually for an oratorio. The score for the *Seven Wonders* was provided by Emil Newman, a top-flight composer of Hollywood. He had his difficulties. When he took over time was short, as it so often is when you work with films. The composition of the music had to be rapid, but we got a magnificent score, provided by Emil Newman in collaboration with composers Jerome Moross, David Raksin, Emil's brother Lionel Newman, and Sol Kaplan. The music written by Jerome Moross is symphonic in character for the biblical sequence.

The correct beginning would have been at the land of Goshen, scenes of today at the place where the Hebrews dwelt during their sojourn in Egypt. But where was the land of Goshen? Nobody knows. There are only inferences.

When Pharaoh, oppressing the Israelites, commanded the destruction of the male children of the Hebrews, Moses' mother placed him in an ark of bulrushes, which she consigned to the reeds along the Nile. This would indicate that the Hebrews dwelt near the Nile, and the belief is that Goshen was in the Nile delta at the westernmost arm by which the river flows into the Mediterranean. The land there would accord with passages in Exodus indicating that Goshen was rich and fertile.

So, for a beginning of the picture, the scenes feature the Nile, busy today with boats as it was in the days of the Pharaohs. The narrative accompanying the picture says: "In Exodus we read how Moses again and again repeated to Pharaoh the command of the Lord: 'Let my people go!'" And the music brings up a chorus of voices in the wailing style traditional to the Hebrew chant.

The route of the Israelites in their flight from Egypt was via the Isthmus of Suez, and there we find an incongruity—a ship traversing the desert, the Suez Canal. Not so long ago that far-famed waterway was a technological wonder of the world. The Israelites journeyed somewhere across this area now cut by the canal, and memories of Moses are mingled with recollections of Ferdinand de Lesseps—incongruous indeed.

He was a French diplomat for years in the consular service, and for some time was assigned to Egypt. There he was inspired by the vision of a canal connecting the Red Sea and the Mediterranean. Nothing came of it until de Lesseps was nearly fifty. Political complications in Paris brought his diplomatic career to an end, a failure which he retrieved by dedicating himself to the dream of a Suez canal. He negotiated a contract with the government at Cairo, rallied the French people to subscribe funds, and presided over the digging of the canal.

Moses was rather different, that mighty figure who, commanded by the Lord, led the children of Israel out of bondage. His engineering was of another sort. It was somewhere on the Isthmus of Suez that the passage of the Red Sea occurred. The biblical account relates how the Lord caused the waters to retire and Moses led his people across dry land, and then the Egyptians pursuing them were overwhelmed by the returning waters. There has been much debate about just where and how this happened. One favorite theory is that the place was a shallow end of the Gulf of Suez, where a strong wind would drive the water off shore.

This was propounded in the last century by Dr. Henry Clay Trumbull, a biblical authority, who pointed out that Exodus states that the Lord sent a strong east wind, which blew the waters all night and made the sea dry land for the Israelites to cross. Dr. Trumbull noted that the winds sweeping into the Gulf of Suez, today, can have something of that effect. This was confirmed for him by de Lesseps of the Suez Canal. Peloubet's Bible Dictionary quotes him as saying:

"M. de Lesseps mentioned to me the extraordinary effects of this kind which he had witnessed in such storms as occur only at intervals of fifteen or twenty years. He had seen the northern end of the sea in places blown almost dry and again had seen the waters driven far overland."

De Lesseps, the creator of the Suez Canal, reflecting on the passage of the Red Sea, makes a beguiling picture.

Just outside Egypt, beyond Suez, there's a jumble of desolate mountains, one of which is Mount Sinai, the mountain of the Ten Commandments. Actually there's some question about which of two lofty peaks it is, but tradition points to Jebel Musa (Arabic, Mountain of Moses), a steep, jagged summit of the Sinai Peninsula. It stands 7359 feet high.

Approached by air, the tall pinnacle of rock is a sight to strike one with awe: "And the Lord came down upon Mount Sinai, on the top of the mount: and the Lord called Moses up to the top of the mount." It was there that the Ten Commandments were given.

Today on the summit there are a small Christian chapel and a small Mohammedan mosque. On the slope are two other chapels, and the Monastery of St. Catherine, where a colony of forty monks reside. In the monastery there is a mortuary where the bones of monks have been piled for centuries and there the skeleton of St. Stephanos sits garbed in monastic gown and hood. These are draped on the sitting skeleton. St. Stephanos died in A.D. 580.

The route of the Israelites, as they wandered for forty years, makes an interesting bit of geography. From Suez they traveled southeast to Mount Sinai, then northeast to the border of Canaan. The triangular-shaped Sinai Peninsula is the wilderness of the Bible, and its craggy desolation deserves the name. Their trail took them to the verge of the Promised Land, Canaan, and they might have marched north into the land of milk and honey.

We read how Moses sent spies into Canaan, all the way to Hebron, where Abraham, Isaac, and Jacob were buried with their wives Sarah, Rebecca, and Leah in the cave of Machpelah. The spies returned with formidable news of the armed strength of the Canaanites and their walled cities. Whereupon the Israelites lost courage and grumbled. They were always longing for the fleshpots of Egypt. So the Lord, in punishment, decreed that they should not enter the Promised Land for many years to come. Aaron, Moses' brother, died on the summit of Mount Hor, almost within sight of the Promised Land. Today, on Mount Hor a shrine marks the traditional site of Aaron's tomb.

This place where the Israelites tarried was the area southeast of the Dead Sea, which extraordinary body of water formed the eastern border of Canaan. With its surface far below sea level and its floor far below its surface, the Dead Sea is along the line of that four-thousand-mile depression beginning with the vast Rift Valley in Africa and extending along the deeps of the Red Sea and the Gulf of Akaba, which connect with the Dead Sea via a desert valley, the Wadi el Arabah. The geological theory is spectacular, and so is the reputation of the Dead Sea.

This ominous name does not occur in sacred Scripture, where the body of water is called "the Sea" or "the Salt Sea," or "the Asphalt Lake." At times chunks of asphalt rise floating to the surface. The name "Dead Sea" occurs only after biblical times. One legend holds that the Dead Sea was formed by the catastrophe that overwhelmed Sodom and Gomorrah, but there's not the slightest evidence for that in the Bible, and all geological knowledge is to the contrary.

The Middle Ages, with their love for dramatic fancy, expatiated on the evil character of that lake which is many times more salty than the ocean. They said no living thing could survive in it, and no bird could fly across it. Actually, in spite of intense saltiness, some primitive marine organisms do exist in its waters, and birds are not bothered by it. Birds, and frogs too, are abundant along its banks. Many travelers find the Dead Sea beautiful, with rippling waters, on which you can recline and read a book!

The final entrance of the Israelites into the Promised Land was made not from the south but from another quarter altogether. They passed around the Dead Sea, on the east, journeying through Moab, in the present kingdom of Jordan, and around the upper end of the Dead Sea. There they faced Canaan near Jericho. But Moses never entered the Promised Land, upon which he gazed from the height of Mount Pisgah.

It was left to his successor Joshua to lead the Israelites into Canaan, and Joshua took Jericho in that famous episode of falling walls. For this our Cinerama narration goes to the Book of Joshua: "And it came to pass, when the people heard the sound of the trumpet, and the people shouted with a great shout, that the wall fell down flat."

From Jericho a historic highway, the Jericho road, leads to Jerusalem, and might well symbolize the rise of Israel to the glory of David and Solomon. The Twelve Tribes fought endlessly against the Canaanites, the Philistines, and gradually won the Promised Land. This culminated with the acquisition of Jerusalem, which thereupon quickly assumed the singular importance that the holy city has had ever since. Jerusalem was not captured by the Israelites from the Jebusites until the time of David, and this coincided with the rise of Israel to the only summit of imperial greatness it was ever to enjoy. Solomon built his Temple at Jerusalem, and that set the seal of sanctity upon the city.

The religious spirit never wearies of singing the wonders of Jerusalem, and historians exhaust their prose in recounting its history. For sheer eventfulness figures will tell the story. Jerusalem has been besieged more than twenty times. Twice the city was utterly destroyed, by the Babylonians and by the Romans. It has passed from one religion to another repeatedly, and was in succession:

Pagan—before the ancient Israelites took possession.
Jewish—with a period of destruction during the Babylonian captivity.

[ 145 ]

Pagan—after the Roman destruction rebuilt as Aelia Capitolina.
Christian—after Constantine.
Moslem—following the rise of Islam.
Christian—under the Crusaders during two different periods.
Moslem—until the present day.

Jerusalem is now divided, the new state of Israel holding the New City, the Moslems retaining the ancient quarter within the walls, where the Mosque of Omar stands on the traditional site of Solomon's Temple. Three temples of the Jews had, in fact, stood there.

Jerusalem was a minor hill fort in a remote era, and is mentioned in Egyptian records of the second millennium before the Christian Era as the seat of a petty principality. The site is of no great consequence for agriculture, for commerce, or for military domination. The history of Jerusalem is to be explained by the power of religion, and the words of the psalmist ring out:

"If I forget thee, O Jerusalem, let my right hand forget her cunning.

"If I do not remember thee, let my tongue cleave to the roof of my mouth."

To the south of Jerusalem, near the shore of the Dead Sea, is a lofty rugged plateau, not unlike a steep mesa of our own American West. This is Masada, which has a tragic place in the history of the misfortunes of the ancient Jewish people.

Masada first comes into prominence with the career of Herod, surnamed the Great and infamous as a savage tyrant. His abilities were as notable as his crimes. He was an Arab of Jewish religion who made himself King of Judea and kept himself in power by a policy of unfailing allegiance to Rome. His father was put into a position of authority by Julius Caesar, and Herod, as a despot in Judea, played the Roman political game with consummate skill.

He raised the power of the Jewish state, suppressed disorder, and rebuilt the Temple. The original Temple of Solomon had been destroyed by the Babylonians of Nebuchadnezzar, and a new shrine had been constructed when the Jews returned from the Babylonian captivity. This had now fallen into disrepair, and Herod built a new Temple with the greatest magnificence.

He was a monster of cruelty, guilty of wholesale murders of members of his family. In the Gospel he is the Herod of the Massacre of the Innocents. On his deathbed he had his son Antipater executed. Josephus, historian of ancient Judea, tells how the dying Herod ordered the killing of many notables among the people, so that there should be grief upon his death, instead of rejoicing.

At Masada Herod built a palace and fortress high on the craggy plateau. The position was one of great strength, and there he could hold sumptuous court and be secure. Today archaeologists have discovered the ruins of Herod's palace on Masada, including a giant cistern cut in the rock where immense supplies of water, collected from the infrequent rains of the arid region, were stored.

Herod flourished by a policy of submission to Rome, but his Jewish subjects never agreed. There were dissensions among his successors, and Rome placed Judea under the rule of Roman governors. Pontius Pilate was a procurator of Judea. There were repeated seditions among the people, leading to the great revolt that brought about the final catastrophe.

The destruction of Jerusalem by Titus in A.D. 70 was one of the major episodes of history. To this day you will see a remarkable memento of it in the Roman Forum. There stands the Arch of Titus, put up to commemorate his victory in Judea. On the arch are bas-reliefs, and one of the sculptured pictures shows a scene in the triumphal processions of the Roman general in which a candelabrum is carried among the spoils of war. It is the seven-branched candlestick from the Temple of Jerusalem.

The city made a defense to the death, and for an epilogue to this there was a similar defense at Herod's old palace-fortress. After the destruction of Jerusalem, a band of Jewish zealots stood siege at Masada. They held out on the summit of the rock until no further resistance was possible. Then they killed their wives, their children, and themselves—a grim final incident in the destruction of the Jewish state and the final dispersion of the ancient Jewish people.

Today, as you fly from Masada eastward, you pass from scenes of rocky desolation to vistas of green fields. This represents modern Israel, with advanced agriculture at communal farms. That color of green is a telltale sign of a unique page of history, the fulfillment of a nineteen-hundred-year-old dream of a people in exile. Nowhere else is anything recorded to compare in historic drama with the restoration of a Jewish state in Palestine.

The modern Zionist movement derives, in one aspect, from an unexpected source—the Dreyfus affair in Paris. In the 1890s, Alfred Dreyfus, a Jewish officer in the French army, was tried for treason, convicted, and sent to Devil's Island. Eventually he was vindicated and found innocent. Throughout the long stormy drama there were anti-Semitic manifestations. From the beginning anti-Semitism was a motive in the prosecution of Dreyfus.

Among the newspaper reporters who covered the trial in Paris was Theodor Herzl, a Viennese journalist. Born in Hungary, he had studied law, then had turned to writing and made a career on the newspapers and as a dramatist in the theatre of Vienna, successful, brilliant, literary. Theodor Herzl might have been regarded as typical of the cosmopolitan Jew in tolerant, easygoing Vienna. He was hardly the kind you'd expect for the role he was to play. Theodor Herzl became the founder of political Zionism.

The anti-Semitism that he witnessed at the Dreyfus trial brought Herzl to a revolutionary conviction. The Jews, he reasoned, must either assimilate and disappear as a people or have a territorial state as their own. He advocated the latter. His experience in the Dreyfus case made him a flaming apostle of Zionism.

Herzl published a pamphlet, *Der Judenstaat*, which made a sensation, and then he went on to rally Jewish opinion to the cause of a Jewish national state. He urged a program of Zionism on chiefs of government, and carried on a propaganda that made Zionism a burning issue of the twentieth century.

There had been religious Zionism down the centuries, and there was a philanthropic movement that settled in Palestine religious colonies of oppressed Jews from eastern Europe. But Herzl's idea was political and in accord with the nationalism of nineteenth-century Europe. He would have been willing to establish a Jewish state anywhere, and the British government made mention of East Africa. There was also talk of the Belgian Congo. But religious Zionism insisted on the ancient land, the two ideas merged, and Palestine was set as the goal of the Zionists.

The rest of it is familiar recent history: how in World War I the British government pledged a Jewish homeland in Palestine, how under British suzerainty this was established, how the Zionists encountered the enmity of the Arabs and became embroiled with the British on questions of Jewish immigration, how the British withdrew from Palestine and the state of Israel was established, and maintained its existence in war with the Arabs. Today Palestine is in a crisis, as it has been so often, ever since the dim days when the children of Israel entered the Promised Land.

Five miles south of Jerusalem is a town of which the Encyclopaedia Britannica says: "Bethlehem has a population of 6600 (5800 Christians), and is a prosperous town with many good houses. The centre of a fertile district, its wine is amongst the best in Palestine." Bethlehem is near the troubled border of Israel and Jordan, on the Jordan side, and is a yearly goal for pilgrims, despite the perilous state of affairs.

Such are the prosy facts about this historical site. For the glory of it we go to the Gospel of St. Luke:

"And she brought forth her firstborn son, and wrapped him in swaddling clothes, and laid him in a manger; because there was no room for them in the inn.

"And there were in the same country shepherds abiding in the field, keeping watch over their flock by night.

"And, lo, the angel of the Lord came upon them, and the glory of the Lord shone round about them: and they were sore afraid.

"And the angel said unto them, Fear not: for, behold, I bring you good tidings of great joy, which shall be to all people.

"For unto you is born this day in the city of David a Saviour, which is Christ the Lord.

"And this shall be a sign unto you: Ye shall find the babe wrapped in swaddling clothes, lying in a manger.

"And suddenly there was with the angel a multitude of the heavenly host praising God, and saying,

"Glory to God in the highest, and on earth peace, good will toward men."

Surely you go to the Gospel to read of the Nativity. But there's another text, of strange tone and character, which has excited a sense of mystery down the centuries. To this day we can only stare and marvel. Forty years before the birth of Christ the Roman poet Virgil wrote:

We have reached the last era in Sibylline song.
Time has conceived and the great sequence of the Ages starts afresh.
Justice, the Virgin, comes back to dwell with us and the rule of Saturn is restored.
The first born of the New Age is already on his way from Heaven down to Earth.
With him the iron race shall end and the Golden Man inherit all the world.
Smile on the Baby's birth, his immaculate Lucina,
Your son Apollo is enthroned at last.

That is from the famous Fourth Eclogue of Virgil, written in the years immediately preceding the advent of—Christianity. He hailed the coming of the Golden Age. In the Roman myth the "rule of Saturn" was the primeval age of happiness, like an era of paradise, which had been followed by the iron age of strife and the sword. Virgil, in one poem after another, acclaimed the new time of peace inaugurated by Caesar Augustus. But in the Fourth Eclogue there is that prediction of the coming of a child, whom he likens to Apollo, and Apollo's mother, called Lucina,

[ 150 ]

is referred to as "immaculate" in the line speaking of the baby's birth.

To this day scholars debate the significance of that famous passage. One supposition, which dates back to antiquity, is that it referred to a child expected to be born to Augustus' daughter Julia, a grandson for the emperor. But that seems none too plausible, considering the tone of the Virgilian prophecy, and it might have been a girl. Scholarship has no definite opinion about the real meaning of the cryptic lines. But the early Christian and the Middle Ages had no doubt. They held that the greatest Roman poet, divinely inspired, had predicted the coming of Christ. You can hardly blame them, when you put two lines together:

"The first born of the New Age is already on his way from Heaven down to Earth." Virgil.

"For unto you is born this day in the city of David a Saviour, which is Christ the Lord." St. Luke.

The Middle Ages regarded Virgil and the Fourth Eclogue with a mystical awe. Sometimes the Roman poet was listed among the prophets. In the *Divine Comedy* it is Virgil who guides Dante through the Inferno and Purgatory.

Nazareth is a flourishing town on the fertile plains of Galilee, now a part of modern Israel. Not far to the east is the valley of the Jordan and the Sea of Galilee, also called Lake Tiberias and Lake Gennesaret. Jesus grew to manhood at Nazareth in the carpenter's home of Joseph and Mary, and most of the events of his early career are placed in the region of the valley, the river, and the lake.

These are of remarkable geological interest, and once again we come to the theme of the Rift Valley, of which they are considered a part, that stupendous depression of fracture and cleavage which we saw beginning in South Africa. The Jordan rises in the mountains of Lebanon, and soon plunges into a deep trough. Two thirds of the Jordan Valley, which runs north and south, is below sea level. The river flows into the Sea of Galilee, which is 680 feet below sea level, then out of the lake and down to the deeper depression of the Dead Sea.

The valley has all the signs of a fracture of the rocks, with cliffs, jagged peaks, and steep craggy inclines. The terrain is so broken that the Jordan, from the Sea of Galilee to the Dead Sea, is one of the most winding streams in the world. The distance is sixty-five miles in a straight line. The river, meandering in serpentine curves, traverses some two hundred miles. Everywhere there are signs of ancient volcanic activity. The Sea of Galilee, though, is beautiful, with pleasant shores, but subject to sudden violent storms because it is set so deep among the rugged hills.

This is all part of the rift that extends along the eastern border of Palestine, one long line of cleavage. Some geologists doubt that it's an integral part of the great Rift Valley in East Africa, and suppose that it may be a separate cleft, formed perhaps at some other time, though along the same line as the East African Rift. But here's a fact that has a curious sound. The Encyclopaedia Britannica says: "There is a close affinity between the fish of Galilee and those of the East African lakes and streams."

This, then, is the region so prominent in the Gospels. There, in the Jordan, John the Baptist, "the Voice in the Wilderness," baptized Jesus. On the Mount of Temptation, overlooking the Jordan, Jesus was tempted by Satan. "The devil taketh him up into an exceeding high mountain, and sheweth him all the kingdoms of the world, and the glory of them." At the Sea of Galilee Jesus walked on the water, and in the blue lake the Apostles cast their nets, and the chief of them was one Simon called Peter, a fisherman. The catch they took in their nets was of those fish of East African type, and undoubtedly the same kinds were involved in the miracle of the loaves and the fishes.

This land is an odd blend of geology and Gospel. Our Cinerama camera caught the craggy aspect of the valley of the Jordan and the fair scene of the Sea of Galilee. The pictures have a decidedly geological look, as they illustrate sites in the New Testament story.

Then on to the culminating phase of the mission of Jesus, which was at Jerusalem, and there the scenes present the Christian tragedy. "Then cometh Jesus with them to a place called Gethsemane," the story of the Agony in the Garden. We proceed into the city through St. Stephen's gate, where Stephen was stoned, the way pilgrims have come for centuries to pray at the scenes named by tradition. Imagination can picture those events when Jesus was led forth to be crucified, as we proceed along the Via Dolorosa, the Way of the Cross, named by tradition as the road to Calvary. Here the narrative accompanying the pictures reverts to the biblical text:

"And there followed him," says the Gospel, "a great company of people, and of women, which also bewailed and lamented him.

"But Jesus turning unto them said, Daughters of Jerusalem, weep not for me, but weep for yourselves, and for your children. . . .

"And when they were come to the place, which is called Calvary, there they crucified him."

At the Church of the Holy Sepulchre the Christian drama comes to its triumph, the scene of the Resurrection, where on Easter the cry rings out: "He is risen. He is risen." Then the Mount of Olives, scene of the Ascension.

In this treatment of the Gospel story music was all-important, and we had the aid of a magnificent chorus. I had heard the Apollo Club of Minneapolis, an ensemble of male voices, the members of which are largely Minneapolis businessmen. In preparation for the Cinerama *Seven Wonders,* I communicated with them, and they were gracious enough to sing for our stereophonic sound a series of choral pieces, religious and patriotic chiefly, which we might use at one place or another in the Cinerama picture.

Our composers, Emil Newman and Jerome Moross, incorporated one of these in the musical score for the Christian half of the Palestine sequence. Then, when the picture was complete, and we screened it, an associate of mine remarked what might be considered a liturgical novelty. On the scene of Bethlehem, the narration that I spoke used the familiar biblical text of the chorus of the angels: "Glory to God in the highest, and on earth peace, good will toward men." This was spoken over the chorus, which thereupon was brought up with resonant tone, as if in response. The hymn was in Latin, and the words at that point

[ 153 ]

were "*Miserere nobis* [have mercy on us]." This might have seemed an unexpected response to the glad tidings.

It might have been that Emil, fitting in the chorus, was not so familiar with his Latin. At any rate, one of those who attended the screening was Monsignor William T. Greene, director of church music for St. Patrick's Cathedral in New York. Emil had consulted him about the music for the papal ceremony at St. Peter's, and he had come to hear how it had turned out. He approved of that part of it, and the associate of mine, who noticed the "*Miserere nobis*" on Bethlehem and the Nativity, asked him about that. The monsignor nodded vigorously—oh yes, that was attributed to Palestrina, the supreme composer of ecclesiastical music in the sixteenth century. He had high approval for the chorus with its refrain, "*Miserere nobis.*"

The Apollo chorus of Minneapolis businessmen had recorded some most erudite music for us, which brought about a liturgical novelty that might have a depth of meaning. It is as if the angels sing "Glory to God in the highest," and the human race replies: "Have mercy on us."

When he came to the music for the end of the Gospel story, Emil was in difficulties. He wanted, naturally, a triumphal climax of orchestra and chorus proper to the Ascension. But the scene picturing the Mount of Olives was not long enough for a great crescendo. So Emil went to Harvey Manger, our chief film editor.

"Harvey," said he, "I need more footage."

"There isn't any more," Harvey replied.

"No more of the Mount of Olives?"

"Not a foot."

"Well, put in some clouds. End the sequence with a beautiful cloud shot, and I can continue the music on that."

"Clouds"—Harvey scowled—"are corny. They use 'em all the time."

"Corny or not," said the maestro, "I've got to have footage."

Harvey knew this was only too true, and they looked up some clouds. What they found was a scene that had been discarded as defective. It was a beautiful shot of a sea of gleaming clouds made from an airplane, but light had glinted on the lens. "Halation," the film men call it, from "halo." There were streaks of light from the top down the middle of the picture. The light streaks made a brilliant pattern with branching streamers, something like a modernistic design rising from the clouds into the sky.

Emil and Harvey looked at each other. The light streaks in the defective shot of clouds might have been symbolism. They might have been a skillfully contrived effect to represent a mystical sign.

Later, when a musical colleague of Emil's saw the picture, he asked: "How did you ever produce that optical effect in the cloud shot of the Ascension?"

It was accidental, but it is glorious.

# Chapter 17

THE FIRST ACCOUNT that classic history gives of India is by
Herodotus, who describes the land as the most populous known
to antiquity. But the Father of History does not dwell on vital
statistics. The duller facts interest him the least. Herodotus gives
us remarkable tales about sundry peoples of India, including a
racy one about how the Indians got their gold. You will note
how he scrupulously attributes the astonishing facts to the
Persians.

"Here, in this desert, there live amid the sand great ants, in
size somewhat less than dogs, but bigger than foxes. These ants
make their dwellings underground, and like the Greek ants,
which they very much resemble in shape, throw up sand-heaps
as they burrow. Now the sand which they throw up is full of
gold.

"The Indians, when they go into the desert to collect this
sand, take three camels and harness them together, a female in
the middle and a male on either side. The rider sits on the female, and they are particular to choose for the purpose one that
has but just dropped her young. . . .

"When the Indians therefore have thus equipped themselves
they set off in quest of the gold, calculating the time so that
they may be engaged in seizing it during the sultry part of the
day, when the ants hide themselves to escape the heat. The sun
in those parts shines fiercest in the morning.

"When the Indians reach the place where the gold is, they fill their bags with the sand, and ride away at their best speed. The ants, however, scenting them, as the Persians say, rush forth in pursuit. Now these animals are so swift, they declare, that there is nothing in the world like them: if it were not, therefore, that the Indians get a start while the ants are mustering, not a single gold-gatherer could escape.

"During the flight the male camels, which are not so fleet as the females, grow tired, and begin to drag, first one, and then the other; but the females recollect the young which they have left behind, and never give way or flag. Such, according to the Persians, is the manner in which the Indians get the greater part of their gold."

That surely would have been a wonder of the world for Cinerama. It was too bad that we could not get on our encompassing screen those ants which Herodotus describes so scrupulously as "in size somewhat less than dogs, but bigger than foxes," the insect army pursuing the camels, with Mama Camel hurrying home to baby.

The first trip to India documented in Western annals, and the one discussed and written about more than any other, was made by Alexander the Great in 327 B.C. It was a classic of imperialism, adventure, and exploration, and presents the young Macedonian hero as insatiable conqueror, daredevil mad for glory and seeker of knowledge.

In great military campaigns he made himself master of the immense Persian Empire. So why bother about India? Well, for one thing, the Persian Empire included a province in India. In the earlier Persian wars against Greece the invading forces included soldiers from India. Herodotus, in enumerating the many nations represented in the host of Xerxes, lists an Indian contingent: "The Indians wore cotton dresses, and carried bows of cane, and arrows also made of cane, with iron at the point." Bowmen from India serving at Thermopylae.

Alexander's political policy was to claim that he was the legal successor of the Persian King of Kings, whom he had overthrown. He assumed the state of an oriental despot, inheritor of the glory of Cyrus and Darius. In this role it was incumbent on him to assert his authority over all the empire, including the province in India.

He campaigned in Central Asia, occupying Persian possessions there. This included daredevil expeditions, for Alexander varied imperial policy with reckless adventure and exploits of war. He subjugated one outlying province after another, and then came the turn of the province in India, the last.

The march into India has long been a problem for scholars. The ancient accounts are copious with place names, but many of these are difficult to relate to present-day names. India is protected on the north by the vast mountain ramparts of the Himalayas. The historic approach is from the northwest, and even today that rugged area is none too well known. Here is the general picture as given in history books:

He led his army across the lofty ranges of the Hindu Kush. This is now Afghanistan. There he divided his forces in two, and sent the main body of troops into India by way of the valley of the Kabul River. He himself led a detachment on a detour through wild passes where there was lively fighting with mountain tribes. After perils and exploits Alexander joined his main force on the banks of the river Indus.

One thing that puzzles me is that the march of the main army into India was by way of the valley of the Kabul River. The great historic highway in these parts is through Khyber Pass, but they didn't go that way. Yet the Khyber Pass is only some twenty-five miles from the place where the Kabul River flows into India.

I myself traveled in the Khyber Pass region some years ago on a trip into Afghanistan, then a closed country. To refresh my memory of topography I consulted a friend, Lauri Shaffi, New York consul for Pakistan. The Khyber area is now a part of Pakistan. He tells me that his country is constructing a great hydro-electric project on the Kabul River at the very place where Alexander's army entered India. He remarked that the better route into India is through the Khyber Pass. Nevertheless it seems that Alexander's main army proceeded along the Kabul

River and then marched across to the Indus, where Alexander joined them.

The Persian province of India was in this region of the Indus, and Alexander might have been content to stop there, but now we have a drama of unbridled ambition. His ideas of the extent of India were hazy. The geographical knowledge of the time was meager, and extraordinary mistakes about distances, oceans, and continents were prevalent.

In the Indus, Alexander saw crocodiles, which existed in that river at the time. To the Greek mind crocodiles meant the Nile, and he thought the Indus must be the headwaters of the Nile, a remarkable confusion of Asia and Africa.

For Alexander the spaces of India that lay before him were, for the most part, the unknown. In spite of this, or because of it, he'd march on. His invasion of India now had the air of high adventure. Never mind imperial policy—march on to the ultimate of the unknown.

Crossing the Indus by a bridge of boats, they were in the Land of the Five Rivers, today called the Punjab. The rivers are tributaries which flow one into another and then into the Indus, and all lay across Alexander's line of march. His invasion of India was a river campaign, from one stream to another, with a series of river crossings.

They were unopposed at the Indus. The king of the nearby city of Taxila was friendly, an ally. But at the second river, the Jhelum, the crossing was disputed by a powerful army. The story of Alexander rings with the valor of Indian King Porus, a giant in stature, a paladin of war. A pitched battle was fought. Porus was defeated and captured, but was restored to his kingdom. Alexander could admire a brave antagonist.

The river next on the line of march was wide and swift with melting snows from the Himalayas. The crossing was perilous and a number of soldiers were swept away. Farther on still another river was crossed, and a violent battle was fought, after which the march continued on to still another stream.

This river was the Beas, not far from the present-day city of Lahore. Beyond it was one more river to go, the Sutlej, and then the approach to the valley of the Ganges. That was a beckoning goal. Today the Ganges is the very symbol of India, and so was it then. Reports told of a numerous population, splendid cities, and powerful principalities with large armies, and Alexander saw new adventures and new glory. But on the banks of the Beas scenes were enacted as tense and dramatic as anything you'll find in history.

Our chief authority for the campaigns of Alexander the Great is Arrian, a Greek historian who wrote in the second century A.D. His sources were earlier histories now lost, including an account written by Ptolemy, one of Alexander's generals on the march into India, who later made himself King of Egypt. Arrian was no dramatic genius at history writing. His preoccupation is more with military matters than with personality and colorful circumstance, and he can be pedestrian. But the drama rises in his narration, as may be seen in these extracts:

"The spirit of the Macedonians now began to flag, when they saw the king raising one labour after another, and incurring one danger after another. Conferences were held throughout the camp, in which those who were the most moderate bewailed their lot, while others resolutely declared that they would not follow Alexander any farther, even if he should lead the way. When he heard of this, he called a council of the officers of the brigades and addressed them as follows:

"'O Macedonians and Grecian allies, seeing that you no longer follow me into dangerous enterprises with a resolution equal to that which formerly animated you, I have collected you together into the same spot, so that I may either persuade you to march forward with me, or may be persuaded by you to return. I, for my part, think, that to a brave man there is no end to labours except the labours themselves, provided they lead to glorious achievements.'"

Then, according to Arrian, he gave them this assurance: "The distance still remaining before we reach the river Ganges and the Eastern Sea is not great."

This presents a truly remarkable ignorance of geography. The distance to the Ganges was reasonably short, but the Eastern

Sea, the Bay of Bengal, was some seven hundred miles away in a direct line and very much more as an army marched. But Alexander seemed to think the opposite coast of India was not far off. Perhaps he was trying to minimize the task ahead, but he was talking not to simple soldiers but to his chief officers, who would be likely to have as much geographical knowledge as he himself.

"O Macedonians and Grecian allies, stand firm," the historian has him continue. "Glorious are the deeds of those who undergo labour and run the risk of danger; and it is delightful to live a life of valour and to die leaving behind immortal glory."

Arrian uses set speeches, as was the convention in classical history writing. It was the rhetorical tradition for representing the gist of what was said. He goes on:

"When Alexander had uttered these remarks, and others in the same strain, a long silence ensued. But at last, Coenus, son of Polemocrates, plucked up courage and spoke as follows [Coenus was one of Alexander's veteran commanders]:

"'O king, inasmuch as you do not wish to rule Macedonians by compulsion, I am going to make a speech. For you yourself see how many Macedonians and Greeks started with you, and how few of us have been left. All those of us whose parents still survive feel a great yearning to see them once more; they feel a yearning after their wives and children, and a yearning for their native land itself. Do not lead us now against our will; for you will no longer find us the same men in regard to dangers, since free-will will be wanting to us in the contests. But, rather, if it seems good to you, return of your own accord to your own land, see your mother, and regulate the affairs of the Greeks. Then start afresh on another expedition, if you wish, against these very tribes of Indians situated towards the east.'

"When Coenus had concluded this speech, loud applause was given to his words by those who were present, and the fact that many even shed tears made it still more evident that they were disinclined to incur further hazards, and that to return would be delightful to them.

"Alexander then broke up the conference, being annoyed at

the freedom of speech in which Coenus indulged, and the hesitation displayed by the other officers. But the next day he called the same men together again in wrath, and told them that he intended to advance farther, but would not force any Macedonian to accompany him against his will. Those who wished to return home were at liberty to return and carry back word to their relations that they were come back, having deserted their king in the midst of his enemies. Having said this, he retired into his tent, waiting to see if any change would occur in the minds of the Macedonians and Grecian allies."

Arrian relates that Alexander waited for three days, but there was no change in the opinion of the army. Still he was determined to go on, and even made the religious preparations customary among the Greeks for any enterprise.

"He none the less offered sacrifice there for the passage of the river, but the victims [the omens] were unfavourable to him when sacrificed. Then indeed, as all things indicated the advisability of his returning, he made known to the army that he had resolved to march back again.

"Then they shouted as a mixed multitude would shout when rejoicing; and most of them shed tears of joy. Some of them even approached the royal tent, and prayed for many blessings upon Alexander; because by them alone he suffered himself to be conquered."

All that is apt comment on the old saw that Alexander wept because there were no more worlds to conquer. On the riverbank in the Punjab he wept because there was indeed a world to conquer straight ahead.

He took his army in retreat. But if his officers and soldiers thought they were on their way home they were mistaken. Turning away from the heart of India, he led them on a down-river march to the mouth of the Indus. This was long and arduous, battles had to be fought, and in the capture of a city Alexander performed one of his daredevil exploits. At the mouth of the Indus he had the satisfaction of taking a boat ride on the Southern Ocean. By now he was well corrected of the mistake of thinking that the Indus was the headwater of the Nile.

This was the farthest length of Alexander's marches, which had begun in distant Macedonia. He made political settlements for territories he had won in India, leaving some under the rule of allied Indian kings and naming a governor for the old Persian province in India. Then he started back for Persia.

Returning, he took a force of soldiers for a frightful journey along and near the coast of what is now Baluchistan. They nearly perished in desolate country without water. At the same time he had a fleet of ships return home under his admiral, Nearchus, on a voyage of exploration from the mouth of the Indus, coasting along Baluchistan and Persia, to the mouth of the Euphrates.

This last phase of Alexander in India was, in fact, a matter of exploration largely. On his return he projected a great voyage to explore the way around Arabia from the Euphrates to Suez, but that was abandoned after his untimely death at the age of thirty-three. His geographical interests are not astonishing. After all, he was the pupil of Aristotle, having had his education with that philosopher as tutor. Setting out on his career of conquest, he had been commissioned by Aristotle to send back examples of things of nature that might be studied at the philosopher's school in Athens. Alexander began Western exploration in the regions of India.

# Chapter 18

OUR CINERAMA expedition into India was less historic, but we did reach the Ganges. Going in advance of the camera crew, I flew from Arabia on a route across the Persian Gulf and along the coast of Baluchistan to Karachi, capital of the great Moslem state created a few years ago when independent India was partitioned. At Karachi I picked up some bits of information for my travel diary:

"Here in Karachi there is a tremendous building boom—and no wonder. Shortly after World War I, I addressed audiences in this city. I was doing a speaking tour of the world at the time. Karachi then had less than 100,000 people. Prime Minister Mohammed Ali has just been reminding me that in those days it wasn't even a provincial capital. Now it's the capital of a nation that has a population of more than 80,000,000, and Karachi itself has jumped to a city of 1,250,000. In fact, some of the newer sections look more modern than most of our American cities.

"It has one staggering problem. On its outskirts there are camping some hundreds of thousands of refugees.

"When the subcontinent of Hindustan was partitioned, a few years ago, by the British, throngs of Hindus fled to India, and a stream of Moslems fled to Pakistan. Many of the latter made their way to Karachi, thinking they might get help there from the new government. They have. Scores of thousands are on relief.

"I saw several units of the Karachi Fire Department go by a little while ago. They looked so primitive that I inquired about them. Why not have up-to-date equipment in a city of over a million—a city which is so modern in its new architecture? No explanation. I guess the city has grown so fast such things haven't kept pace. The Karachi fire trucks even have to carry their own water. In a thousand-gallon tank! You can imagine how much of a fire you could put out with that!

"In the outer harbor, directly in front of my apartment window, is a Japanese liner, the *Ashahi San Maru*. While they were loading it with cotton it caught fire. After it had burned for three days the city firemen decided they couldn't put it out in the usual way—with water and chemicals. So they tried something novel and drastic. From outside the hull they knocked a hole in the bottom. Whereupon the ship sank right here and filled with water. Finish fire. Now, at a cost of four lakhs of rupees—over one hundred thousand dollars—they are trying to raise it.

"I asked Mohammed Ali, the Pakistan prime minister, about the wild country to the north. What is happening to the Mir of Hunza, the Wali of Swat, the Khan of Kalat, and other picturesque princes who added so much color to life in this part of the world? He replied that after the independence of Pakistan nearly all of them stayed on as governors, but without any real power, in the regions where they once had absolute authority. Then he added that within a few months these princes will no longer even be governors. Henceforth they will be princes in name only, something like the vague nobility of France and Italy.

"I wonder how it will all work out. Many of the top men in the Pakistan government have never been in those mountains, which are inhabited by rugged fighting men who may not care for these new ideas, these Western concepts of government. For instance there are some five hundred thousand in one small area in the mountains between Afghanistan and the Vale of Kashmir. I wonder what they and their prince, the Wali of Swat, will have to say about it?"

[ 165 ]

Since my return home I have had occasion to give radio news about revolt among some of the border mountain tribes. Backed by feudal Afghanistan, they demand the status of an independent state, and this constitutes another of those international problems. Apparently the khans who lead the Wazirs, the Afridis, the Mahsuds, and others, are not happy about the status assigned to them by progressive Pakistan.

From Karachi, I took an air liner bound for New Delhi, a trip that inspired the following reflections for my travel diary:

"We have just left Karachi airport, and I have noticed a curious phenomenon aboard this plane which has come through from London. Although, only a moment ago, we flew over one of the great rivers of the world, only one other person, a Chinese, even bothered to look out the window. There are forty of us in the plane. Maybe the others are weary from a long journey. At any rate just two of us looked out and marveled as we crossed the Indus, the delta, and where it flows into the Arabian Sea.

"This flying age is doing weird things to travelers. Men now are catapulted from country to country and from continent to continent without knowing what is beneath them. On the major air lines the pilot or a steward usually calls your attention to any major spectacle you are passing—does this from the cockpit, over a loudspeaker. But you cross the Indus so near Karachi that pilot and steward are still too busy with the technical side of their jobs. In fact, now that we are ten miles beyond the river, the pilot has spoken up and said, 'By the way, as you no doubt know, that was the Indus we flew over a moment ago!'

"Someday I'd like to tell the men who run the round-the-world air lines how they might do a far better job in this connection. It seems shocking to say: 'Oh, by the way, that was the Indus.' The passengers should be told: 'Below us now is the Indus, where Alexander's world-conquering army marched to the Indian Ocean some twenty-three hundred years ago,' and so on."

By way of the ridiculous, I can add a personal reminiscence about the historic river Indus. It happened back in the time when I was on my way to Afghanistan and made a side journey into a section of Baluchistan called Waziristan. Lots of "stan" in those parts. In my book *Beyond Khyber Pass*, I told of the distressful experience as follows:

"To reach this barren, inhospitable country after leaving the railway, you must cross the Indus River. During the spring of the year, when the floods are on, the bridges are washed away, and the usual method of getting over is by swimming on an inflated goatskin. At the time of the rains, the Indus swells in many places, until it is from three to ten miles wide, and swimming across becomes an art. You have to hold one end of the skin in your mouth and keep blowing it up all the time. I tried it, but when I was blowing I forgot to swim and was swept downstream, and when I tried to swim I forgot to blow and nearly sank. So strong and swift is the current that you usually land several miles downstream on the opposite shore."

Puffing and sputtering, I made this goatskin crossing of the Indus, and I'll never forget it.

At New Delhi we made arrangements for filming, and the Cinerama camera proceeded to the Ganges. India is pre-eminently a land of strange religions, with temples beautiful and grotesque, weird ceremonies and incomprehensible customs, and nowhere is religion more astounding than along the holy river. This is true, above all, at the city of Benares, and that metropolis of fantastic shrines and rites was a goal in our quest for wonders.

One obvious procedure was to approach Benares by boat, taking the Cinerama camera for a boat ride on the Ganges. Thus can best be seen the pageant of temples and palaces and the sacred landing places called the ghats. But there was an additional idea for this, an idea mildly Hollywoodian.

On the Ganges we'd have a boatload of girls, good-looking Hindu maidens in their bright costumes, saris of many colors. These in the picture would add a touch of feminine charm to the scene of the river and the city. As Hollywood cheesecake it was pretty tame, but the sex appeal does not come nude in India.

In Benares one task was to recruit the Hindu maidens for the boating party of beauties in saris. Our Hollywood director for these Indian operations was Tay Garnett, but he happened to be away. So the job fell to Bill Lipscomb of London, who found Benares a strange sort of place. Bill gives us the following account:

"I was all alone in the city of wild men and I had to find a boatload of charming ladies in bright saris to be seen crossing the Ganges. In any other town in the world the finding of extras to appear in films would present no difficulties, except for the police to keep the crowd back. Not in Benares. No 'lady' would demean herself by appearing in public in a film.

"But there were 'dancers.' Could one get dancers? Everybody could get dancers. The guide knew them all, the manager of the hotel and that old villain the snake charmer knew dancers —everybody knew dancers. But, like many other promises in India, nobody produced 'dancers.'

"My very fat guide, always in a state of excessive perspiration, at last said, 'You want dancers? I show you.' I didn't like the way he said it, but then I didn't like him anyway. We left the car and went on foot through streets planned by a black-widow spider. The inhabitants grew wilder and the markings on their faces seemed to multiply. We climbed steps three feet high, passed round corners in and out of murderous passages, and came to a room literally not seven feet square.

"I was bidden to sit on the floor. The guide came down heavily beside me. There didn't seem much room left in the place. An orchestra of five got in with their instruments. Dancers would appear. Dancers did.

"The lady who was the prima ballerina had been off diet for a considerable time. She would have filled the room by herself. Sitting on the floor, looking up at her, I had an awful feeling of the infant about to be rolled on by Mama. I thought of the size of boat we should want if we had a dozen of her in it. But there was no way out. She was dancing between me and the door. It became hotter and hotter. The Indian orchestra kept up its reiteration of the one rhythm over and over again. The dancer's gestures became more and more significant, though I hoped I was wrong about them.

"But an even more puzzling feature was the presence of a man who kept washing himself at a small tap in one corner. At first one could imagine that he was somehow part of the performance. But no, apparently it was his washing time, so he washed. A lady feeding a baby leaned into the room occasionally. The baby cried, but that only added another wild note to the orchestra's efforts, and even all this was drowned by the jangling of about two thirds of all Benares' brass anklets and bracelets the lady dancer was wearing.

"The tune being such that there is no earthly reason why it should ever stop, it stops unexpectedly. My fat guide explained that the lady knew no English but her fee would be twenty-five rupees. The lady was furious in any language. Tongues of fire must have come down upon her, for she said in very emphatic English, 'Fifty rupees!' In Hindu she added, 'Or I stamp you to death.' I knew she could do it, too. So she was paid fifty rupees. The orchestra was paid. Even the man who washed himself got something.

"So we had no boatload of dancers. In the end the difficulty solved itself. The proprietor of the hotel had daughters who were modern in outlook. They had pals from the college. So when the time came we had a boatload of very pretty girls who did not mind flouting custom and appearing in the picture.

"Only, of course, they don't; because when we came to the final editing, we were over-length. So the whole scene came out of the picture, anyway. But that's show business."

Bill's efforts in this instance were wasted. When our quest of wonders was done we had much too much film, and had to omit a heartbreaking lot. So our Cinerama boat ride on the Ganges ended with pageant scenes of Benares minus Bill's boatload of girls.

Benares to the Hindus is the holy city. For centuries the great and the rich have built temples and palaces here on the banks of the Ganges. Of temples alone Benares has fifteen hundred. The ghats, the landing places along the river, are sacred, surrounded by legends of the god Vishnu. It's a place of pilgrimage to which the devout by the hundreds of thousands flock to bathe in the Ganges, the sacred water of which will improve their conditions in their next reincarnations.

When you think of Benares you picture vast swarms of people thronging down to the landing places and bathing in the river, Brahmins and ordinary folk, but more particularly beggars and holy men, the lame and the deformed, ascetics of self-torture, the fakir whose legs have withered because for years he has sat cross-legged in the same position, or who has clenched a hand so long the nails have grown into the flesh, or still another with long skewers thrust through his cheeks from one side to the other.

But you will see nothing of the sort in our Cinerama picture. It shows the ghats nearly deserted, with a few scattered people around, loitering or bathing in the river. The scene is handsome, with the empty terraced landing places and the architectural pageant of temples and palaces. The Cinerama camera was not at Benares at a season of great pilgrimage, when the myriads came swarming to the Ganges, and it would have been no use if it had.

The new India is not proud of some of the practices of the old India, and wants to make a good showing in the eyes of the outside world. We would not have been allowed to film the pilgrim swarm at Benares, with its aspects of the horrible, though this has been photographed many times in the past. Even when we were there in the off season, they chased away the beggars and the deformed, banishing the unsightly from the camera. They were careful that we should not get any pictures of the burning ghats, those places along the Ganges where the dead are cremated on funeral pyres.

We took the Cinerama camera through the city. We filmed temple scenes, processions, and street scenes. But everywhere it was the same. The authorities got out of our way the beggars, the grotesque ascetics, the unsightly characters of every sort. Such scenes are now not for export. Our pictures show Benares without a single holy man, not one sadhu, bearded, emaciated,

naked save for a loincloth. That in itself might be construed as
one of the wonders. It's a vivid sign of the new India.

Yet the yogi practicing extravagant austerities, living as a
hermit in the jungle, begging his way across the countryside or
meditating in a shrine, has been a characteristic figure in India
since the earliest times. It will be long before he disappears from
India, if he ever does. After all Ghandi, the architect of Indian
independence, was a saint, a mahatma, completely in the tradition of the mystic and ascetic. He wore the loincloth of the
sadhu, and made the penitential fast a political weapon, with
his threats of starving himself to death. Several hundred generations of holy men will understand in whatever reincarnation
they may be.

One of the most spectacular of ascetics was Kalanos, spectacular for the end to which he came. Seldom has a mortal departed
from this life with such ceremony. He would have called it going to his rebirth, according to the doctrine of reincarnation.
Kalanos, Greek form of some Hindu name, was an ascetic who
accompanied Alexander's army on its return from India. He journeyed all the way to Persia, and there, after a time, took his
departure in a manner that astounded everybody.

In India the Greeks regarded the ascetics with wonder and
curiosity, and called them naked philosophers. Another name
they gave them was gymnosophist, which might signify gym-
nastic wisdom, from the practice of bodily postures and muscular movements in meditation. Alexander, pupil of Aristotle, was
much interested in the naked philosophers, and questioned them
about their wisdom.

One story tells how, when he visited some ascetics, they
greeted him and his companions by stamping their feet on the
ground. Alexander asked them why they did this. They replied
that it was to signify that every man occupies as much earth
as he stands on. Alexander was like any other, though he passed
over great distances, making trouble for himself and other people. But when he was dead he would occupy just enough space
to be buried in.

Alexander approved of this as philosophy. After all, had he

not in Athens applauded Diogenes the Cynic, who went around with a lighted lantern in daylight looking for an honest man? When Alexander visited Diogenes, the surly philosopher told the Macedonian king that all he wanted from him and his companions was for them to get out of his sunlight. So, in India, Alexander could appreciate the plain speaking of the naked philosophers.

He wanted to take one of them home with him. No doubt there could have been interesting discourse between a naked sage of India and the philosophers back in Athens, perhaps with Aristotle himself. But sour Diogenes might have understood better. None of the ascetics was willing to go, until at length Kalanos was persuaded. He traveled with the army on long marches that took him finally to the court that Alexander held in the old Persian domain.

He seems to have been treated with considerable regard. Probably he regaled the Macedonians and Greeks with accounts of yoga, the science of concentration with a system of physical controls to promote a control of mind. They listened with interest, apparently. Arrian tells of Lysimachus, one of Alexander's chief officers, attending the discourses of Kalanos to learn the wisdom of yoga. Alexander himself valued the naked philosopher, as we may judge from Arrian's history.

He relates that Kalanos fell ill and reflected that it was time for him to depart from the present stage of his existence. This, in itself, would not have astonished the Greek mind too much. A decorous suicide would not have been out of harmony with the ideas of Greek philosophers, who could reason sagely about the wisdom of quitting life at an appropriate time. But the way that Kalanos went about it made a sensation.

He announced that he would mount his own funeral pyre and be consumed by the flames. This proposal that Kalanos would burn himself alive seemed rather too extreme. Alexander himself disapproved.

"For a long time," writes Arrian, "the king tried to dissuade him; however when he saw that he was not to be overcome, he ordered a funeral pyre to be heaped up for him. They say that a solemn procession, consisting both of horses and men, advanced before Kalanos, some of the latter carrying all kinds of incense for the pyre.

"A horse was prepared for him. However, not being able to mount the horse, he was conveyed stretched out upon a litter, crowned with a garland after the custom of the Indians, and singing in the Indian language. The Indians say that he sang hymns to the gods and eulogies to his countrymen.

"Before he ascended the funeral-pyre he presented the horse which he should himself have mounted, to Lysimachus, one of those who attended him to learn his philosophy. He distributed among his other disciples goblets and rugs which Alexander had ordered to be cast into the pyre as an honour to him.

"Then mounting the pyre he lay down upon it in a becoming manner, and was visible to the whole army. To Alexander the spectacle appeared unseemly, as it was being exhibited at the cost of a friend; but to the rest it was a cause of wonder that he did not move any part of his body in the fire.

"As soon as the men to whom the duty had been assigned set fire to the pyre, Nearchus says the trumpets sounded, in accordance with Alexander's order, and the whole army raised the war-cry as it was in the habit of shouting when advancing to battle. The elephants also chimed in with their shrill and warlike cry, in honour of Kalanos.

"Authors upon whom reliance may be placed, have recorded these and such-like things about Kalanos the Indian, facts of great import to those who are desirous of learning how steadfast and immovable a thing the human mind is in regard to what it wishes to accomplish."

To the Greeks the sight of the naked philosopher maintaining his equanimity while being consumed by the flames must have indeed been the epitome of the "steadfast and immovable."

The practice of self-immolation by fire has a strange and terrible place in the lore of India. In Benares we filmed a wedding procession, gaudy with painted elephants and ornamented camels, bands of musicians making extraordinary sounds and colorful images carried in the noisy procession. The scene is gay and festive, but the subject of marriage in India brings to mind the practice of suttee, widow burning. This barbaric survival of ancient customs lasted in India to a late date.

In 1817 there were seven hundred and six cases of suttee in Bengal alone. This was at a time when the British authorities were making efforts to stop the practice. They were afraid to prohibit widow burning entirely in the face of fanatical Hindu addiction to tradition, and resorted to intensive persuasion. No suttee was permitted until the prospective victim had been examined by a magistrate, who made sure that she was proceeding of her own free will and urged her to give up her ghastly intention. Only if she persisted in spite of all persuasion could the suttee be performed. In an incredible number of cases the widow did persist.

Various reasons are cited. Ancient belief made this proof of wifely devotion the most honorable act a woman could perform. She would be held in public veneration and her family would be honored. If she survived her husband, widowhood was a most wretched condition in Hindu life. She was urged by relatives, friends, and public opinion, and often enough the victim was in a state of exaltation, determined to accompany her husband in his next incarnation. The word "suttee" is a corruption of the Sanskrit *sati*, faithful wife.

In 1829 widow burning was abolished once and for all by Governor General Lord William Bentinck, who was urged to drastic measures by the great Indian religious reformer Ram Mohun Roy. Suttee became a criminal offense under the penal code. There was opposition from traditionalists, but the law was enforced with the support of enlightened Indian opinion, and the cremation of the living widow with her dead husband became an evil memory.

The great source of information about India in that period is a massive volume, *Hindu Manners, Customs and Ceremonies*, by the Abbé Dubois, a French missionary who spent years in India at the end of the eighteenth century and the beginning of the nineteenth. Abbé Dubois gives an account that he had from an eyewitness of a suttee performed in southern India with royal ceremony. He writes:

"The last king of Tanjore, who died in 1801, left behind him four lawful wives. The Brahmins decided that two of these should be burnt with the body of their husband, and selected the couple that should have the preference. It would have been an everlasting shame to them and the grossest insult to the memory of the deceased had they hesitated to accept this singular honour. Being fully convinced, moreover, that no means would be spared to induce them to sacrifice themselves either willingly or unwillingly, they made a virtue of necessity and seemed perfectly ready to yield to the terrible lot which awaited them.

"The necessary preparations for the obsequies were completed in a single day.

"Three or four leagues from the royal residence a square pit of no great depth, and about twelve to fifteen feet square, was excavated. Within it was erected a pyramid of sandalwood, resting on a kind of scaffolding of the same wood. The posts which supported it were so arranged that they could easily be removed, and would thereby cause the whole structure to collapse suddenly. At the four corners of the pit were placed huge brass jars filled with ghee, to be thrown on the wood in order to hasten combustion.

"The following was the order of the procession as it wended its way to the pyre. It was headed by a large force of armed soldiers. Then followed a crowd of musicians, chiefly trumpeters, who made the air ring with the dismal sound of their instruments. Next came the king's body borne in a splendid open palanquin, accompanied by his guru, his principal officers, and his nearest relatives, who were all on foot and wore no turbans in token of mourning. Among them was also a large number of Brahmins.

"Then came the two victims, each borne on a richly decorated palanquin. They were loaded, rather than decked, with jewels. Several ranks of soldiers surrounded them to preserve order and to keep back the great crowds that flocked in from every side. The two queens were accompanied by some of their favourite women, with whom they occasionally conversed. Then followed relatives of both sexes, to whom the victims had made valuable presents before leaving the palace. An innumerable multitude of Brahmins and persons of all castes followed in the rear.

"On reaching the spot where their untimely fate awaited them, the victims were required to perform the ablutions and other ceremonies proper on such occasions; and they went through the whole of them without hesitation and without the least sign of fear. When, however, it came to walking round the pyre, it was observed that their features underwent a sudden change. Their strength seemed well-nigh to forsake them in spite of their obvious efforts to suppress their natural feelings.

"During this interval the body of the king had been placed on the top of the pyramid of sandalwood. The two queens, still wearing their rich attire and ornaments, were next compelled to ascend the pile. Lying down beside the body of the deceased prince, one on the right and the other on the left, they joined hands across the corpse.

"The officiating Brahmins then recited in a loud tone several mantras, sprinkled the pile with their tirtam or holy water, and emptied the jars of ghee over the wood, setting fire to it at the same moment. This was done on one side by the nearest relative of the king, on another by his guru, on others by leading Brahmins. The flames quickly spread, and the props being removed, the whole structure collapsed, and in its fall must have crushed to death the two unfortunate victims. Thereupon all the spectators shouted aloud for joy.

"On the spot where the deceased king and his two unhappy companions had been consumed a circular mausoleum was erected, about twelve feet in diameter, surmounted by a dome. The reigning prince visits it from time to time, prostrates himself humbly before the tombs, and offers sacrifices to the names of his predecessor and those of his worthy and saintly spouses."

You will read far in the strange record of the human race before you'll find anything as frightful, yet as touching, as the two queens clasping hands on the funeral pyre as the flames were lighted.

# Chapter 19

INDIAN RELIGION presents a baffling contradiction of lofty spirituality and gross superstition. On one hand you find a monotheism going back to early days, the doctrine of the timeless, changeless One, the ocean of existence, the beginning, the end, Brahm. The Hindu Trinity presents the metaphysical concept of Brahma the creator of forms, Vishnu the preserver of forms, and Siva the destroyer of forms. Along with beliefs of that order it is rather shocking to behold an extravagant polytheism, a bewildering multitude of gods, with a fantasy of grotesque idols. It makes India seem a madhouse of bizarre religions.

Accounting for the contradiction is the historical fact that India was conquered some twelve centuries before the Christian Era by northern invaders, Aryans, Indo-Europeans, who brought in the Sanskrit language. They also brought in bright gods, sky gods, similar in radiance to the Olympian divinities of Greece. From these the early monotheistic theology of the Brahmins evolved.

But the aboriginal dark peoples who were conquered had their own gods, which were never conquered, dark divinities and superstitions which in time were accepted along with the official religion of the Brahmins. The doctrine of avatars provided an instrument for combination. Any number of gods might be considered as avatars of a great god. Vishnu returns to earth as Krishna, Rama, and sundry other incarnations.

The contradiction gives us, on one hand, philosophic religious ideas like karma, the moral force that governs the cycle of reincarnations, whereby in life you get what you deserved by merit or demerit in your previous existence. Then there is maya, the veil of illusion, the visible world that hides the ultimate reality. On the other hand, Indian religion includes a nightmare of primitive absurdities.

You'll find them in Benares. We took the Cinerama camera for a drive through the streets of the city—and look out for the sacred cows. Piloting an automobile through any Indian city can be nerve-racking. The sacred cows wander around or lie in the streets, and you pick your way among them. Be careful, don't hit one, or you're in trouble. The drive ended at the Monkey Temple, and there—be nice to the sacred monkeys.

The temple is dedicated to the monkey god Hanuman, and numbers of Hanuman's earthly relations scampered around. There were monkeys in the courtyard, monkeys in the shrine, monkeys having the time of their lives. They are both fed and cherished. In the temple there was a performance by temple dancers, little girls who, to the incomprehensible sounds of an Indian orchestra, went through a ritual dance in honor of the monkey god Hanuman.

It may help our puzzled minds to go to one of the great epics of India, the Ramayana, which tells the story of the hero Rama, an avatar of Vishnu. It's a vast poem, forty-eight thousand lines long, a masterpiece of literature composed some centuries before the Christian Era. Exactly when is not known. In Indian lore such mundane matters as dates are neglected. The Ramayana, like its companion epic, the Mahabharata, ranks high among the sacred writings of India.

It tells how Rama, a royal prince, was deprived of his hereditary right by the machinations of a stepmother, and fled to the forest with his beautiful wife Sita. There they were happy, but the villainous King of Ceylon was in love with Sita, and devised a stratagem to carry her off. To procure the absence of Rama he sent out a magic gazelle, which Rama, being a hunter, pursued. The magic gazelle led him on and on, and while he was away the villain king made off with Sita.

When he discovered this, the grief-stricken Rama sought to rescue his beloved, who had been taken to her abductor's palace in Ceylon. He needed allies, and found them. The monkeys of the forest rallied to his cause, and a monkey army led by a monkey commander, Hanuman, marched with Rama to Ceylon. In the Ramayana the monkeys are called Vanars, and the epic, as translated by Ralph Griffith, relates:

> The Vanar squadrons densely spread
> O'er all the country onward sped,
> While rising from the rapid beat
> Of bears' and monkeys' hastening feet
> Dust hid the earth with thickest veil,
> And made the struggling sunbeams pale.

Hanuman, the cleverest of the monkeys, leaped over the palace wall, made his way to Sita, and comforted her. Rescue soon came. Rama and the monkey army stormed the palace. The villain king was slain, and Sita was restored to Rama's arms.

There's a lot more to the Ramayana, but that's the monkey angle. One supposition is that it may be a distant reflection from the remote era when the Aryan invaders from the north may have regarded the dark people as monkeys of a sort, and Rama's army consisted of aborigines. In any case, Hanuman the monkey commander in the Ramayana now has the status of a deity, and monkeys are sacred.

In the temple at Benares the Cinerama crew did their film job with some grumbling. They had to take off their shoes to go in. They had to walk on stockinged feet, and monkeys are not the cleanest of animals. They had brought a supply of peanuts along, which they fed to the monkeys to keep them in good temper. Altogether, it was an interesting experience. Bill Lipscomb reports:

"Monkeys not only live in this temple, in fact, they own it. But it doesn't make them good-tempered. They'd as soon bite you as take the peanuts you give them. But it's a great tourist sight, and director Tay Garnett fell in love with the incongruity of the spectacle. Being the only Englishman in the Cinerama setup, I was glad to have an illustration of the traditional English stiff upper lip in adversity.

"Whilst we were looking over the place, a most properly dressed Englishman (he must have been a civil servant) and his extremely correct wife came to visit the temple. They submitted, though doubtfully, to the wreaths of marigolds the vendors insist on putting round you. So they stood, wreathed in marigolds, looking a little self-conscious but willing to put up with the notions of the local inhabitants.

"Then the lady felt a violent nudge in her back and naturally turned to remonstrate with whoever it was being so familiar. It was a sacred cow browsing on the marigolds round her shoulders. Her husband whispered fiercely, 'Don't strike it, it's sacred here.' So what was the poor lady to do! Do as any really well-bred lady is expected to do—ignore it.

"So, with stiff upper lip, and staring straight ahead, she endured the sacred cow making a meal off her. I thought it was a masterpiece of restraint. Maybe she was glad it wasn't one of the monkeys."

This was comedy at the monkey temple, but you wouldn't expect amusing entertainment with cobras. The dreaded hooded serpent would hardly seem to be a vehicle for wit and humor. The Cinerama camera filmed the traditional fight between a cobra and a mongoose, and there was nothing funny about that. The agile rodent killed the deadly snake, as it always does, and it's an eerie sight. But in southern India, Mysore, we got a temple dance with cobras, and with it a scene for a smile. This is the more unexpected because it presents the charm of children.

Snake worship has existed in various lands and cultures, and in parts of India the cobra is considered sacred. It's a deadly superstition. India suffers many fatalities from the cobra bite, all the more because so often people will not kill or drive away the sacred serpent. There are shrines in which the cobra figures in the ritual, as in the temple at Mysore. There you see the dancers in their ritualistic postures and movements, while the cobras and the snake charmers perform beside the dancers, playing their part in the act.

The snake charmers of India are an age-old wonder. It is a familiar supposition that they "milk" the cobra of its venom by having it bite into cloth or cotton, which requires, nevertheless, a considerable handling of the murderous reptile. They seem to beguile the cobra with notes they play on a shrill pipe, but the snake, we are told, is deaf and can't hear the notes. The theory is that the cobra responds to the sight of the swaying of the pipe, which the snake charmer moves in a slow rhythm, as he blows into it. In any case the temple dance, which is exotic enough in itself, is made all the more weird by the cobras coiled in baskets and raising their hooded heads high, while the snake charmer sways and pipes.

To go with this Hollywood director John Farrow devised a bit of movie business. An attractive Hindu family attending the cobra dance in the temple, a young couple with a boy and a girl. The little girl is a gem. An Indian motion picture group was working at Mysore, and Farrow enlisted the small daughter of one of the Indian film officials. She turned out to be a remarkable little mimic. At the cobra dance she does an imitation of the dancers with a childish grace and drollery. The adjective seems hardly one to go along with cobras, but people will say, "It's cute."

Cinerama operations in Indian cities were bedeviled by crowds of the curious, people gazing at the ponderous camera setup, pushing in for a close inspection, and getting in the way of the pictures. Jim Morrison, a member of the expedition, tells me that on one occasion they rigged up a dummy camera and made a play of shooting pictures with it to draw the crowd away from the real camera. It worked. The fake was more potent in attracting people than the genuine article, as is often the case in life.

Cameraman Gayne Rescher tells of a danger of air photography in India—a peril of vultures.

"We were flying low coming in at Delhi, and I was behind the camera in the nose of the plane, shooting pictures. Ahead there was a big flock of vultures circling around, huge birds. If you hit one at two hundred miles an hour, it might crash through the windshield and kill somebody inside. Paul Mantz, at the controls, called to me, and said we might have some trouble—watch out. I was looking over the camera, and he'd yell: 'Duck.' Well, it wasn't a duck, it was a vulture, which we were about to hit. So I'd duck, until we had missed the bird. Then I'd get up, only to hear Paul yell again: 'Duck.' That kept me going up and down like a jumping jack, until we were clear of the flock of vultures. Luckily we didn't hit any, the camera kept running, and we got our pictures."

# Chapter 20

OF THE SEVEN WONDERS of the Ancient World, two were dedicated to sentiment in marriage: the Mausoleum, monument of a wife's devotion to the memory of her husband; the Hanging Gardens of Babylon, erected by a husband for the happiness of a favorite wife. Among the wonders of the modern world, one of the most famous commemorates a husband's devotion to a wife. It is, of course, the incomparable Taj Mahal, the tomb that Shah Jehan created for the beauteous Mumtaz Mahal, at the city of Agra, in India.

The Taj Mahal, built in the seventeenth century, was hardly completed before its breath-taking beauty became legendary in Europe as well as in Asia. The French traveler, François Bernier, who toured the East three centuries ago, was in Agra during the 1660s, saw the building when it had been up for less than twenty years, and wrote in his journal: "Possibly I have acquired an Indian taste; but I am of the opinion that this monument has much more right to be included among the wonders of the world than the pyramids of Egypt."

This was high praise coming from a cultivated European whose homeland was the France of Louis XIV, but later generations have endorsed Bernier's opinion. Some critics have gone beyond him, declaring the Taj Mahal to be the most beautiful edifice ever erected by man. Everyone can judge for himself since the Taj, unlike the Hanging Gardens and the Mausoleum, still stands, an ethereal vision in marble and sandstone, the brightest jewel in the crown of the new Indian nation, maintained with loving care just as it was, first by the Moguls and then by the British.

Shah Jehan was one of the Mogul emperors who reigned over India in golden splendor. A Moslem, he practiced the polygamy ordained in the Koran, which permitted four wives, not counting the concubines whom it was customary for an Islamic potentate to have in his harem. Mumtaz Mahal, young, dainty, and beautiful, was the favorite wife. The Taj Mahal, therefore, is a monument to romantic sentiment in the harem, a husband's devotion in polygamous family life.

This to the Western mind may be unexpected. We are accustomed to think of true love in terms of monogamy and of marital devotion in the system of one mate. The harem might seem to us to be an institution of sensuality devoid of sentiment. Yet the story of the Hanging Gardens cites the matrimonial sentiment of Nebuchadnezzar, and a Babylonian king would have a monstrous harem. It is not clear if King Mausolus had only one wife. He was a Greek by culture, and the Greeks were monogamous, but he was a vassal of the Persians, and they were enthusiastic polygamists. So it is more than likely that Queen Artemisia built the Mausoleum of Halicarnassus for a husband who had other wives.

The truth is that romantic love flourished in the harem with an abundance of moonlight and roses. Some scholars, in fact, hold that the extreme romanticism of the Middle Ages, with the knight dedicated to his lady, was derived from the Moslems in Spain. There is endless evidence in the form of love poetry in Arabia, verses celebrating the worship of the beauteous one by a lover who had an ample harem.

The Taj Mahal is the masterpiece of Mohammedan art. That it arose on Indian soil is explained by history. The Moguls came originally from Central Asia, their name being a variant of the word "Mongol." They were Moslems, and they conquered India. The founder of the Mogul Empire was one of the remarkable men of all time. In martial ardor and ability to command, Baber may have been a typical princeling of Tartary, but he was also a man of culture, the author of perhaps the best political memoirs ever written by a reigning monarch.

In December of 1525 he led his army into India along the classic route through the Khyber Pass, pushed rapidly on toward Delhi, and met the forces of the local ruler on the field of Panipat. The battle took place on April 12, 1526, and proved to be one of the decisive conflicts of world history, for Baber won the victory that gave him a permanent foothold in the land that was to be ruled by his descendants.

Baber did not finish the work of integrating an imperial domain. Moreover there was a recession toward anarchy under his son Humayun, who inherited none of his ability. But the Moguls were lucky in the next representative of their dynasty, who resembled his grandfather rather than his father—Akbar, known to history as Akbar the Great.

He introduced a new system of government, bringing all the land under his direct authority, naming his own viceroys, setting up a comprehensive tax levy, keeping the provincial military forces in the pay of the central treasury to prevent local rebellions before they could get started. He thus centralized his sprawling realm as a single political entity.

Akbar's greatest coup, the thing that gave stability to his throne as nothing else could, was his abrogation of the old distinction between Moslems and Hindus. The custom of the victors of Islam was to levy a special poll tax on infidels, and in India that tax fell on the Hindus, who naturally resented it bitterly and were ready to intrigue with the enemies of their masters.

Akbar saw that good sense dictated a removal of the Hindu "second-class citizen" stigma. He abolished the poll tax on the Hindus and treated them as the equals of his Moslem subjects. They repaid him, as he saw that they would, with steadfast loyalty during his subsequent wars.

Akbar was something of a philosopher. Early in life he became accustomed to listen to priests and shamans of various faiths. Theological disputation became a passion with him. The emperor could sit and listen to debaters wrangling about the fine points of their religion. The heat and venom of these sessions, with each doctor defending his own version of religious truth, and pouring scorn on the others, helped to dilute Akbar's Mohammedanism. He welcomed men of other faiths, Hindus from his own domain, Zoroastrians from Persia, even the Christian missionaries who made their way to his court.

The moment of Akbar's religious crisis came in the midst of a hunt. On April 20, 1578, he ordered a *battue* on the immense scale native to India—hundreds of beaters streaming through the forests driving thousands of terrified animals within range of the royal hunting party. The slaughter was rising to a climax when the emperor suddenly ordered an end to the hunt, told the beaters to go home, and said that no more beasts should be killed. He had experienced a revulsion against killing.

The British historian of India, Vincent Smith, wrote: "Akbar was by nature a mystic who sought earnestly, like his Sufi friends, to attain the ineffable bliss of direct contact with the Divine Reality, and now and again believed, or fancied, that he had succeeded. His temperament was profoundly melancholic, and there seems to be some reason to suspect that at times he was not far from the danger of falling into a state of religious mania. His ambition and intense interest in all the affairs of this world saved him from that fate, and brought him back from dreams to the actualities of human life. He was not an ordinary man, and his complex nature, like that of St. Paul, Muhammad, Dante, and other great men with a tendency to mysticism, presents perplexing problems."

The upshot was that Akbar, attracted to all religions but convinced entirely by none, decided to appoint himself the supreme theological authority in the Mogul Empire. He published an "Infallibility Decree" that virtually made him pope as well as king. It stated that henceforth he would decide between conflicting opinions on matters of faith, with everyone bound to accept his decision as the truth.

Akbar lived in a period of great European nation-builders—

Queen Elizabeth in England, Henry of Navarre in France, Philip II in Spain—but he was greater than any of them, a wiser statesman, a better administrator, a more refined patron of the arts. At his death (1605) he left behind an empire so closely knit and organized that it could continue in much the same form for another century. He also left behind a tradition of building on the magnificent scale, for he studded his cities with his own edifices. By patronizing artists and architects he forwarded the development of style and skill to the point where, under his grandson, the miracle of the Taj Mahal became possible.

Akbar was succeeded by his son Jahangir, the potentate to whom the title of "The Great Mogul" was first applied—a title that has become part of our everyday speech, as when we talk of "movie moguls."

During his reign travelers from the West started to turn up in India with greater frequency. The Portuguese, of course, had arrived earliest. They followed in the wake of their great sea captain, Vasco da Gama, who rounded the Cape of Good Hope and sailed to India in 1498. Twelve years later they captured Goa, built up a thriving commerce, sent out missionaries, and regarded the subcontinent as their own private preserve. This was the heroic age of Albuquerque and St. Francis Xavier.

As time passed the Portuguese found that they could not keep out other Europeans. The Dutch, the French, the English, were all anxious to tap the source of wealth uncovered by Da Gama. The imagination of the West was inflamed by stories of the beauty, power, luxury and oriental splendor of the Mogul Empire. Merchants, travelers, ambassadors, missionaries—all helped to fill in the picture of the Great Mogul and his kingdom.

One visitor to the court of Jahangir deserves special mention. Sir William Hawkins arrived there in 1609. Hawkins was no polished or philosophical observer. He was, on the contrary, a bluff English seaman in the pay of the East India Company, but during his voyages he had picked up languages and was able to speak to the Moguls without an interpreter. He also had learned to drink deeply, a habit to which Jahangir was addicted.

[ 187 ]

The English sailor became a boon companion of the Great Mogul, their drinking bouts extending far into the night.

Hawkins gives us a classical description of excess and grandiosity. He estimates Jahangir's yearly income at fifty million pounds, and the number of servants who waited on him at thirty-six thousand. The emperor wore garments spangled with gold and resplendent with jewels of fabulous wealth and size, while he was surrounded with courtiers hardly less glittering.

Sir William Hawkins won from Jahangir commercial rights for his company, an important point since it was the first step toward British influence in India.

Jahangir died in 1627 and the throne passed to his son, Shah Jehan, he of the Koh-i-noor diamond, of the Peacock Throne, of the Taj Mahal. Shah Jehan was something of a throwback to Akbar, amiable and accessible to his subjects.

Under his popular rule the Mogul Empire reached its height. His reign was remembered for its order, security, and justice. Agra, his capital, was a thriving metropolis; one European traveler estimates that by itself the city could put an army of 200,000 men into the field if necessary, and that the standing army of the empire boasted cavalry numbering 144,500, excluding elephants.

One extant symbol of wealth and beauty is the Koh-i-noor diamond—the "Mountain of Light." Its origin is shrouded in mystery, but it came from the Golconda diamond mines of Hyderabad, in southern Hindustan, and was presented to Shah Jehan by an official of the district. The Frenchman Tavernier saw it when it was still a prize possession of the Moguls. He was staggered by the size, weight, and brilliance of the jewel—186$\frac{1}{16}$ carats before being cut. The Koh-i-noor quickly became proverbial, the most sought-after of diamonds. Carried off by the Persians in 1739 when they invaded India, it then passed from hand to hand in a circuitous route until it came into the possession of the British. In 1849 it was presented to Queen Victoria, who added it to the crown jewels.

The Mogul emperors naturally had several splendid thrones, but Shah Jehan wanted something special. He put his craftsmen to work and they produced the legendary Peacock Throne. Tavernier tells us that it was six feet long and four feet wide, with three cushions to support the emperor as he sat in state before his court. The three closed sides were covered with a canopy, above which stood an artificial peacock flanked by artificial flowers. The Peacock Throne coruscated with gold and jewels. Tavernier counted 108 rubies, and even more emeralds, many of the largest size. Diamonds and pearls decorated the underside of the canopy. The peacock was fashioned from gold inlaid with gems, particularly blue sapphires; from its breast dangled a pear-shaped pearl. Tavernier's guess at the cost of the throne comes to perhaps twenty million pounds in modern currency.

The Koh-i-noor diamond and the Peacock Throne—two marvels that would add luster to any royal court. Yet both are of secondary consideration when the reign of Shah Jehan is in question. Both must give place to his masterpiece, the Taj Mahal.

In 1612 he had married Arjumand Banu, a cousin, and their wedded bliss until her death in 1631 constitutes one of the great love stories of the world. It was not dimmed by the fact that Shah Jehan, in Moslem fashion, had a harem of other wives. She was his favorite, the one he called Mumtaz Mahal, or "Ornament of the Palace." A powerful influence with him, she was largely responsible for his orthodox Mohammedanism, for she held strictly to the tenets of Islam. Mumtaz Mahal bore her husband fourteen children, the last of which caused her death on June 17, 1631.

Shah Jehan reacted to the tragedy as did Artemisia on the death of Mausolus. He was so inconsolable that it was feared he would die of grief. In fact he never recovered from the shock, although he did rouse himself because he wanted to venerate the memory of his wife with a suitable monument. The greatest thing he did during the rest of his reign was to build the Taj Mahal.

As a site he chose a high bank of the Jumna River, one of the holy rivers of Hindustan, where it bends around at Agra. He summoned the finest architects and craftsmen from all over his empire and had them submit plans for the proposed building. The Portuguese Jesuits in Agra reported that the man who won was a Venetian, Geronimo Verroneo, and that this Westerner actually erected the Taj. But that story has been rejected by some later scholars on the grounds that the building shows no European influence. Other accounts name a Turk or a Persian.

In any case many experts worked on the Taj. The monumental *Cambridge History of India* makes the interesting suggestion that the structural design was mainly the work of Moslems, the decorations of Hindus.

The basic material used was white marble, with the wall and gates of red sandstone; a color scheme that has the remarkable effect of showing different tints at different times of the day. The building stands on a 186-foot square with the angles cut to form an octagon. Beneath it is a raised marble platform extending all around and marked by delicate minarets at each corner. Above swells the great dome, about two thirds of a sphere, surmounted by a crescent and flanked by smaller domes. Each of the walls is cut by arches of a similar but not at all monotonous pattern; rather, they contribute to the unity of the whole. Light enters through marble screens.

There is an old saying that "the Moguls built like titans and finished like jewelers." The Taj Mahal proves the truth of the remark. Looked at from a distance, its appearance is indeed dreamlike, with a grace and balance that make us wonder how human beings ever achieved so miraculous a result from marble and sandstone.

But as you come close you begin to see the work of the jeweler, decorative patterns of exquisite refinement beginning on the outside and rising to the summit of glory on the inside where the cenotaphs of Mumtaz Mahal and Shah Jehan now repose. The Taj has four chambers. The walls are inlaid with marble plates six feet high, on each of which flowers are portrayed in dazzling gems. Floors and ceilings show elaborate tracery and pattern design. Trelliswork in marble breaks up the bare extent of the rooms.

The cenotaphs are of simple design, yet of extreme beauty

*A close-up of the entrance to the Taj Mahal shows the delicately wrought pattern of the decorations.*

*From his prison in Agra Fort, Shah Jehan could gaze at the Taj Mahal in the distance, the tomb where he would rejoin Mumtaz Mahal in death.*

*Boating on the sacred river Ganges in the shadow of the temples and palaces of Benares.*
                                                                                Photo by Edwin W. Sippel

*The bathers wash their sins away in the water of the holy river, but the lads look like kids in swimming anywhere.*
                                                                                Photo by Edwin W. Sippel

*Elephants blocking the right of way are an old story, ever since the Darjeeling Railroad went into operation back in the last century. The boy mahout is called upon to get the pachyderm off the track.*

The traditional combat between the mongoose and the cobra. The nimble rodent is not immune to the lethal poison of the hooded serpent, but always wins through tactics and agility.          Photo by Edwin W. Sippel

One of the legendary wonders of India, the snake charmer, as he fascinates the cobras.          Photo by Edwin W. Sippel

*Street scene in Benares. No sacred cows visible here, but they're a definite traffic hazard.*

Photo by Edwin W. Sippel

*At the Monkey Temple the child dancers are accompanied by an orchestra making music mystifying to Western ears.*

*Darjeeling, at this lofty altitude, has great tea plantations, from which we get Darjeeling tea.*

Photo by Edwin W. Sippel

*Air view of Darjeeling, mountaintop resort in the Himalayas.*

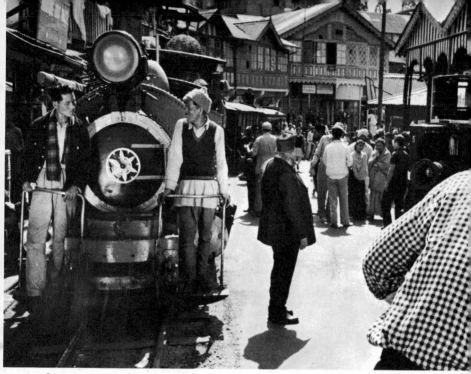

In this quaint wonder of railroading, the train starts out from a station down in the plains of sweltering India. It's rather like a toy train, and no part of it is less than seventy-five years old.          Photo by Edwin W. Sippel

Photo by Edwin W. Sippe

*Climbing the steep Himalayan slopes to lofty Darjeeling. Moe and Joe are sanding the tracks. If it were not for the sand, the wheels would not get traction up the steep grade.*

and worthy of the building that holds them. That of Shah Jehan lies off center. He had intended the Taj for Mumtaz Mahal alone, and planned his own tomb in contrasting black marble, for the other side of the river. But it was never built, and his son decided to make the same tomb do for both, which was appropriate enough, for the husband and wife who were so closely united in life deserved to be united in death.

Beyond the Taj Mahal itself stretch wings running north and south. They have gardens, ponds, and entrances for visitors. On one wing stands a mosque which would be an outstanding architectural achievement anywhere else, but which pales beside its overwhelming companion.

The Taj gains much from its setting. From the front it has the beauty and majesty of the man-made approach. The rear takes on a special ethereal quality from the reflection in the Jumna, which makes the building seem to be floating between water and sky. The Taj is thus one of the most satisfying of all structures, avoiding anything like sameness or monotony, offering the observer ever new visions of the sublime depending on the time of day and the direction. It draws the traveler back again and again. I, for example, have made exactly thirty pilgrimages to the Taj. The thirtieth when I went there with our Cinerama crew.

The Taj Mahal occupied the labor of some twenty thousand men over a span of eighteen years. Completed in 1648, it had strained the Mogul genius to the limit. After it nothing superior was possible; on the contrary there was a falling off in the architecture of Hindustan, as if creative thought had been used up. The emperors continued to build, but signs of stiffness and formality became more and more evident.

This was in harmony with political developments. After Shah Jehan the Mogul Empire had no place to go except downward. This great ruler lived to see the first bitter fruits of failure, for his sons rebelled against him, and the one who came out on top, Aurangzeb, deposed him and threw him into prison. Then Aurangzeb moved the capital of the Mogul Empire from Agra to Delhi.

For seven years Shah Jehan remained in a cell in the fort at Agra, protesting against the unfilial behavior of the new emperor, and spending much of his time gazing across at the Taj Mahal where the symbol of his best days lay buried. Shah Jehan died in 1658 and finally left prison to lie by the side of Mumtaz Mahal in her glorious tomb. Many an hour I have spent at the great "Red Fort" in Agra, sitting where Shah Jehan sat, looking out across the Jumna at his masterpiece.

Aurangzeb hastened the downfall of the Mogul Empire because he was a bigoted Moslem with no respect for Hinduism. He reimposed the poll tax, and that touched off riots among his subjects. He stimulated the dormant fanaticism of the Hindus by destroying their temples. He tried to hold his dominions together by force instead of by the political good sense of his predecessors.

Aurangzeb maintained his throne for fifty years, the last Mogul of any consequence. On his death in 1707 fierce fighting among his sons broke out. The family produced one weak ruler after another, nonentities whose main business seemed to be to preside over the dissolution of the empire. Final ruin came in 1739 when the powerful King of Persia, Nadir Shah, invaded Hindustan, pillaged Delhi, and took home as part of his booty both the Koh-i-noor diamond and the Peacock Throne.

From then on the Mogul Empire of Akbar, Jahangir, and Shah Jehan was but a memory, but it had left behind a colorful page of history climaxed by the enduring monument that attracts and charms visitors to this day, that wonder of the modern world, the Taj Mahal.

It's a glory to photograph, but it provided plenty of trouble for Cinerama. Both of our cameramen, Harry Squire and Gayne Rescher, had their difficulties. Gayne Rescher, who was with Paul Mantz's air photography unit, was assigned to get some ground shots of the Taj, and relates:

"We never had such hard luck in our lives. The weather was bad, foggy with an overcast, but it was never bad enough to keep us from going out. We'd make the trip from our hotel in Agra to the Taj, and set up our cameras, but it would cloud up, and we'd wait and wait. For four days we had these disappointments. Then, one morning, the weather was perfect, and we said we'd really get it today. But when we got there we found they had emptied the reflecting pool. They were cleaning it. No reflecting pool, no Taj. However, we finally got some shots."

For Harry Squire the weather was okay, but Harry says: "The pond bent."

The reflecting pool, which as you approach mirrors the exquisite dome, is a perfect oblong. But it got out of shape, "the pond bent" like a figure of odd geometry.

This was because of the peculiarities of the multiple Cinerama camera with its three lenses. At some angles a straight line passing from one lens to another will bend. At the same time, the choice of angles is tricky, because of the "match lines." On the screen, the junction of the three films may show up as vertical lines. The way to minimize that is to get something dark where a match line would occur.

At the Taj Mahal, the angle that was right for the match lines was wrong for the reflecting pool. It took some experimenting before Harry was able to overcome both difficulties. Finally he got an angle from which a tree covered an offending match line, and the pool preserved its correct geometrical form.

# Chapter 21

THE CITY OF AGRA still retains some of the majesty of its imperial days. The Taj Mahal is only one example of magnificent Mogul architecture, and the Red Fort, which was begun by Akbar, still looks frowning and formidable with its great length of sandstone walls. In the city you see street signs in English, and that tells a story—how the British Raj succeeded the great Moguls. British influence still persists, though the British Raj, too, has gone.

The streets of all Indian cities are lined with signs in English. In our Cinerama picture one strikes your eye particularly in Benares. In huge letters—H A M L E T. The British motion picture of the Shakespearean tragedy was playing in India while we were there. The name of Hamlet was spread across a building, while the sacred cows ambled in the street. This may well suggest that Hamletlike character so great in the establishment of British domination in Hindustan. Clive of India was as perplexing a character as Hamlet, as dark of mood as any Melancholy Dane.

Clive's biography shows a moody, introspective pessimist, given to spasms of despondency, fretful about the treatment he received from the world, one who three times tried to commit suicide and succeeded on the last. It is not fanciful to read something of Hamlet into Robert Clive, who also spent a good deal of his time pondering the question "To be or not to be?"

Clive's reputation for singularity began in childhood. Born

in Shropshire in 1725, he was sent to a variety of private schools to be educated, but he seems to have resisted the process successfully. His masters called him an idler, although he impressed them as one of potential ability, who would not put it to its proper use. That he was courageous to the point of foolhardiness is indicated by one story of how he climbed to the top of a church steeple and frightened the townspeople by sitting astride an ornamental waterspout.

At this time he also manifested the beginnings of a genius for devious operations, forming a gang of bullies and threatening the windows of any shopkeeper who refused to buy him off —in short, young Clive had discovered the art of "protection" long before the gangsters of twentieth-century America took it up. His capacity for duplicity was to reach its consummation years later when he was able to take over Bengal largely because he knew how to outmaneuver a blackmailer.

At the age of seventeen Clive was given a job with the East India Company. His father despaired of anything better for him. So he shipped out to Madras as a writer, meaning a clerk, whose business was accounts, ship cargoes, and all the usual routine. Arrived at Madras, he was domiciled along with the rest of the British colony in Fort St. George, one of the European oases that stood isolated from the seething millions of Hindus and Moslems.

It was a critical moment in the history of Hindustan, for the massive Mogul Empire was breaking up.

The big power in India was France, whose forces were under the command of a soldier of vision and energy. The Marquis Dupleix had long-range plans for grandiose conquest. Macaulay tells us in his essay on Clive, "The man who first saw that it was possible to found an European empire on the ruins of the Mogul monarchy was Dupleix. His restless, capacious and inventive mind had formed this scheme at a time when the ablest servants of the English Company were busied only about invoices and bills of lading." Dupleix was already moving to create a French raj.

As for Clive, he was but another writer for his company during the early 1740s. He was unhappy at Fort St. George, for he was a stranger without friends or money and he did not mix well with his new acquaintances. The depth of his homesickness is evident from one of his letters, which says in part, "If I should be so far blest as to revisit again my own Country, but more especially Manchester (the centre of all my Wishes) all that I could hope or desire for would be presented before me in one view." He began to frequent the governor's library, which was thrown open to him, and it was at this time that he absorbed the knowledge that was to help him in the career that lay just ahead.

But his fits of despondency became worse until he fell into the depths of despair and decided to commit suicide. He loaded his pistol, placed the muzzle against his temple, and pulled the trigger. Nothing happened. He repeated the act; still the gun refused to go off. He was mulling over the meaning of this when a friend entered his room. Clive asked the friend to point the pistol out the window and fire. This time it responded properly, at which Clive said with some excitement that he believed Providence had some grand design for him. He was right. War with the French was about to break out; soon he would leave the countinghouse for the battlefield.

The French took the offensive, Dupleix driving up from Pondicherry and capturing Madras. The British there were made prisoners, Clive among them. With some others he escaped to Fort St. David, another British inclave, which was filling up with refugees and had become a wide-open, brawling, drinking, gambling mecca for those who were willing to see their world disintegrate as long as they could have a good time. Clive gambled heavily, fought a duel over an issue of cheating at cards, gained a reputation for turbulence, and caned a chaplain for mentioning it.

Then came the French attack on Fort St. David. Immediately Clive's innate military ability showed itself. He was made an officer, took part in the fighting, planned and directed the defeat of the French. He captured Arcot and held it during a memorable siege of almost two months. He made a name for himself. An uneasy peace supervened, with British fortunes on the rise, French on the downgrade.

At this point romance enters the life of Clive in a manner characteristic of his romantic, impulsive nature. A friend of his showed him a picture of a sister, and Clive was so struck by it that he burst into the exclamation that he would marry the lady if he could. He did. She came to India to visit her brother, was introduced to Clive, and they were married shortly afterward. Then they sailed for England.

His fame had preceded the young commander. He was welcomed by his family, by the Company, and by the country. He even won a seat in the House of Commons, only to lose it through the political chicanery typical of the eighteenth century. Then he returned to India.

By this time Dupleix was gone, moved from his post and called back to Paris, thus depriving France of the best man she had in India. Beating the French was no longer the main British concern; dominating the sultans and rajahs and turning them into clients was.

The ruler of Bengal, Surajah Dowla, seized the British colony of merchants at Calcutta, took them prisoners, and threw them into a dungeon. Their incarceration lasted but one night, but that was enough to give it a permanent place in the history books, for the dungeon was the infamous "Black Hole of Calcutta." Almost one hundred and fifty persons, including some women, were placed in a room twenty feet square with but two small barred windows. It was the hottest period of the year, with the cell a stifling, scorching inferno. The result was a crazed melee, a frantic struggling for air. The weak were trampled underfoot, and the rest began to collapse as the night wore on. When the "Black Hole" was opened in the morning no less than 123 of the victims were dead.

The news sent a wave of horror through the rest of the British in India and a demand for retribution. Clive led an army into Calcutta. He was determined to get rid of Surajah Dowla by placing another candidate on his throne. One of those in on the conspiracy was a Sikh banker who at the critical moment threatened to reveal it, if he were not promised a fortune to remain silent. Here the devious side of Clive's character came out. He caused two documents to be drawn up, one with the stipulated promise, the other without it. The first satisfied the Sikh, and he signed it. But Clive used the second, thus making it unnecessary to pay the blackmailer anything. Clive's defenders have argued that after all he was dealing with a criminal, but the truth is that the British admiral on the scene refused to be party to so perfidious a scheme. Whereupon Clive coolly had his name forged.

While these maneuverings were going on Clive was preparing for battle with Surajah Dowla, who had gathered an enormous army. The odds were twenty to one when the two armies met on the field of Plassey, but Clive made skillful use of his forces and of European techniques of warfare to win one of the key battles of world history. The Battle of Plassey in 1757 is the true beginning of the British Raj. Clive, the first of the great British proconsuls, was named governor of Bengal in 1758.

He visited England in 1760, was received by the king, and was honored with the title of Lord Clive of Plassey. He remained at home for about five years, until the pull of India became too strong. He was a great and powerful potentate abroad, with wealth for the asking. No wonder London could not satisfy him. Besides, the Company wanted him to go back.

The subcontinent was still not settled. Sir Hector Munro had won the Battle of Buxar, but even so there were disorders everywhere. Clive remarked on his arrival, "Tomorrow the whole Mogul power is in our grasp," meaning that the very existence of chaos indicated that there was no power capable of withstanding his forces.

When Clive left India for good in 1767 he had placed Britain firmly in power, moving steadily toward full domination. Arriving home, he soon discovered that his countrymen were not so willing to venerate him as in the past. The Ministry was beginning to take more interest in India, and one of the first questions that arose was Clive's behavior out there.

He was bitterly attacked in Parliament by a committee graced by the presence of General Burgoyne, who a few years later was to suffer one of the great catastrophes of British arms when the American colonists defeated him at Saratoga. However, there was no premonition of Burgoyne's fate when he opened the assault on one of Britain's most successful commanders.

Clive was accused mainly of abusing his position to build a fortune for himself. Complaining that they were treating him like a sheep stealer rather than as the conqueror of an empire, Clive defended himself with great energy. He did not deny that India had made him wealthy, but he did deny that he had been greedy or venal. Before the bar of the House of Commons he expostulated in ringing tones: "Consider the situation in which the victory of Plassey had placed me! A great prince was dependent upon my pleasure: an opulent city lay at my mercy; its richest bankers bid against each other for my smiles; I walked through vaults which were thrown open to me alone, piled on either hand with gold and diamonds and jewels! Mr. Chairman, at this moment I stand astonished at my own moderation!"

Enough members were swayed by his defense to refuse to condemn him. Parliament said it could not accept everything he had done in India, but it went on to add the rider that "Robert Clive did, at the same time, render great and meritorious services to his country."

The tribute came too late to do its object any real good. During the long-drawn-out proceedings, when he heard the most venomous insults hurled at him by gentlemen who had never been close to India, his bouts of desperation returned more frequently. The feeling that he was being badly treated became more intense. The hopelessness that he had known at Fort St. George, back in the days when it seemed that the future of Hindustan belonged to France and when he himself was but a writer in the service of the East India Company, returned. Says Macaulay, "His strong mind was fast sinking under many kinds of suffering. On the twenty-second of November, 1774, he died by his own hand. He had just completed his forty-ninth year."

And so the Hamlet of British India gave his own answer to the question, "To be or not to be?" Life was simply not worth living for the former accountant who turned soldier in a moment of crisis and went on to found an empire without the loss of a single battle. But long before his tragic end he had placed an indelible mark on the history of India, of the British Empire, and of the world.

# Chapter 22

THE HIMALAYAS have an average height, valleys included, of 20,000 feet above sea level, and a whole series of peaks rise above 25,000 feet. Mount Everest, the world's loftiest peak, is more than 29,000 feet high, and Mount Godwin-Austin, K2, is only 890 feet less. Yet the Himalayan rocks are sedimentary, formed by sediment deposited in water. In remote geological ages this loftiest of mountain ranges was part of the bottom of the sea.

Some titanic force over a long period folded the sea-bottom rocks upward, thrusting them aloft to become the highest pinnacles on earth. The process seems to be still going on. They say Mount Everest is growing higher. One sign of mountain building is earthquakes, and the Himalayas are an earthquake area. Several years ago in the eastern Himalayas occurred earthquakes so violent that the very face of the earth was changed.

Southern India, with the plateau of the Deccan, does not consist of sedimentary rocks laid down in the sea. The signs are that southern India was never under water. This, with the ocean-formed Himalayas, constitutes a geologic pattern.

A classic explanation is that southern India is the remains of an immense continent that reached from India to Africa. They call it Gondwanaland, after a district in southern India. To the north was a sea, where the Himalayas are now. In the dim past the Gondwanaland continent foundered and sank under the ocean, leaving only the plateau of southern India above water.

This continental catastrophe, incidentally, was what caused the cracking of the Rift Valley in East Africa and western Asia. The Himalayas were created when sea bottom to the north of Gondwanaland was folded up by the thrust of immense forces generated by the sinking of a continent.

So geology tells us with its wonder story of continents and oceans in vast ages of time. History, that brief moment, tells us that in the nineteenth century the British in India applied trigonometry to the measurement of Himalayan peaks. In 1854 they calculated the height of a mountain, the snowy tip of which could be seen in the far distance thrust above the lofty line of the Himalayan ranges. The figures indicated that this was the highest of mountains. Its altitude is 29,140 feet. The calculation was made by an Indian computer. The survey was the project of Sir George Everest, an eminent geographer engaged in Indian survey work, and the peak was named after him.

Mountain climbing is a modern avocation which began as a sport in the Alps and there culminated with the conquest of the Matterhorn in 1865. The Himalayas were the greatest challenge, and Mount Everest the supreme goal. That loftiest of summits was, however, so remote that it was an exploit to get to it at all. Everest climbing did not begin until the early 1920s, when the mountain was reconnoitered for climbing and the first attempts on the summit were made.

The history of brave men versus the highest of mountains is one of tragedy and triumph. Nothing could be more heartbreaking than the expedition of 1924, when two of the foremost of mountaineers went up on the climb to the topmost pinnacle. They may have reached it. They may have conquered the highest point on the globe. Nobody knows. They never came back. In the extremest contrast, nothing could exceed the jubilant glory of the expedition of 1953. The circumstances were almost unbelievable in surrounding a victory with splendor.

The tragedy of 1924 is related by Captain John Noel, the official photographer in the party of British climbers, in his book *The Story of Everest*. The attempt on the mountain was made by the northern approach, which was considered the most practicable. The party went in through Tibet, and began a systematic ascent, establishing camps at various levels. Thus they climbed their way to within striking distance of the top. The final assault was made by Mallory and Irvine from a camp at the twenty-seven-thousand-foot level. To support them Odell and Hazzard, with Sherpa porters, were stationed at twenty-five thousand feet.

Others of the party waited at a lower level. The summit of Everest was hidden by clouds. Two days and nights passed with nerve-torturing suspense. Endlessly they peered through a telescope. They could see the camp of the support party, and then came the black moment. It had been agreed that blankets would be used for signaling, and now they saw Odell and his companion lay six blankets on the ice. The design was unmistakable —a cross. It meant—death.

"I remember the moment vividly," Captain Noel writes. "I saw this signal through my telescope. I saw plainly it was a cross. We all looked. We all tried to make it different. But it was plainly a cross on the white snow."

Presently the support party descended and joined them. They told how Mallory and Irvine had started from their camp at the twenty-seven-thousand-foot level, and began on the final dash, while Odell and his companions waited at the twenty-five-thousand-foot camp. The pinnacle of Everest was covered by a dense mist, into which the two climbers disappeared. But then, as Odell watched, the wind cleared the mist away from the final summit of Everest.

"Suddenly," Odell related, "I noticed high up in the almost perpendicular wilderness a moving black spot silhouetted. Then I saw another speck move up to join the first. It was none other than Mallory and Irvine, within six hundred feet of the summit."

As Odell watched the two black specks, he believed they would surely reach the top for the conquest of Everest. But then the wind blew the mist across the scene and the summit could be seen no more. He waited and watched, but had no further glimpse of the pinnacle and the two black spots.

The next day Odell, with two Sherpas, climbed up to the top-level camp, from which Mallory and Irvine had set out. He thought he'd find them there, but the tents were empty. On the following day he made another ascent to the camp at twenty-seven thousand feet. But again there was no sign of the two climbers. It was then that the support party laid out the blanket signal in the form of a cross—death.

They were now utterly exhausted, and after two days and nights there was no chance that Mallory and Irvine could have survived. Odell and his companions then made their way to the lower camp and told the story.

"I think," Odell concluded, "that it is quite possible, and even likely, that Mallory and Irvine reached the top and were overtaken by the night in the descent, exhausted and frozen to death."

Mallory and Irvine found their tombs in the glacier that crowns Everest. Somewhere their bodies rest, probably below accumulated snow and ice. They have never been seen.

For some years after that there was no further attempt to conquer Everest. This was partly because the tragedy at the summit was interpreted by the native peoples as a sign that the Goddess of the Mountains was angry. In 1933 a British party in two airplanes flew over Everest and made motion pictures of the summit. In 1936 another climbing attempt was made and failed.

In 1953 there were two Mount Everest expeditions. The Chinese Reds were in control of Tibet, and that closed the northern approach to the mountains, which was considered the best. A southern approach through Nepal was more difficult, it was thought, but there was no better route. A Swiss expedition made its way far up the slope but failed to reach the summit. Then a British party toiled up the steeps of glacier and rock, and the climax came in June, almost exactly twenty-nine years after the tragedy of 1924. We can best appreciate the event, perhaps, if we take it as it then appeared in the news. My broadcast record reads:

"All that Coronation festivity in Britain today turns out to be something unique—the like of which has never been known before. I can think of few moments in history to approach it—for sheer drama. The glowing pageant of royalty, with all the splendors of centuries past—combined with an historic exploit, the achievement of one of mankind's most difficult and perilous ambitions, the conquest of Mount Everest.

"Imagine Ferdinand and Isabella celebrating some sort of magnificent jubilee, when in walks a sea captain with a party of sailors. Christopher Columbus—announcing the discovery of America!

"Tonight, while all Britain sings, 'God Save the Queen,' they are also acclaiming Hillary, the New Zealander, and Tensing the mountain man of the high Himalayas!

"Queen Elizabeth was aroused from sleep to hear about it. She had retired on the eve of her Coronation, and was to arise in a few hours for the great event. But she was got out of bed—to be informed of the exploit, which, from the beginning, had been intended as a Coronation gift to her.

"Actually, the topmost pinnacle of Everest had been climbed on Friday, but it was only tonight that the news got through—from the lofty reaches of the world's highest mountain—then sent on to a point for communication to the outside world.

"The climbers had been beaten back on previous attempts, but had stuck to their camp at the 27,000-foot level, for one more 'go' at that ultimate summit—which no human being had ever scaled before and come down to tell the tale, as far as is known. They had to make it now or never because the monsoon was closing in, the rains which mean huge snows high in the Himalayas. Moreover, they were determined to do it in time for the Coronation.

"The final victory over Everest was won by a thirty-four-year-old New Zealand beekeeper—E. P. Hillary, who learned mountaineering by climbing the magnificent peaks of the south island of his own native New Zealand. He was accompanied by a fabulous native guide—named Tensing—a Sherpa tribesman who, time and again, has accompanied Everest expeditions. Tensing, the Sherpa of Nepal, had taken part in more attempts on Everest than any other man in the world.

"What a tremendous feature to accompany the pageantry of

royalty in London. Far off in the Himalayas, the conquest of Everest."

In our Cinerama quest for wonders, we did not get Mount Everest. Our idea was to have Paul Mantz fly into the mountain world of the Himalayas and make a pageant of the world's loftiest summit. But the Indian government said no. Everest is in Nepal near the border of Tibet, and Tibet is now dominated by the Chinese Reds. India would permit no flying whatever anywhere near the frontier of Communism, and this included most of the higher line of the Himalayas.

There was nothing to do but accept the facts, make the best of things, and get what we could. It may sound like an absurd anticlimax to say that we got the Darjeeling railroad, but that Himalayan wonder was, in its way, as much of a goal as things far grander.

In *This Is Cinerama* the "scream" was the roller-coaster ride, the Cinerama camera taking the theatre audience through the ups and downs and whirling gyrations of a Coney Island thriller. The screams in the audience were a shrill token of the effectiveness of the Cinerama medium for taking people into an experience. A thriller of the same sort was a must in the *Seven Wonders*.

Moreover we wanted some comedy in the picture, and I knew the Darjeeling railroad. Back in the twenties I had made a film of India, to follow my Allenby-Lawrence of Arabia show. It was in the silent picture days, and the film equipment would seem primitive now, but I had the latest type then, a skillfully made French camera which did excellent work. My motion pictures of India may have been no Cinerama fantasy, but they were quite a production for the time. One sequence always got a laugh— the Darjeeling railroad.

The historical background of that prodigy of railroading reverts to the early part of the nineteenth century. The East India Company ruled in Hindustan, and was rounding out the British Raj there. In the Himalayan region to the north of Bengal there was a war between the principalities of Nepal and Sikkim, and the latter seemed about to be conquered. The Company did not approve, and intervened. Later the British would establish protectorates over both Nepal and Sikkim, but for the time being the East India Company was content with stopping the war and obtaining some concessions.

In negotiating a settlement a British envoy went up to Sikkim, where he noticed a village on a lofty Himalayan ridge looking out on a superb panorama of towering mountains and deep valleys. This was Darjeeling. He thought that, with its cool bracing climate, it would make a first-rate hill station for invalided British soldiers, a relief from the sweltering plains of Bengal. So, as part of the settlement, he obtained a lease on the agreeable site, together with a strip connecting it with Company-controlled Bengal. This was a reasonable concession from the potentate of Sikkim, grateful for being saved from the Nepalese. Soon the lease on Darjeeling and the strip was turned into outright possession.

That began the history of Darjeeling as a hill station, and in time it became the summer headquarters for the government of Bengal. There British officials went to escape the appalling heat of the plains just below. There travelers from abroad sojourned. Darjeeling, a resort of renown, where life went on in the raciest tradition of Kipling. Tea cultivation was introduced on the surrounding hillsides, and Darjeeling tea became world famous.

So Darjeeling was quite a place when the era of railroading came, and there could be no doubt that the mountain paradise for Bengal officialdom should have a railroad. The project was undertaken in 1879 by British engineers, who performed prodigies. Mountain railroading can be difficult, and this was like a nightmare, especially in the early days of the technology of rails and trains. The general geographical fact is that these Eastern Himalayas rise suddenly from the sea-level plains of Bengal and soar abruptly to those great heights.

The Darjeeling railroad is only forty miles long, and in that short distance it climbs from the lowlands of Bengal to its lofty terminus, and attains an altitude of 7400 feet. The grade is as high as one in twenty, which means that in the distance of a mile of track it rises sometimes 250 feet. The road bed meanders around steep slopes and craggy heights. The track winds back and forth in tight curves, and makes remarkable loops, one of which has a radius of 59 feet, the rail line doing a sort of tight spiral. In places it climbs to the edge of cliffs that look down into chasms as deep as 6000 feet. The gauge had to be narrow, two feet between the tracks.

The rolling stock is correspondingly small, small enough to remind you of a toy train. Locomotives and cars are of the style of seventy-five years ago. On the front of the locomotive two men must be stationed to sand the tracks. Along the road they drop handfuls of sand on the tracks, without which the locomotive wheels could not get traction for the steep grades. The train attains a speed of twelve miles an hour, and you get to Darjeeling in maybe four hours, if there is no delay.

But the line has an imposing name—the Himalayan-Darjeeling Railroad. Going up, it carries rice, hotel provisions, tea-planting supplies, vacationers, and tourists. For the return trip it takes on loads of garden vegetables and tea. Sometimes there have been disturbances because of tigers and leopards. On one occasion the Darjeeling train had to turn back because a herd of wild elephants pre-empted the tracks and threatened locomotive and cars.

Such was the Himalayan-Darjeeling Railroad nearly three quarters of a century ago. Such it was when I filmed it in the twenties, and such it remains today. To my mind it offered rare possibilities. The country it traverses takes your breath away, and it's a most amusing railroad. So the instructions to the Cinerama crew were—get the Darjeeling railroad for thrills and comedy.

Our London playwright associate W. P. Lipscomb devised a scenario. Some people take a train trip to Darjeeling—Hindus and an American tourist, Drowsy Dan, who sleeps all the way. The mere railroad journey is high comedy. In the dinky locomotive the fireman shovels coal into a firebox with a shovel that might go with andirons. Out in front Moe and Joe strew sand on the tracks. The train rounds curves and loops that are a laugh in stupendous Himalayan scenery.

Then there's trouble. The train comes to a halt—elephant on track. Ahead a mama pachyderm lies asleep across the track, baby elephant beside her. Trainmen and passengers get out to shoo them away, but it's no go. The elephants won't budge. Then comes rescue. The great elephant hunter with a high-powered rifle? No, it's Sabu the elephant boy. An absurdly small lad climbs on the back of the monster, gives a command, and the elephant gets up and shambles off, followed by the baby elephant.

The trainmen and passengers out in front of the locomotive watch this, and then they hear an alarming sound. They look around and see the train backing downhill. Something has gone wrong with the brakes, and it's a runaway train speeding backward down Himalayan slopes. They think they may intercept it at one of the slopes, but it's too late. The runaway train goes whirling around bends and loops, two hundred miles an hour, three hundred miles an hour. It's camera technique of course, but it sure creates excitement on the Cinerama screen, a super roller coaster. The train finally comes to a stop at its starting place, and Drowsy Dan, who has been asleep all the time, thinks he has arrived at Darjeeling.

All this caused considerable activity along the Darjeeling railroad for some ten days. The Cinerama crew hired a train for the job and painted the locomotive brightly so that it would show up better in the pictures. On occasion they'd tie up traffic and hold up scheduled trains for hours at a time. But the Indian authorities were understanding. They want to develop Darjeeling as a tourist resort, with the little railroad as an attraction. So we got our comedy and thriller.

# Chapter 23

BEYOND THE HIMALAYAS from Darjeeling is Tibet, and in Tibet is Lhasa, with the Potala. The Chinese Reds had closed that land of Buddhist monasteries, and there was no chance of taking the Cinerama camera to the city of the Dalai Lama. Paul Mantz had a wild idea of making a sneak flight into Tibet —go winging over Lhasa and buzz the Potala—but discretion was as much the better part of valor as it usually is.

During my trip to India in the twenties, I planned to make the journey to Lhasa. Recently I was rather amused to note how carefully I had planned. Among old belongings stowed away I found a long page of calculations, listing the equipment and supplies I should take for the Himalayan journey, all itemized in detail, with costs. I was being properly methodical about the presumptive adventure. One important problem was that of getting into Tibet. Lhasa had a long history as a forbidden city.

But all that went the way of futile dreams, it seemed. Other concerns intervened, briefly I thought. But time went by, and there I was on the radio, nailed to the mast, nailed to the microphone of a nightly, year-around program. Then, at long last, the opportunity came. I had my first vacation from the radio program.

When I had done that planning in India those many years before, I had a wife and a two-year-old boy. Now I had the same wife, but the tiny lad was a near six-footer, off on expeditions of his own. So we made the trip to Lhasa together.

Tibet is a vast plateau, with an average altitude of 16,000 feet. The valleys range from 12,000 to 17,000 feet. The passes through the mountains are up to 19,000 feet. Agriculture at these altitudes is sparse and primitive. The people are largely herdsmen, and their principal means of life is that invaluable animal the yak. Yet in Tibet you see magnificent buildings, monasteries, and the chief of these is the shrine of the Living Buddha.

I'll never forget the moment when Lowell Junior and I, having been on the craggy Himalayan trail for several weeks, emerged through a valley, and there before us was Lhasa and the Potala. The palace-monastery is on the summit of a steep hill that dominates the city. It is built up the slope and on the top of the summit. Rising along the sides and crowning the top, the Potala seems to have grown out of the rock. With its many stories of brilliant white and red, it soars more than 900 feet, two thirds as high as New York's Empire State Building, and gleams with the gold of gilded rooftops. The construction of the Potala was begun in 1741 and would have been a remarkable exploit of engineering for the architects of Rome, Paris, or London at the time, let alone the builders in this lofty land of Central Asia.

The climax of our story in Lhasa came when we were received in audience by the Dalai Lama. Lowell Junior has described it in his book, *Out of This World*. Our immediate impressions were given in tape recordings we made for my radio program back home. We kept a spoken diary throughout the trip, and the rolls of tape were sent out by Himalayan caravan to India, and from there by transoceanic airliner. Here is the account I gave of the visit to the Potala and the call on the Living Buddha.

"Two hours before time for the audience," I related, "our escort arrived. It was headed by two nobles of the court, Rimshi Kypup, and Dorje Changwahba. In their bright red and gold gowns and hats, and with turquoise in their ears and hair, they were most impressive.

"Off went our cavalcade with all of us mounted on gaily caparisoned horses and mules. Ahead pranced two outriders in wide scarlet hats, to clear the way. Next rode our two nobles, to whom all the common people bowed low as we passed. Then came the two of us; strange beings at whom everyone stared.

"Behind us rode four of our entourage who had come all the way with us from Sikkim on the other side of the Himalayas. They were carrying for us the presents we had brought, which included genuine tiger skulls, teeth, snarl, and all, set in silver and gold. These I had bought in Siam, from a Bangkok silversmith, one for the Dalai Lama, and another just a shade smaller—for the regent. A folding traveling alarm clock, and a new-type raincoat, from America—for the Dalai Lama. Also they carried a bag of coins, in a white scarf, a symbolic gift you must always take.

"It would be an unthinkable breach of etiquette not to bring presents. Then when we leave Tibet we understand the Dalai Lama and the regent will send presents to us.

"Arriving at the palace gate, dismounting before the stone dragons, we entered with a stream of monks and nobles—all in robes and hats of red and gold.

"We walked up an avenue of flowers, and in an outer court we sat for an hour—drinking tea, also watching the lamas, the priests, the cabinet ministers, and other nobles file into the audience chamber. They have to be there every morning, to greet His Holiness, although they never utter a word, but merely drink yak-butter tea, bow low many times, and chant.

"Monks on the roof blew weird tenor notes on trumpets of brass, then deeper notes on conch shells, until they worked up to the deep rumble that came from brass horns eight or ten feet long—so long and heavy they were supported on a golden stand. These gave forth deep, thundering, monotonous tones—like what you might expect to hear announcing the end of the world.

"A line of a dozen or so monks formed at the entrance. We were told to fall in behind them, also our servants with the presents. After us fifty or more Tibetans, eager to receive the blessing of their ruler whom they regard as the reincarnation of Buddha.

"Inside, through a haze of incense, we could see the Dalai

Lama on his throne. He smiled, and to our surprise kept smiling at us all during the ceremony.

"In a moment I was standing directly under him, holding a white silk scarf across my hands. In less time than it takes to tell about it the lord chamberlain placed certain symbols on the scarf. These the Dalai Lama took, one after the other. The first, shaped like three cones, or mountains, we later learned was to represent the world. The others were placed on my scarf and then whisked off by the Dalai Lama with such speed that I didn't even see what they were. But one was an image to represent the body, another a book, to represent the mind; and a pyramid to represent the spirit, and then he took my silk scarf. After which he touched his hands to my head—giving me his blessing. The same for my son, who followed me. Next we went through the same ritual with the regent, who sat on a lower throne nearby.

"And all through the ceremony the great horns thundered from the roof.

"From cushions on the floor, near the throne, we watched the others in the line—shuffling along—none daring to look up. Instead of touching these with his hands, the Dalai Lama flicked them with a tassel. He touches only monks and distinguished visitors. All common folk, and all women—even including wives of nobles and cabinet ministers—get the tassel treatment. One nun is the only exception—the Diamond Sow, or the Thunderbolt—who presides over an all-male monastery. She is the only female regarded as one of the reincarnations of Buddha. Her monastery is at Yamdok Tso, the Turquoise Lake.

"As the Dalai Lama flicked the tassel he smiled repeatedly at us. Only a few Europeans and Americans have been granted an audience with a Dalai Lama. Since he is only a fifteen-year-old boy, I suppose he was as curious about the strange white visitors as we were about him.

"One of the most colorful moments came after the shuffling line of Tibetans had been hustled from the room. Monks brought us bowls of rice. We flicked a few grains to the right. Then one taste. That was all. Merely ceremonial.

"Next our official host, Dorje, sat cross-legged—like Buddha—before the throne. Into his own wooden bowl, which he brought from under his robe, a monk poured yak-butter tea. Dorje downed it with one gulp and then prostrated himself three times before the Dalai Lama, bumping his head on the floor. Only after this was over did the Dalai Lama drink some of the same tea. Dorje, we learned later, was acting for us. His was the responsibility of proving to his lord and sovereign that the tea contained no poison. In the past there have been Dalai Lamas who have been poisoned.

"The lord chamberlain placed red scarves around our necks—which we were told was a special distinction. One of His Holiness' seven-foot bodyguards roared out a command, and the formal audience was at an end.

"We then spent an hour with the Dalai Lama in the palace garden, taking motion pictures of the number one Living Buddha, the fourteenth Dalai Lama, who comes from Kumbum, near Lake Koko Nor, along the undefined Tibet-China border. His full name is Getson Nwgang Lobsang Tengin Gyapso Sisunwangyur Tshungpa Mapai Dhepal Sangpo."

Yes, that was an experience of a lifetime. It was followed a week or so later by another experience that I don't want again in this lifetime or any other. Our stay at Lhasa was all too short, but I had to get back to my radio job in New York. My leave of absence from my sponsors at the time was limited. We were on our way out, then luck went bad. It was Lowell Junior who made the report to the news program back home. He spoke it for the tape recorder at a remote outpost in the Himalayas:

"This is a report I wish it were not necessary to make—but it is, in that it will explain why my father will not be back on the job in New York for several weeks.

"It happened a week ago this evening—just after crossing Karo Pass, on the return from Lhasa to Calcutta; we were five days out of the holy city and two days from Gyantse—making much faster time than on the way in, thanks to a swift ride down the swollen Kyi Chu in skin coracles—a ride that carried us bobbing southward the forty miles to Chushul in six hours instead of the two and a half days it had taken us earlier by trail. My dad and I had every hope of continuing the rapid pace and of landing at New York before the first of October.

"I remember we had just been discussing how soon we might be home—then it was that luck left us in the lurch. In Tibet it is customary to dismount and walk going downhill; for they have a saying that 'he's no horse if he doesn't carry you to the top of the hill, and you're no man if you don't get off and walk going down.' So it was that we had just finished the long hike, leading our animals down to the Ralung plain from that 16,600-foot pass.

"I was in the lead when my dad, a few yards behind, decided to remount his steed. Suddenly there was a commotion and a scuffle, and I turned in time to see Pop sailing through the air to land on a pile of rocks. He had had one foot in the stirrup, the other halfway over the saddle, when his horse whirled and bolted, throwing him violently to the ground—the first time any such thing had happened on our long journey to the Tibetan capital.

"My dad was unable to get up—completely out of breath, white as the snows above us, and struggling to keep consciousness. Such a mishap at an altitude above that of Europe's tallest peak—where there's a lean mixture of oxygen—can spell the end quickly. A weaker heart might not have stood the shock. He had landed on his hip—on some sharp stone.

"This turn of fate caught us pretty much off guard. We had no doctor, and our first-aid kit was some miles behind with our slow-moving caravan. It was getting late—only another hour till dark—and Ralung, the nearest habitation and our immediate destination, lay more than four miles across the plain. What to do? The nearest medical help was in Gyantse, more than two stages away, and even that was doubtful. We could do nothing but wait there on the trail, hoping that our caravan would arrive before darkness.

"Fortunately, we didn't have to wait long for the sirdar and his mules and yaks. Unloading our bedding, we got Dad wrapped up in a sleeping bag and onto an army cot. But large as our first-aid kit was, there wasn't anything to relieve his agony, nothing to ease the effects of shock—no morphine.

"Four hours later, after a painful ride through the darkness and the cold that goes with nights at these altitudes, riding that flimsy cot carried by six coolies, my father at last reached shelter. Only with the utmost difficulty and with pain to him was I able to get that cot up the rickety ladder that led to the sleeping quarters of the peasant home we were to stay in.

"That first night was one of the worst Pop has ever known—the effects of shock and exposure took the form of a high fever, accompanied by faintness; his injured hip, which we thought must be broken—gave him the very devil; no position was comfortable for him—sleep impossible; it was a long gasping night of agony and worry in just about the most out-of-the-way spot you can find—in a land whose people don't believe in doctors, who rely solely on the lamas to cure their ills through prayer.

"Next morning when Tsewong, our interpreter, and I hiked to the Ralung telephone office—and incidentally the presence of a phone was a lucky thing, for only a few villages along the main route from Sikkim to Lhasa are connected with a single strand of wire—I prayed that the line was not down, as it frequently is for days and weeks at a time; and that I could contact the Indian army doctor in Gyantse who's based at the Mahratta garrison, and further, that I could persuade him to come to the rescue. We certainly were treading on thin ice! It was almost a matter of life and death. Without a doctor to do something to Dad's leg, I could see no way to ever get him home.

"The lineman managed to rouse Gyantse, after much shouting and blowing into the ancient battery-driven outfit. Though Gyantse was only thirty-three miles away the connection was so poor that everything had to be repeated three and four times before being understood. Yes, Dr. Pal was there, but still in bed; then someone went off to wake him up. A half hour later the doctor's voice was on the other end, and I tried frantically to make him understand who I was and what had happened, but no luck; only Tsewong, talking to his brother, a clerk at the Indian Trade Agency in Gyantse, was able to get the message through. The doctor's reply was that he'd try to come if permission for him to leave could be arranged with the Tibetan trade agent. Dr. Pal, like all his Indian colleagues, is allowed to go only seven miles beyond Gyantse—the terminus of the Indian mail courier system; so special permission had to come from the Tibetan government if he was to come to our assistance.

"Happily, the Tibetan trade agent gave the nod and the good doctor that same day made a forced march the thirty-three miles to Ralung. Never has anyone been more welcome than Dr. Pal when he entered our cold stone hut that night at nine. Besides the necessary medical equipment, he brought something even more valuable to both of us—mental relief! Without an X-ray machine (and there's no such thing anywhere in Tibet) he could not tell for sure whether Dad's hip was fractured, but he felt fairly certain that the injury was only muscular—torn muscles and a severe sprain—a most reassuring opinion.

"Three more days of agony on a stretcher, jouncing over a narrow rock trail that at times was so dangerous it took ten coolies, at a snail's pace, to keep Dad from plunging down into the river far below; hour after hour, strapped to the stretcher, his leg in a splint. When the sun was out he nearly roasted, when it ducked behind clouds and a cold wind brought rain, he nearly froze.

"The first night, at Gobshi, we had to borrow Tibetan tents, sleeping out in the cold, for a detachment of soldiers had arrived just ahead of us and taken over all available space in the village—and in Tibet no one dares raise a finger to the soldiers, who are accustomed to making up their deficit in salary by helping themselves to anything. The next night was better. We put up at the country home of a man who could have been a king but preferred life as a Tibetan country gentleman.

"Jigme Tering, one of our hosts in Lhasa, of royal Sikkimese blood, was to have been the next Maharajah of Sikkim, but he passed it up. At a party our last night in the Hidden City, Jigme had invited us to spend a night at his estate seven miles out from Gyantse. How much better his soft beds were than the narrow cots of the previous night in that cold yak-haired tent, I cannot describe! The following morning brought us to the Indian garrison in Gyantse. There Dad spent ten days in bed under the watchful eye of Dr. Pal.

"There is probably no more primitive or remote military outpost of a modern nation than that tiny Indian station behind the tallest mountains in the world, in the forbidden kingdom of Tibet. But even so, it seemed like the comforts of paradise after those first grim days of stretcher, tent, and cots.

"And so, there's the explanation why that familiar voice won't be with you, except in recordings, for a few more weeks. The doctor thinks Dad's leg will let him take to the saddle again in a fortnight; then he'll soon be at third base—Calcutta, where a Pan American clipper will help him make the steal home."

That was followed by day after day of travel through mountain passes. I had to be carried on a stretcher, and sometimes the trail was so narrow it seemed as if the stretcher, with me on it, was about to go over a chasm a few thousand feet deep. It took a couple of weeks of that before we were down in India, where at Calcutta I was able to have an X-ray examination which showed the thighbone smashed, eight fractures at the junction with the hip. Even then I didn't have the fractures set until we had flown back to New York.

We were the last Western visitors to make the journey to Lhasa. Soon the Chinese Reds invaded the Himalayan land and took control. For centuries Tibet was closed to the outside world by the desire of its own people for seclusion. Now it is open to Communism and closed to the West. One wonders how the Buddhist monks in the monasteries will take to the doctrines of the Reds.

We had got excellent motion pictures in color of the Tibetan trip. These were the conventional 35-millimeter kind, not Cinerama, which had not yet appeared. But they did provide something for the *Seven Wonders*. We took from the film a clip of the Potala which I used as a still picture in the prologue, remarking that it was a pity we could not take Cinerama into Communist-dominated Tibet and film the palace of the Potala and the Dalai Lama for the great curved screen.

North of Tibet lies China, and there they have the largest man-made wonder—the largest many times over. The Great Wall of China has a reputation to match the Pyramids of Egypt as a monstrous construction. But the Great Pyramid is a pigmy in comparison, in the amount of stone it contains. The rampart of masonry extends from near Peking westward into the middle of North China. With all its windings, it is 1900 miles long. Its height is from 20 to 40 feet. Width, 15 feet. Along the entire top are two parapets, one for either side, and between them is a roadway 12 feet wide. A man could drive the entire 1900 miles in a chariot and be shielded from the missiles of enemies by the parapets all the way. At regular intervals there are tall watch-towers on top of the wall, 24,000 towers in all. The Great Wall traverses mountainous country and goes uphill and down valley —never mind the terrain. It climbs mountains, at one point a summit five thousand feet high.

The amount of treasure and toil it took to construct this prodigy is incalculable. The garrison needed to man it as a regular fortification would run into fantastic figures. Stationed a yard apart, it would have taken three million soldiers to line the Great Wall of China. No doubt the method of defense was to keep a watch and mobilize troops at a threatened point.

The Emperor Shih Hwang-ti, who founded the Chin Dynasty in the third century B.C., is famous for two things principally. He burned the books and he built the Great Wall.

In seizing the throne, he overthrew the political system maintained by the scholars who followed the tradition of Confucius. He reckoned that the principles of that philosopher, who had flourished several centuries earlier, were inimical to his regime, and ordered the destruction of the Confucian classics. This was the famous Burning of the Books.

The Emperor Shih Hwang-ti built the Great Wall to protect his domain from the barbarian tribes on the plains of Mongolia. These were the age-old enemies of China, forever invading.

No two things could have been more useless. After the emperor's death his anti-Confucian system collapsed. The scholars brought back the classics, copies of which they had hidden and saved from the Burning of the Books. Confucianism was restored as the official philosophy down the centuries, and Shih Hwang-ti got no more than an evil reputation from the scholars, who were the historians. As for the Great Wall, it failed to prevent barbarian invasions from the north, and China was conquered repeatedly.

One can imagine the rampart scaled by ladder with the aid of movable towers, or some other sort of military engineering the ancient peoples had. In any case the tribes from Mongolia got over the rampart many times, and they may have breached it, or gone around it. The Great Wall of China stands, a monumental futility.

It would have been magnificent if we could have flown the Cinerama camera along a hundred miles or so of this prodigy, but here once again was the impenetrable will of Communism, rather more effective than the Great Wall. Red China was forbidden land. There was no use, in fact, of thinking of Wonder hunting in the Communist world at all. The Porcelain Tower in Nanking, with its architectural grace and splendor, would have been an excellent subject, and so would the Kremlin in Moscow with one of those monster military parades in Red Square. But we might as well forget Soviets and satellites and Red China.

The last time I saw China I was on a quest, and never was failure more complete. I was chasing General Jimmy Doolittle, and flew around the world trying to catch him. The pursuit included China. And Jimmy Doolittle, onetime speed king and daredevil of the air, was a hard man to overtake.

It was in the Second World War. I was traveling around war fronts in Europe, and encountered General Jimmy, then commander of the Eighth Air Force in the bombing of Nazi Germany. The war in Europe was about over, and the Eighth Air Force was to be transferred to the Pacific. I had known Jimmy since the early days, and he invited me to fly with him to the war fronts in the Far East. He was going via the Mediterranean and southern Asia, starting out in a week or so.

I accepted gladly, but had to return home briefly. I said I'd fly to New York, spend a few days, and then take a plane back to Europe. Jimmy and I made a date to meet in North Africa the following week, and then we'd proceed on the trip to the Far East. You could fly fast and far in these days of transoceanic aviation, and the trip from Europe to New York and back across the Atlantic to North Africa in a week was nothing special. But I was delayed a bit at home, and when I got to Casablanca Jimmy had gone on, leaving word for me to follow and catch up with him.

That's what I tried to do. I flew in an army plane, which took the same route that he did. I thought I might catch him in Egypt, in India, but at each stop Jimmy Doolittle had already left.

When I got to Calcutta, I saw a brief newspaper item in the *Statesman,* saying that General Doolittle had just arrived in Washington. He had been called home for emergency conferences. He sure was far ahead of me, and that was how I failed to catch Jimmy Doolittle.

Having missed out on that, I decided to make a detour across the Himalayas to China, a flight over the Hump. That was a vivid experience of those wartime days. The trip was in a DC-4, all the bucket seats of which were occupied. Several of the passengers were State Department officials. Sitting beside me, a cavalry colonel. The others were Air Force personnel returning to bases in China. Much of the flight was made at altitudes above twenty thousand feet. The cabin of the plane was not pressurized, so each of us wore an oxygen mask.

The thing I remember most vividly about the flight was that while the older men looked out the windows, enjoying the grandeur of the Himalayan scenery, some of the young airmen spent most of the journey down on the floor, rolling dice, paying no attention at all to the majestic peaks below us, one of the most inspiring mountain sights I had ever seen.

The cavalry colonel told me that upon our arrival at Kunming his assignment was to proceed to a distant part of China, along the Tibetan border. Our people at that time were helping Generalissimo Chiang Kai-shek's army round up thousands of small Central Asian horses to use for transporting supplies and equipment to the areas that could not be reached by air. He invited me to go along.

This again turned out to be a flight that I will never forget. We had two planes, both DC-3s. The one I was in was piloted by a veteran China National Airways flier, a Captain Pottschmidt.

From Kunming we flew northwest over as wild a region as I ever expect to see. We crossed the gorges of some of the great rivers of Asia, the Salween, the Mekong, the Yangtse, and the Yellow rivers. They were comparable to the Grand Canyon of the Colorado.

During the flight we landed on some pasture land near the walled city of Sichang. Here we encountered two Tibetans named Gunga and Donga, who had brought a string of horses from Tibet and were about to make the long return journey overland, some hundreds of miles, to their home. We were going that way. So Captain Pottschmidt offered to give them a lift. In a mere few hours they could fly over a region which otherwise it would take several weeks to traverse.

We took off with the two Tibetans, Gunga and Donga, and ran into stormy weather. It looked for a time as though we were lost, and might be obliged to bail out. "Potty" came back from the cockpit with a solemn look on his face. He said he had just been checking on the number of parachutes; and that we had enough for the crew, the cavalry colonel, and myself; but none for Gunga and Donga. Then a smile came over his countenance, and he said:

"Ah, I have it. We're not so far from their territory. I'll open the door of the plane, and say, 'Here we are, boys. Here's your home, but look out for that first step!'"

We were forced off our course for hundreds of miles to the east, and wound up on an airfield outside the walled city of Chamdo. Gunga and Donga had a long trip overland, after all.

At that time I hadn't the tape-recording way of keeping a travel diary. I gave reports for my radio news program back home directly by short wave, and that could be uncertain. Sometimes the reception was bad, or maybe you couldn't get through at all. Once in Cairo, as I found out later, I could not be heard

The skyscraper city of Shibam in the desert of southern Arabia. The tradition is to erect tall buildings, the main ingredient being mud. Situated in the midst of a rugged, barren wilderness, this towering metropolis is a most unexpected wonder of the modern world.

The Temple of Solomon once stood here, now the Mosque of Omar, where at the fountain Moslems perform their ritual ablutions.

The Mount of Olives, scene of the Ascension. Save for the tall tower in the distance, the scene must be pretty much as it was in biblical times.

Photos by Edwin W. Sippel

*Above*—child dancers at the Monkey Temple of Benares. *Below*—the Cobra Dance with a snake charmer and the deadly hooded serpent.

Photo by Edwin W. Sippel

The sacred Ganges and the ghats (landing places) at India's holy city of Benares, where there are fifteen hundred temples and palaces.

Painted elephants are a feature of any Hindu ceremony. Here they're in a wedding procession passing through the streets of Benares.

You can turn this picture upside down and get almost as good a
view of the Taj Mahal, so perfect is the reflecting pool. Many consider
this the most beautiful building in the world.

Among the ruins of the Khmer civilization in Cambodia, which until recent years were buried in the jungle. Buddhist monks revive ancient ceremonies at the great temple of Angkor Vat.

Photos by Edwin W. Sippel

Ancient ritualistic dances are performed in the courtyard of a ruined temple in Cambodia. Note native orchestra.

Fuji Yama is the classic type of mountain. With an almost perfect cone, it rises in solitary grandeur from a plain along the sea.

The huge Kamakura Buddha in Japan. The drapery with trim folds illustrates the ancient Greek influence on Buddhism.

Japan is a land of attractive young women, and this scene in a Japanese garden illustrates the age-old quality of charm.

The great statue of Christ overlooking the harbor at Rio. Fashioned of white concrete, it stands on the lofty summit of Corcovado.

Flying down the gorge of Iguazu Falls in South America, near where the borders of Argentina, Brazil and Paraguay meet. The falls are a series of giant cascades.

Among the wonders of the modern world, the Empire State Building
has its lofty place. Rising among the skyscrapers of Manhattan, it
is the tallest building in the world.

The Grand Canyon, the world's most extraordinary phenomenon of its kind, where the Colorado River has wrought stupendous sculptures of Nature.

Among the famed Wonders of the World, Niagara Falls is not to be omitted, no matter how often it has been pictured. This is the mighty cataract of the Canadian Falls.

in the United States, but was picked up clearly at an outpost of the French Foreign Legion deep in the Sahara Desert, where most of them didn't understand English anyway. However I did manage to get through all right from time to time, with the following from China:

"Here I am, still on the other side of the world. Although I have tried many times to get through by short wave from Chungking, the Chinese International Broadcasting beam isn't so very international. I doubt if it covers half of China. The head of it, Mike Pung, told me we would get through easily, to the states. But later I learned that not a word got through; the station was not powerful enough. And in hot Chungking, at six forty-five in the morning, that's discouraging.

"Well, in the ten days or so that I've spent in China, I visited by air and by jeep the provinces of Yunnan and Sikang, both about as remote as any parts of this vast country; and also the provinces of Szechwan, Kweichow, and Kwangsi.

"The ranking American general in the field in China is Major General Bob McClure, a stocky, ruddy-faced, tough, hard-bitten veteran. He asked me to accompany him on a trip, by jeep and by munitions carrier, to one of the wildest parts of China, the mountains of Kwangsi, where a lot of recent fighting has been going on.

"One object of the trip was to take General Ho Yin-chin, former Minister of War, and now Chief of Staff of the Chinese armies, down to that corridor. Also General Yu Fei-peng, Minister of Communications.

"General Yu Fei-peng is a Chinese notable of large dimensions. If he wore the silk coat of a mandarin of old, and if you put him in a sedan chair, he would look just like an old Chinese print.

"It was blazing hot. The road was bumpy and dusty. General Yu, in his jeep, perspired copiously, and fanned himself furiously. Every time the jeep would pull up because of a road block caused by pack trains or water buffalo, General Yu's aide would run to the nearest stream or paddy field and bring back a basin of water wherewith the great man would refresh himself and get ready for the next lap with its clouds of dust and the bumps that were mighty hard on the sacroiliac of General Yu Fei-peng, and General Ho Yin-chin, and your humble radio reporter.

"At Machang we found a detachment of our American lads living in a Chinese temple, and then on to Tuyun, Tushan, and Nantan. I'm getting a lot of practice pronouncing Chinese names that will come in handy when I return home.

"We were in the country of the chocolate-drop mountains, thousands of separate peaks like green rice croquettes on a great platter; with paddy fields in between. Until recently Europeans never came here, except an occasional missionary, carried in a sedan chair.

"An American aviator recently had a miraculous escape in these mountains; Lieutenant Colonel William E. Blankenship, second in command of a P-51 fighter outfit. The colonel had been strafing the Japs at Liuchow. In this sector even pursuit planes carry bombs. Blankenship, coming in low over Liuchow, spotted a camouflaged area. Releasing a bomb, he hit the bull's eye, and up went an ammunition dump. With the tremendous explosion not only up went the dump but down came Colonel Bill and his plane. A wing was coming off. But it held till he could climb a thousand feet or so, and then he bailed out. Whereupon the air colonel came down kerplunk in the mud of a rice paddy. Half devoured by mosquitoes, it was four days before he located a friendly military outfit in those chocolate-drop mountains."

# Chapter 24

From india the Cinerama route led across southern Asia, and there the chief wonder was a monument of a lost civilization, a lost empire. Indo-China was in the turmoil of advancing Communism. The Reds had seized great areas of the dominion long held by France, but in inner Cambodia the peace of isolation brooded over the jungle and the ruined metropolis of another era.

Two names are to be noted, Angkor Thom and Angkor Vat. The former denotes a royal capital, with palaces, shrines, monuments, and battlements. The latter, a temple outside the confines of the city. It is the best known of the great ruins because it is the best preserved. All were abandoned long ago and left to the invasion of the jungle, were half forgotten and brought to light again only during our own time.

What was this glorious kingdom? It was the empire of the Khmers, which rose about the sixth century of the Christian Era, and became the dominant power in Southwest Asia, holding sway over most of what is now Indo-China and Siam. The Khmers were of uncertain origin, perhaps derived in part from India. History finds them first a people subject to a neighboring kingdom, but in time the Khmers won independence and empire.

Their legends dwell on King Yacovarman, who came to the throne in the ninth century A.D., at a time when the Vikings were ravaging in northern Europe. Of his prowess remarkable tales are told. He could vanquish a tiger or an elephant without the use of weapons. His accession to power was disputed, and he had stubborn seditions to deal with. So, to be secure, he built a fortress city for his capital, Angkor Thom, as splendid as it was strong. From this he ruled his empire.

The Khmer civilization was derived from India, whose culture swept the shore lands of southeastern Asia and the islands of the Indies. Hindu art set the style, and was modified by the Khmers into forms of their own. The religion of the Khmers was brought from India, the cults of Shiva and Vishnu.

The Khmer Empire had its vicissitudes and culminated in the twelfth century with a warrior sovereign, Jayavarman by name, who raised the state to the height of its power. He was the ruler who completed the building of Angkor Vat, a late masterpiece of Khmer architecture and sculpture, which is now heralded as a world wonder. Then, after a glorious reign, he abdicated his authority and retired to the life of meditation of a Buddhist monk. This fact signalized a religious change. Buddhism had come to the empire of the Khmers.

Splendor continued, but decay set in. The glory of the Khmers was going the way of empire. The Siamese, the Thais, long their subjects, revolted successfully, and Siamese power rose. The Khmer Empire was overthrown and vanished. Angkor Thom, the palace city, was abandoned in the fourteenth century. King, court, priests, and people left in the face of a successful enemy. Angkor Vat, the great temple, was deserted. The jungle crept in, the devouring jungle of the tropics. Creepers climbed up walls. Plants sprouted in cracks between stones. Trees reared themselves in sacred enclosures, and embraced statues and architecture with tentacles of green. In a century or so Angkor Thom and Angkor Vat were ruins, the spoil of the jungle, and all but forgotten.

More centuries later French influence in Indo-China began in the eighteenth century with the work of missionaries, who had great success at first. But in time there was an anti-French, anti-Christian reaction. There were martyrdoms of French missionaries and massacres of native Christians, until the French intervened in 1858, and in time gained control of Indo-China.

This opened the way for French scholars to study the remarkable ruins in Cambodia. The engulfing jungle cleared away, a lost civilization, a lost empire, was revealed for archaeological investigation. The shrine of Angkor Vat at long last was opened to the gaze of all, as a wonder of the world.

From the monuments, the images of the gods, they discerned a religious transition in the Khmer Empire—from Shiva, the ferocious Hindu divinity of destruction, to the amiable Vishnu, and finally to Buddha of eternal compassion. Today the ancient creed of the Light of Asia prevails in Cambodia, and the Cinerama camera filmed yellow-robed monks and a Buddhist ceremonial dance at Angkor Vat.

Our trail from Southwest Asia led via Hong Kong to Japan. Here, for a time, I went on ahead of the camera crew, and made sundry arrangements. The plan was simple. Our primary goal was that wonder of nature, Fuji Yama.

You might guess that some cosmic sculptor had created that perfect mountain. He knew how to pick a site, flat land on the shore of a bay with no surrounding mountains to obscure the grandeur of a solitary peak. He was also versed in geometry. The ideal shape for a mountain is a cone, and Fuji Yama is almost a mathematical cone with a flattened top. Every proper mountain should be snow-clad, and the summit of Fuji is draped beautifully with gleaming white. Our cosmic sculptor had a proper sense of decoration. He was Vulcan, lord of volcanoes, who builds mountains by hurling forth subterranean fire and lava.

Fuji Yama is so nearly perfect it's no wonder the Japanese regard it as their sacred mountain. It fits their style of art, so neat and decorative. Long generations of artists, in Japanese prints, have delighted in picturing the geometrical cone with a flattened top rising all alone from a level plain and crowned with eternal snow.

But Fuji Yama proved a stubborn wonder of nature for the Cinerama camera. It was a primary goal for director Walter

Thompson and the camera crew. No use of going to Japan if you don't get Fuji Yama in some scenes. But, like so many mountains, Fuji has a way of being veiled in clouds, and this by hard luck was the case when they were in Japan. Day after day they went out hoping the clouds would clear. Film business has a way of producing exasperating delays, and this was it. But then came a favorable half hour. Luckily they were in position with the camera set. In the sweep of a fickle wind the clouds opened, as if trying to imitate a theatrical curtain, and there was Fuji Yama in full glory, as if posing for the picture.

Along with this they filmed a sequence with emphasis on charm, that curious quality of grace and quaintness which the Japanese have. Nor could they miss the fact of U. S. Armed Forces in Japan. Director Walter Thompson applied to Army public relations in Tokyo, and recruited a couple of G.I.s and then Cinerama went with them, seeing the sights in Japan. Naturally, Walter rounded up a party of Japanese children. What would G.I.s be without the kids? So the sight-seeing was done by Joe and Bill from the U.S.A. trailed by youngsters in the bright costumes of old Japan. Although this sentimentality was designed for a light touch, it did illustrate one aspect of affairs in Japan.

In Tokyo, I noted the good will so apparent between the Japanese and Americans. This was well known, of course. On the radio job I had recited innumerable bits of news about Japan as our postwar ally. Remarkable changes of foe to friend and vice versa are to be expected along with the bedlam violence called war. But, even as long as nearly ten years later, it was surprising to see at close range the amicability between such bitter enemies who had fought each other so savagely in warfare without mercy.

On my 1945 trip to Far Eastern battle fronts, I reported the following on my radio program:

"I am broadcasting this from the base of a famous volcano, right at the front door to Japan. The name of the volcano is Suribachi. From that you will know this is coming through by short wave from a spot that has cost us more lives for its size than any place on earth, the island of Iwo Jima.

"The Marines came in here last February 19. It was on the twenty-third that they took Suribachi. They raised the flag just a few yards from this mobile transmitter, the truck from which I am broadcasting. That was the day the photograph was taken with which you are all familiar (the picture published everywhere of four Marines raising the American flag on the summit). Up to March 16 some four thousand of our boys had been killed here, and more than fifteen thousand were wounded and missing.

"Since then they have been digging Japs out of the caves that abound on this mountain that juts out of the sea. They have killed thirty-six hundred of them. Bringing the Japanese dead on Iwo Jima up to around twenty-five thousand. All dead; except less than two hundred taken prisoner.

"I flew in here yesterday with the Chief of the Army Air Forces, General Arnold, and the man who commands our Air Forces fighting the Japs in this part of the world, General Barney Giles. One of the first things General Arnold did, before we climbed to the summit of the volcano, was to decorate some of our airmen. The Japs remaining in the caves still make raids here on Iwo, suicide raids. Jap planes didn't come over last night, by the way. But here is the way one citation reads—it has to do with a surprise Jap attack:

"'Upon being awakened in the early morning by the sound of heavy fire, Lieutenant Coons (Lieutenant Joe Coons from Minnesota is a tall broad-shouldered airman, with high cheekbones and deep-sunken eyes) discovered that the enemy had begun firing and throwing grenades into the tent area. With total disregard for his own safety, Lieutenant Coons opened fire on the invaders with his pistol from inside his tent.' Then the citation tells how he went on out of the tent to get a better shot. In fact he moved from one enemy position to another, throwing hand grenades and firing his pistol. Crawling over the rough lava surface (this island is all lava), he crawled to within a few feet of an enemy entrenchment containing about twenty-six Japs. Of

[ 229 ]

these he proceeded to kill more than half. For this General Arnold awarded him a Silver Star."

From Iwo Jima I went on to Okinawa, and there the picture was similar, according to my radio report:

"I was on the island, or watching the fighting from the air, at the time when the Japs were making their last stand. The Marines and doughboys were cutting them up into smaller and smaller pockets, with heavy losses on both sides.

"I was there when General Simon Bolivar Buckner was killed. In fact I had just missed the general at his headquarters that morning, or I would undoubtedly have been with him. But I was delayed, and his chief of staff, Brigadier General Elwyn Post, asked me to stay and talk and have lunch and await General Buckner's return.

"The G-2, in charge of psychological warfare, joined us, and told us the Japs were beginning more and more to surrender. Even their officers at last showed a distase for committing suicide by throwing themselves off cliffs, walking into the sea, or making futile banzai charges. Although some were still dying blindly, organized resistance had been broken.

"About the death of General Buckner; his number evidently was 'up.' For the Japs had only one gun, one mortar, still in action. With it they lobbed over one shell, and that shell got the general. Then they sent over six more, doing still more damage. Delayed, I was with his staff at the moment their chief was killed. My schedule had called for me to be with him. Dame Fortune has smiled on one of us.

"The general's office had been moved that morning. His name, Lieutenant General Simon Bolivar Buckner, was there on his desk as I stood before it, with his colleagues, Generals Post, Schick, and Dumas of the army, and Oliver Smith of the Marines. The office and desk that Simon Bolivar Buckner never had a chance to use."

What I saw and heard in those days at places like Iwo Jima and Okinawa gave one an evil feeling of how masses of human beings can hate each other with a rage for collective murder. Normally American soldiers in war are about as decent as is possible in organized killing. But the Jap atrocities, their fiendish treatment of helpless prisoners, forced our people in the Pacific battles to be almost as merciless as the Japs themselves.

A few weeks after I returned home from wartime Iwo Jima and Okinawa one of the greatest headlines in history broke. Referring back to my broadcast notes, I can experience again the excitement and sense of history that the news evoked:

"It may be that, according to the evaluation of future history, this should be marked down as the beginning of the atomic era. Reverberations from around the world indicate that the human race realizes that the atomic bomb that hit Japan marked the beginning of an epoch in which the affairs of man may be determined by the control of the deepest force of nature, the primordial and elemental force in the atom.

"As for the actual havoc wrought by the first atomic bomb, we hear that evidence is now being studied and assembled for quick release. One earlier report was that photographic observation planes, on the job shortly after the cataclysmic blast at Hiroshima, had been unable to penetrate the cloud of smoke and dust that hung over the devastated area.

"The Japs speak in tones of vague panic of the thing that hit them. They intimate that great destruction was caused, and are saying that there were several of these missiles. But we know from definite statements by the American side that only one atomic bomb was let loose—the first in the history of mankind."

On subsequent days, my broadcast record shows:

"Our own Air Force surveyed the damage at Hiroshima and reported that more than four square miles of the city had been utterly destroyed, razed to the ground by that one mere 400-pound bomb. The casualties, according to the American estimate, might be over a hundred thousand. That figure would now seem to be an underestimate—according to what the Japs have to say.

"Tokyo today announced that a new-type bomb 'completely destroyed' Hiroshima. The words 'completely destroyed' are from a Japanese account, which states: 'The impact of the bomb was so terrific that practically all living things, human and animal, were literally seared to death by the tremendous heat and pressure engendered by the blast.'

"Tokyo indicates that sixty per cent of the city was damaged, burned and disintegrated into rubble. Buildings, factories, leveled to the ground by the force of the exploding atoms. The magnitude of the devastation is indicated vividly by the fact that the Japanese today, several days after the explosion, were not yet able to ascertain the full extent of the havoc."

Such was the frightful culmination of the hate-filled war in the Pacific. As we know, another atomic bomb was dropped—this time on Nagasaki—and Japan surrendered. You might have thought the hatred would linger for generations, as has so often happened between nations, the victor and the vanquished, the conqueror and the conquered. It was generally supposed that the subjugated Japanese, with their country occupied by the enemy, would be filled with an impotent bitterness and that they in their fanaticism might resort to terrorist tactics.

Some while after the war I was talking to General George Kenney, who had been wartime air chief to General Douglas MacArthur. He told me that during the last weeks of the conflict MacArthur had made a study of what he'd do, the role he'd play, when the war was over. Obviously, he'd be the commander of the conquered country.

Kenney noted that MacArthur, after years of experience in the Orient, understood the oriental mind. He reckoned that the Japanese, for all their war mania and for all their bitter-end courage, would accept the fact that they had lost the game. It was in the oriental tradition to have a due regard for the victor, and the Japanese would respect superior power. MacArthur understood, likewise, that the Japanese were accustomed to revere a transcendent overlord. Their worship of their own Mikado was evidence of that. The benevolent despot is historically a favorite figure in the Orient.

So MacArthur prepared himself for the role. With the hatreds and furies of war still rampant, he schooled himself for a quick change from enemy commander to benign autocrat. He had the temperament and the personality for it, not to forget the imposing presence. When the time came, MacArthur assumed the part of the master, aloof in authority and integrity, and the conqueror became the idol of the conquered.

Of course G.I. Joe had something to do with that too. The Japanese must have expected rough treatment from American soldiers, the kind of brutality that their own army was accustomed to inflict on a vanquished people. But the G.I.s fell in with the situation amiably, and forgot their hatred for the previously odious Jap. Altogether it made one of the most singular transformations that war and armistice have ever produced. In Germany, to be sure, the Western occupation troops got along well enough with the conquered Germans. But the European war had not been as remorseless as the conflict in the Pacific, and Germans welcomed the Western invaders in preference to the Soviet Russians.

So in our Cinerama picture we have the two G.I.s and the little tots with an abundant supply of Japanese charm. There are scenes of the countryside in its pastel shades and Japanese gardens quaint and lovely. Geisha girls were not omitted. Walter Thompson rounded up a good-looking lot. But more than that he filmed a Japanese musical extravaganza. Nor do Joe and Bill from Kankakee and Kalamazoo neglect the venerable shrines of Japan. Still trailed by the children, they visit Shinto temples and Buddhist shrines.

At Kamakura, now a seaside resort, there's a shrine with a giant statue of Buddha. The bronze effigy is more than forty feet in height, weighs more than one hundred tons, and the height is all the more impressive because it is a sitting Buddha. In gigantic proportions the Kamakura Buddha reposes cross-legged and smiles with an enigmatic serenity.

Buddhist countries abound in representations of Buddha of every sort—statues, bas-reliefs, paintings. Buddhist art revels in the human semblance of the Blessed One. Yet in the earliest Buddhism there were no images of the founder. He was never shown as a human figure.

In the sixth century B.C. Prince Gautama, scion of a royal house, having grown disillusioned with the world, taught a doctrine of salvation from life and self, an escape from the cycle of birth and rebirth, the wheel of reincarnation. He was the Buddha, the Enlightened One. His followers developed an extremely abstract philosophy of Nirvana, the extinction of self, the absorption into infinity, or perhaps nothingness. This was high in clouds of metaphysics.

Buddhism was, in general, a reaction against the elaborate religious system of the Brahmins. It rejected caste and accepted all men on equal terms. It disdained spectacular rituals and practiced a simplicity of ceremony. It denied the extravagant polytheism of Hinduism and recognized none of the gods, although in time Buddha came to be regarded as a divinity. Most emphatically Buddhism cast off the rank idolatries prevalent in India then as now, and would have no image to be worshiped.

In accordance with this iconoclasm, there were no statues or pictures of Buddha. He might be represented by a symbol, the lotus flower. In a place where you would expect the person of Buddha, the lotus signified the idea. Artists used various devices to avoid the human figure. In a scene out of the legend of Buddha his followers might be shown in attitudes of worship, but the presence of the Blessed One would be indicated by an empty throne. The symbol took the place of the human image. In their anti-idolatry the early Buddhists went to extremes in avoiding statues and pictures of Buddha.

Today, complete contrast. Images of Buddha are familiar around the world. Everybody knows the conventional figure, rather plump, sitting in the conventional cross-legged Indian posture and meditating with a slight smile. Something happened somewhere along the line to produce so remarkable a change.

For a clue we can go to the giant effigy in Japan, the Kamakura Buddha. We may note the way the figure is clothed. The garment is drapery, the bronze sculpture reproducing draped folds, neat and formal, which harmonizes with the serene repose of the seated figure. The drapery is Greek in origin, akin to the formal folding of robes in classic Greek sculpture. The Kamakura Buddha in Japan gives evidence of Greek influence on Buddhism, and this goes back to Alexander the Great.

Alexander's conquests resulted in the spread of Hellenism far and wide in Asia. After his death his chief generals contended for the inheritance of empire, and one of them, Seleucus, won a realm that included most of the old Persian domain, with territories on the border of India. The Seleucid kingdom included Bactria, which coincided more or less with modern Afghanistan. Many Hellenic cities are said to have existed in Bactria and Greek was the prevalent language.

In time an ambitious Greek governor of Bactria, Diodotus, made himself an independent monarch. He and his successors enlarged their domain, and a brilliant Greek empire of Bactria flourished. Its history is obscure, known largely today from abundant and splendid coins. One Greek historian calls it "the empire of a thousand cities." This Greco-Bactrian realm expanded into the valley of the Indus. Later, a Greek kingdom was established in India, and a Greek dynasty ruled over an Indian state.

Hellenic glory on the border of India, and in India, lasted during the several centuries after Alexander. The Greek kingdom in India was overthrown by the Scythians about the beginning of the Christian Era. During that period Greek culture exerted a large and abiding influence. There was a fusion of Greek and Indian civilization, and this was particularly evident in Buddhism.

The Greeks were attracted to Buddhism, and introduced into it their own Hellenic ideas. To them the ban on human images of Buddha was incomprehensible. They were the reverse of iconoclasts. They were wedded to their great art of sculpture, and to them it seemed in the nature of things that a god should be represented in marble. Greek Buddhists thought of the Enlightened One as a divinity to whom sculptured statues should be reared.

Thus it came about that the first images of Buddha were fashioned by Greek sculptors. A tradition was formed, mingling Greek and Indian elements. The cast of features of the sculptured Buddha might be oriental, the cross-legged posture was oriental, but the manner of sculpture was Greek.

The classical tradition of Hellenic art was one of moderation and repose, which accorded with the meditative quietism of Buddhism. The art of Hinduism was extravagant and violent, as in the grotesque of a multiarmed Siva contorted in a frantic dance. The Greek effigies of Buddha were serene.

Greek tradition prescribed the garments of the sculptured Buddha, draped neatly and skillfully carved. In Athens, Apollo might be nude, but Zeus, the chief of the gods, would be robed with careful folds. Hence the draped Buddha, in contrast to Hindu gods, who might be garbed with a bizarre ornamentation.

Gradually throughout the Buddhist world the prohibition against the use of the human form to represent the Enlightened One was forgotten, and Greco-Buddhist art set a style for statues of Buddha. The faith of the Sage of India spread across southern Asia and was carried through Bactria to Tibet, to China, and on to Japan. Everywhere there's a familiar type of Buddha showing the Greek influence. In the great draped Kamakura Buddha in Japan you'll perceive characteristics that take the story back to Alexander of Macedon.

From Japan the trail was homeward across the Pacific. The camera crew would complete their circumnavigation that way. I preceded them. The transpacific flight was uneventful, and I could only think of the last time I had returned home from Asia via the Pacific. That had been during Far Eastern journeyings in World War II.

It really started at Chungking, where I was told that the Air Force was going to try a night flight out of China to the Philippines, then on to the islands of the mid-Pacific. I was invited along, and they flew me to another remote walled city called Luliang.

There a group of us, all in uniform, were taken into a hut. The door was locked, and an Air Force staff officer briefed us. He said we'd take off that night, and would not leave the room until time for departure.

Then he described the country over which we were to pass.

First, a wide area inhabited by primitive tribes who had lived in these mountains since long before the Chinese had invaded that region. These people were called the Lolos and the Meows. Next we were to pass over a thickly populated section of China, where, if we had a forced landing, we might come down among friendly people. Beyond that, we would be above a coastal area occupied by the Japanese army. He said that in our jackets, which were passed out, were drugs that it might be advisable to take rather than be captured. From the coast we would fly over the China Sea, and for this part of the journey we were told what to do if we came down in the water. All this briefing went on for more than an hour and was far more harrowing than I have indicated here.

Shortly after dark the door was unlocked, and we were marched directly to the plane. The chief pilot, a major in the A.T.C., as he strode up the aisle, leaned over and introduced himself. He asked me if I had ever heard of the name Wenerick. I replied that I had indeed; that my mother had told me of a schoolmate named Laura Wenerick to whom her family was distantly related. Said the pilot: "She was my mother!"

He showed me a bunk that I could use. Shortly after we left the ground I fell asleep. Next morning, at dawn, Major Wenerick shook me and said that we were about to fly over Corregidor, at the entrance to Manila Bay. And a short time later we were landing at Clark Field.

Eleven aboard the plane were American airmen, who had been shot down over China. They had succeeded in avoiding capture, had eventually reached a Chinese army outpost, and now they were being flown back to join their squadrons somewhere on the islands of the Pacific.

Strange things could happen in wartime, with Americans in service all over the globe. But I doubt whether there were many stranger coincidences than this: flying out of China, by night, on the first run over the Japanese-occupied mainland of Asia—piloted by a distant relative!

I flew on to Guam, and there the homeward voyage was interrupted. Parked next to our plane was a shiny DC-4 on the front of which I read: *Argonaut IV*. I knew this meant that the commander-in-chief of the American Air Forces, General Hap Arnold, was there. We were old friends.

When he was a young officer and a staunch supporter of the inspired and controversial General Billy Mitchell, he was exiled to an Army cavalry center in Kansas. I visited him there and he started to fly me to Oklahoma. On the way we had a forced landing when his single-engine suddenly went to pieces.

As a result of this episode we became pretty well acquainted. So when he found that I was in Guam he insisted that I join him on a tour of inspection of our Pacific air bases; then finish my flight around the world with him.

That brought about a long detour, which included visits to the battle fronts on Iwo Jima and Okinawa. Then finally it was homeward bound for our uneventful flight with General Arnold across the Pacific.

# Chapter 25

Suppose columbus had not discovered America. Suppose he had been compelled to turn back to Spain before he sighted San Salvador. Or suppose he had never returned. Suppose his three small caravels, the *Pinta, Niña,* and *Santa María,* had foundered in a West Indian hurricane. Suppose the epochal voyage of 1492 had never been made. What would then have happened? Would America have been discovered? If so, when? And by whom? It is possible to answer these questions precisely.

If Columbus had failed, America would have been discovered on April 22, 1500, by Pedro Alvares Cabral. This is an historical probability that is virtually a mathematical certainty. Here is the logic of events:

In 1415 young Prince Henry, third son of King John of Portugal, distinguished himself at the siege of Ceuta. Portugal was waging war against the Moors, who still held part of Spain. Ceuta was at the point of Africa opposite Gibraltar, and its capture was a military headline of those days. Prince Henry of Portugal was an able soldier whose military reputation, begun at Ceuta, was enhanced in subsequent years. On one occasion or another he was offered the command of the army of the Pope, of the King of Castile, the German emperor, the King of England. His mother was an English princess, granddaughter of Edward III. But he rejected military glory and is known to history as Prince Henry the Navigator.

His youthful exploits, his start in life, had been at Ceuta in Africa. There, somehow, Africa had got into his blood and become the dominant interest of his life. He was not the last to be lured by the mystery of the Dark Continent. He set in motion a prolonged effort to disclose the secrets of Africa, and the prime secret of those days was—where did the continent end? He launched and directed a maritime campaign to explore the African west coast and seek a way around the southern point.

His motives were partly those of a crusader, seeking to extend Christianity. There was always the lure of the legend of Prester John, a supposed Christian potentate in Asia, Africa, or wherever. Nor did the Portuguese prince ignore the mercantile advantage of a trade route around Africa to India and the Spice Islands. The spice trade was ever a golden objective. But he had a geographical interest, which in that late medieval period set a style for modern exploration, the expansion of knowledge of the earth.

Prince Henry the Navigator made no voyages himself, but sent ship after ship down the African coast, pressing ever farther to the south, extending the knowledge of the shore line little by little. At Cape St. Vincent, where Portugal projects farthest to the southwest, he set up a center of geographical study, where charts were evolved and information collected, the new knowledge brought back by the ship captains.

They rounded Cape Blanco and pushed on to Cape Verde. They sailed to islands off the coast, the Azores, the Madeiras, the Cape Verde group. They rounded the bulge of Africa and were nearing the Equator when, after forty years of this African coastal exploration, Prince Henry died in 1460. Scarcely half the route to the tip of Africa had been traversed.

The project lived long after its creator. The Portuguese Crown continued the sending of ships. They sailed through the Gulf of Guinea, past the mouth of the Congo, past Cape Frio. There seemed no end to the African coast, which trended ever southward. But in the end the dream of Henry the Navigator was fulfilled.

In 1488, Bartholomew Díaz, with three ships, was engaged in

the usual business of pressing farther south. He was out of sight of land, having swung out to sea for better sailing. This was the practice of the Portuguese mariners. They didn't hug the shore. The better to deal with wind and current, they'd keep out to the west until they reached an intended latitude. Then they'd veer east and close with the coast. Sailing south and out of sight of land, this was the purpose of Bartholomew Díaz. But, when his three ships turned east, they couldn't find the coast. There was no Africa.

They sailed well east of where the African coast should have been, and then turned north. Then they encountered the coast, but it did not run north to south. Instead, it extended west to east. Bartholomew Díaz had rounded the Cape of Good Hope without being aware of the historic exploit.

He followed the coast eastward, and then it turned north. He followed it on and on, until he was convinced he was on the east coast of Africa. He had found the way round the continent and achieved the purpose of Prince Henry the Navigator. He had shown the way to the sea route to India and the Spice Islands. Today the fame of Bartholomew Díaz is not as great as it should be. He is a neglected hero of the great discoveries.

After the long voyage from Portugal, his three ships were in no condition to sail on to India. That would have meant another great length across the northwestern quarter of the Indian Ocean. So off the east coast of Africa he turned back, and in the voyage home discovered the Cape of Good Hope.

This showed the way to Portugal's imperial career in the Indies. The program would begin with the sending of an imposing expedition around the Cape, a Portuguese armada sailing to India. This would be the magnificent voyage of Vasco da Gama. But it did not happen for another nine years. Bartholomew Díaz rounded the Cape of Good Hope in 1488. Vasco da Gama sailed from Lisbon in 1497.

In the meantime, Columbus discovered America. When his three tiny caravels reached the New World in 1492, Spain was on the way to a golden empire across the Atlantic. The voyage of Columbus had little effect on Portuguese prospects. Portugal and Spain promptly made an amicable arrangement dividing East and West between them. If Columbus had failed, if there had been no Columbus, Portugal would have gone ahead, exploiting the sea route to the Indies. The events in this were virtually automatic.

Vasco da Gama with his armada made the first sea voyage from Europe to India, and found golden prospects of trade and plunder. Doing a profitable business in India, he sent a ship back to Portugal with a report, and recommended that another expedition be sent out. Another armada was prepared and set sail from Lisbon. Its commander was Pedro Alvares Cabral.

This voyage was planned to be routine. In his recommendation, Vasco da Gama had sent detailed sailing instructions for the course from the North Atlantic on. These were to sail to the Cape Verde Islands and then swing westward, which would make the best of trade winds and ocean currents. It would avoid the doldrums on the eastern side of the tropical Atlantic and the impediment of currents along Africa. Previous navigators exploring the African coast southward had kept well out to sea, and it was by swinging to the west that Bartholomew Díaz had missed the Cape of Good Hope.

Cabral followed the instructions sent by Vasco da Gama. Sailing to the Cape Verde Islands, his armada took a southwesterly course. But the trade winds and ocean currents can play tricks. Sailing on for days, his course was farther to the west than intended. By accident of the elements he veered too far out, and the result was historic. He sighted land to the west. This accidental landfall, on April 22, 1500, would have made Pedro Alvares Cabral the discoverer of America, if Columbus had not already discovered it.

The land was the coast of Brazil, south of Cape São Roque, the easternmost projection of South America. It was completely unexpected. Columbus' discoveries had been in the West Indies, far to the west. Nobody could suspect the existence of the great eastern bulge of South America, the longitude of which is less than twenty degrees west of the western tip of Africa. Previous Portuguese navigators swinging out in the Atlantic on their way south must have come within easy sailing distance of South America. In the regular maritime traffic around the Cape to India, somebody someday was sure to swing far enough to the west to sight land, and that one was Cabral. He interrupted his voyage to India briefly to investigate.

We are all familiar with that climax in Columbus' discovery—the three small caravels, the signs of land, birds, and drifting weed, the sighting of land at daybreak of October 12, 1492, the going ashore at San Salvador of Columbus and his Spaniards, the discoverer taking possession in the name of Ferdinand and Isabella. If that had never happened, the discovery of America would have been something like this:

Cabral's armada of numerous noble ships was sailing on a southwesterly course, when drifting seaweed was observed, which sign of land surprised officers and crews. On the following day, toward the west a mountain was sighted. Cabral thought this might be an island, and was curious to ascertain its character. The ships approached, and the shore where the mountain stood could be seen extending afar. Cabral and companions landed and set up a wooden cross, claiming the land for his sovereign King Manuel of Portugal.

They were greeted by natives described later by the King of Portugal writing about the discovery to the King of Spain. This is quoted by Samuel Eliot Morison in his invaluable monograph *Portuguese Voyages to America in the Fifteenth Century*. King Manuel stated that Cabral "reached a land which he newly discovered to which he gave the name Santa Cruz. Therein he found the people naked as in the first innocence, gentle and peaceable; wherefore it seemed that Our Lord miraculously wished it to be found because it is very convenient and necessary for the navigation of India."

The peak that Cabral sighted was Mount Pascoal, a lofty landmark along the coast. The name of Santa Cruz, or Vera Cruz, which he gave to his discovery, later became Brazil. He sailed along the shore far enough to make sure that it was not an island but mainland. Then, having delayed for eight days, he continued a successful voyage to India.

So if Columbus had not discovered America, Cabral would have. As it was the Portuguese navigator discovered little or nothing. He didn't discover South America, on the mainland of which Columbus landed in his third voyage, 1498. He didn't discover Brazil, the present territory of which had been reached by Spaniards earlier in 1500. But Cabral did give Portugal its claim to Brazil. The western part, where he landed, was on the Portuguese side of the line of demarcation agreed upon in the treaty with Spain, and Spain never interfered with the huge Portuguese expansion in Brazil.

This theorizing about discovery is made with the knowledge that the Norsemen were in Greenland centuries before Columbus, and Greenland is a part of the Americas, in addition to which there is the question of the voyage of Leif Ericson. Moreover there are Portuguese theories that Portuguese navigators had been to Brazil before Columbus, but that the discovery was kept a secret by the Portuguese government. This seems to be thoroughly disproved by Samuel Eliot Morison in his masterly study of the Portuguese voyages.

Subsequent Portuguese exploration of the coast of Brazil produced a comic absurdity of geographical naming. A ship captain, sailing along, spied a magnificent bay and supposed a river flowed into it. The month was January. So he named the place the River of January. But there's no river there and it's not January all year round. Nevertheless the capital of Brazil retains the name, Rio de Janeiro. To be consistent they should divert a river through their city and call every month January.

This absurdity is quite in the spirit of Rio, a city of gaiety and paradoxes. It lies along the beach and among the hills. The higher you live the lower the rent you pay. The rich prefer the low-lying real estate, and the slums are on the slopes. The poor live high.

Rio is, perhaps, the most spectacular city in the world, a city for a cameraman. In air shots the threefold camera swept in to get a matchless pageant of suburb after suburb among the hills and then the long line of the Avenida with a cliff of tall buildings on one side and beach and surf on the other.

Carnival time was on, and we got ground shots of a street full of dancing hurly-burly, and the music is the impetuous rhythm of a Brazilian samba. Then the camera takes to the air again, and for stunning contrast goes winging to the great statue of Christ the Saviour on top of Corcovado, a mountain overlooking the city. The Saviour stands with arms outstretched as if in blessing. Rio sometimes needs a blessing.

This superb metropolis might be called the capital of the jungle. Brazil contains a lot more than equatorial wilderness, but most of its enormous area consists of the valley of the Amazon, which is the green hell of the tropics almost ad infinitum. Paul Mantz was flying to Rio when he spied an unexpected wonder of nature, and the Cinerama camera went into action. Along the coast, a battle between the sand and the jungle. The yellow of sand advancing inexorable against the green hell. The scene is vivid and graphic. Long spears of yellow into the green. The sand winning against the jungle.

The story of the Amazon has a similarity to the drama of the discovery of the source of the Nile. In the case of the Nile, a bitter personal quarrel. In the case of the Amazon, personal recriminations even more savage. In one instance, Burton versus Speke. In the other, Gonzalo Pizarro versus Francisco de Orellana.

The Amazon rises in the Andes and flows four thousand miles to the Atlantic. With its tributaries it is a river system draining by far the greatest area of jungle on earth. It is a network of huge rivers which finally unite, and to speak of one original source might be fairly meaningless. The great exploit of river exploration would be to start in the Andean area and proceed downstream to the Atlantic. The remarkable thing is that this was accomplished in the earliest days of the Spanish conquistadores on the west coast of South America and in the course of their first expedition across the mountains.

In 1532, Peru was conquered by Francisco Pizarro, who made his brother Gonzalo Pizarro the governor of a northern part of the subjugated empire of the Incas. In 1541, nine years after the beginning of the conquest, Gonzalo Pizarro led an expedition across the Andes. He marched from his city of Quito, now capital of Ecuador, traversed the lofty ranges, and descended the eastern slopes. He had a well-equipped party of conquistadores and a large force of Indians. His second in command was Francisco de Orellana.

One lure of the adventure was Eldorado, the mythical Golden One who reigned in a treasure city beyond the mountains. This was according to stories told by the Indians, who in South America, North America, everywhere had a knack of regaling the white man with tales of gold, what the white men wanted to hear.

But there was another lure—cinnamon. Reports told of immense groves of cinnamon trees beyond the mountains. That condiment was treasure. It was one of the valuable commodities of the Spice Islands. So there was the dream of Eldorado and the vision of the Spice Islands rolled into one, enough to drive conquistadores across any mountains and through any jungles.

The crossing of the Andes was in February 1541, and they suffered severely from cold in the snowy, icy passes. Reaching the lowland, they were in a wilderness of thickets, morasses, and swampy streams. Their march was a random search hither and yon at the verge of where the Amazon River system begins. Indians were friendly and Indians were hostile. Food resources in the jungle were meager, and they were eating up the abundant supplies they had brought along. They continued this meandering month after month, until eleven months had elapsed since their departure from Quito.

Needless to say they never did find Eldorado, or any golden treasure. Neither did they discover the Spice Island wealth of cinnamon. They did encounter cinnamon trees, but these were few and scattered, a mere mockery of wealth of the cinnamon groves they had expected. The hard reality forced itself upon them—they were chasing an illusion. By now they were less concerned with gold than with food. Their supplies were nearly exhausted. The Indians they encountered had little food, and they were faced with starvation in the wilderness.

They came upon a large river, now called the Napo, and there the decision was made that brought about the drama which followed. The Indians of the vicinity declared that a few days' voyage downstream there was populous country with many villages and an abundance of food. The decision was to build a ship for navigation downstream to the country of abundant food, instead of hacking a way through the jungle.

The ship was built of timber felled in the equatorial forest. The conquistadores could perform prodigies of that sort when it was necessary. The large party included soldiers with maritime knowledge, who could direct shipbuilding. The vessel is called a brigantine, which means that it was a two-master, but apparently the masts were not set up. Oars would be used for river voyaging. It turned out to be a sturdy enough craft.

The project was to send the brigantine downstream to load up with food, while the main party remained behind. Aboard were fifty or sixty men, including seven who were sick. The commander of the brigantine was Gonzalo Pizarro's lieutenant, Francisco de Orellana. On the bank of the Napo River there was fervent leave-taking, as the voyage began.

The brigantine never came back. Orellana never returned.

That was the fact of the bitter dispute. Gonzalo Pizarro charged that his lieutenant deserted him, that Orellana had made off with ship and equipment and left his comrades to starve. He said that Orellana had schemed to save himself. The bitterness of the accusation can be understood. The main party waited until they lost all hope of ever seeing Orellana and the brigantine again. Then they made a frightful march back across the mountains. Some perished of starvation, and the ones that got back to Quito were a woebegone remnant of the brave expedition of conquistadores who had set out in search of Eldorado and cinnamon.

Orellana's account says that the brigantine proceeded downstream for several days, and they looked in vain for the rich country of villages and food. The riverbanks showed no signs of human life. They deliberated on whether or not to return but decided to continue some distance farther in the hope of finding the rich country with food.

Then, as they went on for several more days, they began to realize they would have difficulty in returning. The river current had grown swift, and the task of rowing the brigantine upstream would be hard. They had taken little food along and that was soon gone. Hunger beset them. They grew so famished they ate leather straps boiled in spices. They halted along the riverbank, and some ate jungle herbs which made them ill or afflicted them with a species of madness. Some were in a state of collapse from hunger.

Eight days after leaving the main party they came upon an Indian village on the bank, and there they procured food. The Indians were susceptible to the lure of trinkets brought along for trading, a familiar story everywhere in the early exploration of the Americas. The Spaniards were able to satisfy their hunger, though this was no fat land abounding with provisions to stock the brigantine. They remained at the friendly village for days, and this was the time of the crisis.

Orellana gathered his followers and proposed that they now turn back upstream to rejoin their comrades. The men refused. They said it would be impossible to row the brigantine against the swift current of the river. Their comrades would probably have gone by the time they got back. Their only hope was to continue downstream and try to reach the coast. Orellana was compelled to abide by the decision of the others, and the die was cast.

This was Orellana's version, and he affirmed it at the Indian village with legal formalities. He had formal papers drawn up stating that the decision had been made by his companions against his own intention. These documents he later presented in his own defense. In any case, they were now committed to a voyage down-river to the sea.

They hadn't much idea of where they were or how far it was to the sea. Actually they were on a tributary of the upper Amazon, only a tiny fraction of the distance from the Andes to the Atlantic and several thousand miles from the mouth of the Amazon. They had no notion of what kind of country they would traverse or what kind of people they would meet, friendly Indians or hostile. They could only board their brigantine and push on.

One of those aboard was the Dominican friar Gaspar de Carvajal, who later wrote an account that is the chief source of information about Orellana's voyage. He tells how the first stage after they left the hospitable Indian village was fortunate. The brigantine, aided by oars, drifted downstream without mishap. They came upon deserted villages, from which the Indians had fled in alarm, and there they seized food. At other places friendly Indians brought them turtles and parrots to eat.

They came to a great river which joined the Napo on which they were navigating. This was the main stream of the Amazon, which they now entered, voyaging thereafter on the mightiest current that flows on any continent.

Their fortunate experience thus far culminated at a large village where the Indians made hostile gestures, but where Orellana was able to parley with them and score a triumph by telling them a tall tale. He had, Friar Carvajal indicates, a great facility for conversing with aborigines of unknown tongues. There's a universal sign language at which travelers among primitive people become adept. Orellana had a gift for that, and readily picked up native words in addition. The pious friar could preach a spiritually enlightening sermon in Spanish, but the Indians understood what Orellana told them better.

Frair Carvajal, as translated by Bertram T. Lee, relates that the village headman asked who they were, and Orellana replied that they were travelers—but what travelers!

"He told him more, namely," relates Carvajal, "that we were Children of the Sun and that the object of our journey was to go down that river. . . . At this the Indians marveled greatly and manifested great joy, taking us to be saints or celestial beings, because they worship the Sun and hold him (i.e., the sun) to be their god, whom they themselves call Chise. They then told the Captain that they were his servants and that they wished to serve him."

There was a legend widely prevalent in pre-Columbian America, of a white god who had gone off toward the rising sun.

Perhaps Orellana's yarn was justified by the whoppers the Indians were always telling Spaniards.

As Children of the Sun Orellana's men were welcome indeed and this gave them an opportunity to put into effect a project which they had already planned—that of building another ship. It would be a safeguard if they lost their present brigantine, which was showing signs of rotting timbers. Using jungle lumber, they constructed a second craft of the same type, but larger. They had tools for ship carpentering, and used cotton for calking. The Indians provided them with gum from trees for tar. The labor was long, and they stayed at the village for nearly a month. Then they had two brigantines.

The villagers wanted the Children of the Sun to remain with them forever. But, since the divine personages had to depart, they did what they could for them. Their headman was a potentate of some consequence, and he arranged for food to be available at villages downstream as far as his influence extended. He wouldn't want the Children of the Sun to starve.

Under the sweep of oars the two brigantines moved off with the Amazon current. Good fortune continued for a few days, and Indians in canoes brought them food. When this ceased they knew they were out of the territories of their friend the tribal overlord. Thereafter Orellana was not able to play the game of Children of the Sun.

Friar Carvajal writes: "From here on, we endured more hardships and more hunger and [passed through] more uninhabited regions than before, because the river led from one wooded section to another wooded section and we found no place to sleep and much less could any fish be caught, so that it was necessary for us to keep to our customary fare, which consisted of herbs and every now and then a bit of roasted maize."

When they came to inhabited country again, the Indians were hostile. The brigantines were attacked by tribal warriors in canoes, and there were lively engagements, arquebus and crossbow against flights of arrows. The roar of the arquebus frightened the Indians, the usual effect of gunpowder on primitive people when they first encounter firearms. When the voyagers went ashore to procure food they were received by Indians in hostile array, and there was often hard fighting before they could capture a village and seize what edibles they could find.

They passed the mouths of great tributaries flowing into the Amazon—the Rio Negro, the Rio Madeira. Then they came into the most remarkable country of all:

"We were proceeding on our way," writes Friar Carvajal, "searching for a peaceful spot to celebrate and to gladden the feast of the blessed St. John the Baptist, herald of Christ, when God willed that, on rounding a bend which the river made, we should see on the shore ahead many villages, and very large ones, which shone white. Here we came suddenly upon the excellent land and dominion of the Amazons.

"These said villages had been forewarned and knew of our coming, in consequence whereof they (i.e., the inhabitants) came out on the water to meet us in no friendly mood. When they had come close to the Captain, he would have liked to induce them to accept peace, and so he began to speak to them and call them, but they laughed, and mocked us and came up close to us and told us to keep on going and [added] that down below they were waiting for us, and that there they were to seize us all and take us to the Amazons."

Orellana ordered the two brigantines to put to shore for a landing to seize food in a village. The Indians resisted with showers of arrows. Arquebus and crossbow felled a number of them, but they fought on. Five Spaniards were wounded, including Friar Carvajal, who was struck by an arrow in the side. The landing party had a hard fight on shore, the Indians defending themselves in a hand-to-hand melee. Friar Carvajal explains:

"I want it to be known what the reason was why these Indians defended themselves in this manner. It must be explained that they are the subjects of, and tributaries to, the Amazons. . . . We ourselves saw these women, who were there fighting in front of all the Indian men as women captains. These latter fought so courageously that the Indian men did not dare to turn their backs, and anyone who did turn his back they killed with clubs right there before us, and this is the reason why the Indians kept up their defense for so long.

"These women are very white and tall, and have hair very long and braided and wound about the head, and they are very robust and go about naked, [but] with their privy parts covered, with their bows and arrows in their hands, doing as much fighting as ten Indian men. Indeed there was one woman among these who shot an arrow a span deep into one of the brigantines, and others less deep, so that our brigantines looked like porcupines."

In the battle for the village seven or eight Amazons were killed, the friar avers, and the Indians were driven from the village. But that did not suffice to win the day. Other warriors from other villages were swarming, and a fleet of hostile canoes was approaching. Orellana in alarm ordered the landing party to hurry back aboard, and the two brigantines went rowing away as fast as they could. The realm of the Amazons was too much for the conquistadores.

They still had an ambuscade to get through, a fleet of canoes darting out from hiding places along the jungled riverbank and showering the brigantines with arrows. The soldiers aboard took refuge behind their shields in the rain of missiles, and Friar Carvajal relates mournfully:

"They hit no one but me, for they planted an arrow shot right in one of my eyes, in such a way that the arrow went through to the other side, from which wound I have lost the eye and [even now] I am not without suffering and not free from pain, although Our Lord, without my deserving it, has been kind enough to grant me life so that I may mend my ways and serve Him better than [I had done] hitherto;"

Farther downstream Orellana took the opportunity to question an Indian whom they had captured.

"The Captain," Carvajal relates, "asked him what women those were [who] had come to help them and fight against us; the Indian said that they were certain women who resided in the interior of the country.

"The Captain asked him if these women were married: the Indian said they were not. The Captain asked if these women bore children: the Indian answered that they did. The Captain asked him how, not being married and there being no man residing among them, they became pregnant: he said that these Indian woman consorted with Indian men at times. When that desire came to them, they went off to make war, and by force they brought men to their own country and kept them with them for the time that suited their caprice.

"After they found themselves pregnant they sent them back to their country without doing them any harm; and afterwards, when the time came for them to have children, if they gave birth to male children, they killed them or sent them to their fathers. If female children, they raised them with great solemnity and instructed them in the arts of war."

What are we to make of all this?

Friar Carvajal was a man of integrity and sound sense. Later in Peru he held posts of high responsibility in the ecclesiastical hierarchy, and became head of the Dominican Order in Peru. He wrote his narration for no purpose of romantic entertainment. His account, prepared immediately after the end of the adventure, was a report on the events of Orellana's voyage. The style is hasty, plain and factual, sober and without storytelling artifice. It gives the impression of a lucid mind, an accurate memory, and systematic habits of thought.

The tale of the Amazons occurs repeatedly in the annals of tropical American exploration. Columbus himself began it by reporting women warriors on a West Indian island. Carvajal's account has abundant corroboration, more than many an accepted fact of history.

Yet the Amazons were an illusion.

Carvajal says he actually saw Amazons in the fight and that seven or eight of the women warriors were killed by the Spaniards. This may be explained by the fact that it was common among the Indians, as among other tribal peoples, for women to join the men in battle, urging them on, or perhaps participating in the conflict. He says they were seen using clubs to encourage the males, which might have been the case. It might be true that the women were powerful archers. Carvajal describes them as "very white and tall." They may have whitened their faces and been of good stature. Or are these alleged personal observations to be explained, in some degree perhaps, as illusions based on a firm belief in Amazons?

The remainder of Carvajal's account is hearsay, the recital by the Indian prisoner under questioning by Orellana. It follows in general the ancient Greek legend of the Amazons, and includes the classical statement that the women warriors lived without men, consorting with them once a year to procure offspring, of which they retained the females to continue the race of Amazons. In the exploration of Paraguay a similar account was given by an Indian, who added another detail from the classical legend—that the Amazons removed the right breast so as to handle bow and arrow better. You'd think those aborigines had read Greek literature.

It would seem that in these cases the Spanish interlocutor was asking leading questions, having in mind the classical legend of the Amazons, which was a favorite in the Middle Ages, and the Indian informant was taking the hint and humoring the white man. You can imagine Orellana asking the Indian, "Are these Amazons thus and so? Do they do this and that?" The Indian replying, "Yes," and embroidering on the affirmative. Add to this the fact that the dialogue would be partly in the sign language and partly in the little of the Indian's native tongue the Spaniard might know. With a delusion about the Amazons to begin with, Orellana and his companions would be confirmed in it.

In any case, that is how the great river got its name. At its mouth it had already been called the "Sweet Sea," because of the vast expanse of fresh water. The river was also given the name of the Marañón, but Orellana called it the Amazon, and that, as we know, is the prevailing name it has today.

From the land of the women warriors the voyage continued through hostile country to a continuous accompaniment of hunger and enemies. An evil climax was reached when they

*The CINERAMA ride featured a dazzling whirl of the train running backward, and now it's back where it started.*     Photo by Edwin W. Sippel

*A boatload of Hindu maidens who were to have added a colorful touch to the approach of Benares but had to be left out of the film.*

*At Angkor Vat, an integrated system of buildings reclaimed from the jungle shows the massive style of Khmer architecture.* Photo by Edwin W. Sippel

*The Khmer civilization of Cambodia adopted Buddhism, and its great temple of Angkor Vat abounds in images of Asia's great religious teacher.*
Photo by Edwin W. Sippel

*Young ladies of Japan at the airfield in Tokyo.* Photo by Edwin W. Sippel

*The ocean front at Rio, the magnificent beach lined with tall apartment houses. In the background at the right, the familiar landmark, "Sugar Loaf."*

Photo by Moore-McCormick

*Hoover Dam, which backs up the largest man-made lake, is a technological wonder of the world.*

*The immensity of the Grand Canyon is illustrated here by the perspectives.*

came upon Indians armed with poisoned arrows. One soldier was struck by a shaft and soon died. Later, when attacked by a fleet of canoes, they sustained another casualty, as Friar Carvajal relates: "They killed another companion of ours, named Garcia de Soria, a native of Logrono; and in truth the arrow did not penetrate half a finger, but, as it had poison on it, he did not linger twenty-four hours and he gave up his soul to Our Lord."

However, there was compensation when, in this engagement, a marksman with an arquebus killed two Indians with one shot.

They were now navigating through a length of the river where there were signs that raised their spirits. There were indications of a rise and fall of water—the tide. On the Amazon, tidewater extends far inland, but they were nearing the ocean. There were many islands, but the riverbanks were lost in the distance. The Amazon is two hundred miles across at its mouth.

Then, as they approached the sea, utter disaster seemed at hand. In putting to shore to capture a village for food, the smaller brigantine rammed a log, a plank was smashed, and the vessel was swamped near the bank. Invading the village, they encountered a large force of Indians and had to fight for their lives. In this crisis Orellana divided his forces in two, one party holding off the Indians while the other salvaged the brigantine and made repairs.

In that way they were able to escape. But they got no food, and were so near starvation they rationed what maize they had, counting it out by grains. Then came an unexpected bounty, as Friar Carvajal relates:

"Once again, while we were in the midst of this suffering, Our Lord manifested the special care which He was exercising over us sinners. One day toward evening there was seen coming (i.e., floating) down the river a dead tapir, the size of a mule. When the Captain saw it he ordered certain companions to take a canoe to bring it in, and they did bring it, and it was divided up among all the companions in such a way that for each one there turned out to be enough to eat for five or six days. . . .

This tapir had been dead for only a short time, because it was [still] warm, and it had no wound whatsoever on it."

At an uninhabited island they prepared the brigantines for an ocean voyage. They set up the masts for sailing, for which they had had no occasion hitherto. They stitched blankets for sails, and made cordage for rigging out of vines of the forest. Setting sail for the mouth of the river, they came upon Indians who had encountered white men previously, the Spaniards who had been exporing in those parts. They were friendly and provided supplies of maize and roots. The brigantine took aboard fresh water and sailed out into the ocean.

Their river voyage had lasted eight months. Some of the company had been lost in the hardship and encounters with hostile Indians, but most of them had survived the Amazon journey from near the foot of the Andes to the Atlantic. This, so soon after the first Spanish conquests in the Andean regions, constitutes one of the most remarkable adventures of mortal man.

Now there was an ocean voyage in the two jungle-built brigantines with stitched blankets for sails and twisted forest vines for rigging. They knew there were Spanish settlements on the northern coast of South America. It was a long distance. They steered northwest along the coast and then became separated at sea. Each party gave the other up for lost, but each made its way to a Spanish-held island off the coast of Venezuela, and they met again. Their troubles were over.

To this day there is no agreement about the rights and wrongs of Orellana's voyage. Gonzalo Pizarro made a furious charge of betrayal against his former lieutenant, and put this in a letter to the King of Spain. Friar Carvajal is not conclusive about the decision made at the village on the river, when it was determined to go on downstream. Spanish historians, writing in the period of the exploration, generally hold that Orellana could and should have returned to his chief, and speak of his "treason."

The story became embellished with statements that Orellana, leaving in the brigantine, made off with a treasure of gold and jewels, which is manifestly absurd. Recently, about the beginning of the twentieth century, a South American historian, José

Toribio Medina, published a close study of the evidence and found Orellana's conduct to have been justified.

Orellana himself returned to Spain, where obviously no blame was placed upon him. The Crown authorized him to explore lands in northern South America and rule them as governor. Orellana led an expedition that failed disastrously, and he perished in the jungle.

# Chapter 26

A CONTINENT of great rivers is likely to have spectacular waterfalls, and South America has more than its share. There's Iguazu, in a remote corner of Argentina, near an angle where the borders of Brazil and Paraguay meet. The Iguazu River, broad and deep, comes to a line of cliffs, where some knife of nature, it might seem, had sheared the rock to form perpendicular walls. The result is a broad front of giant cascades. Iguazu has a combined rim twice as wide as Niagara, and is half again as high. In the spring the water flowing over it is twice the volume of Niagara.

This was a mark for the Cinerama camera, and Paul Mantz flew down into the gorge for dazzling pictures of that combination of brilliance and movement that only the tumbling waters can present. But, talking about Iguazu, you should say it in Spanish, or with the magniloquence that comes naturally in Spanish. There's a resort hotel at the falls, with a register in which visitors give their impression of the cataract. One entry is by a Chilean lawyer, Humberto Malina Luco:

"Looking at Iguazu Falls . . . moved by such beauty, such grandeur . . . we wish we had been born poets so as to sing with inspired verse the imposing sound of the waters . . . the pearl of its lymphs, forming the rainbow upon being struck by the golden rays of the sun . . . the spotless whiteness and purity of the currents, pure as the conscience of good men, and so render homage to their Supreme Creator, One Who more properly ought to be called the Great Architect of the Universe."

Any mighty wonder of nature in the Americas is likely to suggest the question—who discovered it? The New World was disclosed by prodigies of exploration. Here in this part of southern South America the story of exploration is curiously connected with that of North America, Canada, the United States. Recalling our schoolbooks, we of the United States are surprised to find familiar names.

The first great exploration of the Argentine interior was by Sebastian Cabot, son of John Cabot, who was the first to reach the North American continent. John Cabot, Genoese navigator in the service of England, sailed to the coast of Canada in 1497, five years after Columbus' first voyage. Sebastian Cabot accompanied his father on a second voyage to North America, and later embarked on an exploration career of his own. He transferred from the service of England to that of Spain, and went on a voyage to southern South America. In 1526 he entered the Rio de la Plata, which had been discovered previously, and sailed far upriver into the remote wilderness.

"Argentina" means silver, and the word "plate" in the name of the river signifies the same thing. Yet the country never was a great producer of precious metal, nor the river a highway for treasure ships with cargoes of silver, the "plate ships." The misnaming occurs because Sebastian Cabot heard the usual tales of treasure, and did find examples of silver among the Indians, as he navigated by river deep into the continent. It appears that the articles of silver came from distant Peru, where Pizarro was soon to find and conquer the treasure land. The precious metal made its way by trade among the Indians. Sebastian Cabot's dream of discovering incalculable wealth went for nought, but the silvery name stuck to the country and river.

The Iguazu Falls were discovered by Cabeza de Vaca, who was also the discoverer of Texas. School children in other parts of the United States may be ignorant of his name, but not in Texas. It is typical that in the realm of the Lone Star the schools teach Texas history as well as American history, with some emphasis on the former, and Texas history begins with Cabeza de Vaca.

Fourteen years before he caught sight of the swirling cascades in the remote wilderness of the Argentine that paladin of exploration had landed near what is now the city of Galveston. This had occurred in the course of an almost unbelievable journey from Florida to the Pacific coast, traversing virtually the entire width of the present-day United States.

Cabeza de Vaca's exploration in South America was in essence a spiritual consequence of his years in Texas. There he had been a slave of the Indians, a proud hidalgo of Spain serving aboriginal masters in the wretchedness of abuse and toil. This had brought about a reformation in the Spanish soul of Cabeza de Vaca, and thereafter his ambition was to prove a moral point. His career in South America was that of a visionary seeking to demonstrate an ideal—the ideal that had come to him in Texas.

His odd name, meaning "head of a cow," was a warrant of his aristocratic origin. The story told how, in the old days when the Christians were fighting the Moors in Spain, a Castilian army could not advance because of mountains, and won a victory only because a mountaineer showed them a way through by marking a pass with the skull of a cow. In recognition the King of Castile granted him high honor and gave him a new name of honor, "head of a cow." Thereafter the family of Cabeza de Vaca flourished as soldiers in Spain. Don Alvar Nùñez Cabeza de Vaca began his career with military service in the Spanish wars in Italy, and was a soldier of consequence when he sailed for America. He was then near his fortieth year.

An expedition was to be made to Florida, which had been discovered by Ponce de León, who had sought the Fountain of Youth and had found, not youth, but death. This time the goal was treasure, which was to be equally futile. It was the usual case of insistent tales of gold, fostered by the Indians. What are now Florida and Georgia were envisioned as another Mexico, another Peru. After all, had not Cortez and Pizarro conquered treasure beyond all dreams? Bound for Florida, a fleet of five ships set sail from Spain, and Cabeza de Vaca went along. He had the dignified post of treasurer, which also had a promising sound, as if in anticipation of gold in Florida.

The commander of the expedition was an interesting personality, Pánfilo de Narváez, who had had a ludicrous misfortune with Cortez in Mexico. Cortez had gone to the conquest despite the governor of Cuba, who presently sent a military force to Mexico to bring the insolent adventurer back in chains. Narváez commanded that effort, landed with his soldiers in Mexico, and lost them to Cortez, who induced them to desert. This occurred in a comic-opera battle. Narváez went back to Spain, where his good connections procured for him the command of the treasure hunt in Florida. He is described as brave but imprudent, which judgment he would soon vindicate in Florida.

The expedition proceeded via Santo Domingo and Cuba and after some vicissitudes stood off the west coast of Florida near present-day St. Petersburg. There were four ships and a lugger, four hundred men and eighty horses. A landing was made, and the conquistadores marched around inland, looking for treasure. None was found. The Indians seemed to indicate that the gold was farther north. The ships had no good anchorage along that part of the coast. The belief was that there was a great sheltered bay to the north. Actually they might have found Tampa Bay a short distance south. The decision was to proceed north.

What transpired now was a monstrous error. The sensible thing would have been to board the ships and sail north. Treasurer Cabeza de Vaca says he urged this course. But Narváez differed. He ordered a march to the great bay to the north, while the ships sailed north along the coast. There would be a rendezvous at the supposed bay. There was no such bay, and there was no meeting of land party and ships. They never found the ships, and the ships never found them. They marched for weeks, seeking the rendezvous, and never saw the ships again.

They were marooned in the Florida wilderness, without food, surrounded by hostile Indians. They marched north hoping to find the fair land of the treasure. They never found that either, only wretched Indian villages. For several months they wandered through miasmal swamps, through swarms of insects and showers of Indian arrows, and reached the border of present-day Georgia. Then, having lost the hope of finding another empire of Montezuma or the Incas, they doubled back to the coast. How to get out of this land of hell?

They performed a prodigy. On the coast of the Gulf of Mexico they built ships. They had no proper tools. All equipment of that sort had been left aboard the missing vessels. They had to fashion tools. Making charcoal for metallurgy, they smelted iron, the stirrups of saddles, the iron parts of crossbows and firearms. They forged axes and other implements, and built five ships. These seem to have been, actually, large barges to be rowed with sweeps, each craft capable of holding about forty men. They now numbered some two hundred, of the original four hundred. Some had been left aboard the missing ships, and others had perished in the frightful marches.

Did they, rowing their ponderous barges, proceed south along the coast of Florida to Cuba? That was a long way, and they thought Mexico was nearer, Mexico which Cortez had conquered, as Narváez knew only too well. It was a monstrous error of geography, which illustrates the meager knowledge of American coasts in those early days. Anyway, they were soldiers, and had left the navigators aboard the missing ships. They thought they'd soon find Mexico and the Spaniards not far to the west, and the five barges proceeded that way along the coast. Treasurer Cabeza de Vaca commanded one of them.

The voyage had the familiar ordeals of the sea. They were caught in a storm, but the barges weathered it, and took refuge in what is identified as Pensacola Bay. Their supplies of fresh water ran out, and they were tortured by thirst and hunger. They went ashore from time to time, and sometimes friendly Indians gave them water and food, sometimes the Indians were hostile. Toiling at the oars day after day, week after week, expecting to reach Mexico at every turn, they proceeded along the coasts of western Florida and Alabama. They passed the mouth of the Mississippi River, then along the shores of Louisiana and Texas.

At a point off the coast of Texas they decided to go ashore for food. They were down to rations of half a handful of maize per day per man. It was a dangerous shore with heavy surf. At night, while they were waiting for morning, Cabeza de Vaca's barge was caught by a wave and hurled ashore. The royal treasurer and his companions crawled onto land. They were on an island, identified now as San Luis Island, southwest of Galveston.

Another of the barges were driven ashore on another part of the island. The two parties found each other, and there were eighty castaways on the island. Their barges were now useless wrecks, and they were marooned. The other three barges continued on and were lost somewhere on the Gulf of Mexico. In one was the commander, Narváez, who had always been unskillful and unlucky.

There were Indians on the island, and at first they were hospitable. They were skillful fishermen, and provided food. Four of the survivors got over to the mainland and started overland to reach Mexico and send help. Mexico was always just beyond the horizon. The four were never seen again.

It was winter, and the norther blew cold on the coast of Texas. Food ran short on the island, and a plague broke out. At first the Indians thought the visitors might be medicine men, and Cabeza de Vaca went through motions of magic. But death struck both Indians and Spaniards, and presently only fifteen of the castaways were left.

This brought Cabeza de Vaca to the depths. His sorcery a failure, the Indians made him a slave. In the spring they migrated from the island and took him along, leaving the other survivors behind. He was set to the meanest tasks, digging roots in the marshes, a task for women, carrying loads of driftwood on his back to camp, bearing burdens when the camp was moved. He was whipped and buffeted, and reduced to eating rats and lizards.

After a year of this ordeal he got away to another tribe, and became a trader, bartering primitive merchandise—sea shells, deerskins, flints, red pigment—from tribe to tribe. Then he fell into servitude again, and went through another year and more of abuse by Indian masters.

This was his time of spiritual crisis, the first step of a moral reformation. He knew the atrocities the Spanish conquistadores inflicted on the Indians, the massacre, the torture, the enslavement. The Spaniards were remorseless in their lust for gold. The glitter of wealth had been the goal of the proud company with which Cabeza de Vaca had set out in quest of treasures, and now—what had happened to them? The revulsion of the recent treasurer is expressed by Morris Bishop in his illuminating volume, *The Odyssey of Cabeza de Vaca.*

"Pride had been their sin and their undoing, pride and the lust of mundane vanities. They had forgotten that this world is but a short road to the next, that our pleasures here are brief, but our pains in hell eternal. God had taken from them first their presumptuous dreams of wealth; then he had stripped them of their weapons and fine armor and all their worldly goods; then he had treated them to the tortures of purgatory; and when the lesson was finished, he had put them one by one to death. If Cabeza de Vaca was yet alive, it could be only because his lesson was not yet completed. Still some scrap of pride persisted, still some protest. He could not die until he should withdraw his protest, and recognize that God's wisdom was infinitely good, until pride, self-will, and selfhood were dead in his heart. There were darker defiles yet to be traversed in the valley of the shadow; there was an ultimate despair reserved for his training in humility."

He encountered three other survivors, two Spaniards and a Negro, the last of the group he had left at the island where they had been cast ashore. The others had perished, and the three were slaves of the Indians, as Cabeza de Vaca was. Of the brave company of conquistadores, three white men and one Negro were all that was left, and they were serfs of the red men.

Their misadventures in Texas had taken them southwestward along the coast, and they were now near the Guadalupe River. Presently they planned an escape, but there was another year as beasts of burden before they were able to steal away and get clear. This was near present-day Corpus Christi. They had now been in Texas for five years.

From this point, as the fugitives trudged along the coast, the story changes. Indians they encountered took them for medicine men, and once again Cabeza de Vaca tried his hand at the sorcery of healing. This time, successfully. The Indians were highly susceptible to the tricks of the witch doctor, and more than one proclaimed himself cured. The method of magic was to perform some mumbo jumbo and recite fervent prayers in Church Latin. Their reputation spread, and they were welcomed as they passed from tribe to tribe.

They traveled on, once again seeking Mexico and the Spaniards. Their course took them to the Rio Grande, then across into northern Mexico. They reached a point where several hundred miles more to the south would have taken them to Spanish outposts. But the exigencies of geography and their relations with tribes sent them west and north into Texas again. They traversed the westernmost part of Texas, and passed on via the present site of El Paso. Then ever westward, bearing south, until they came to the Gulf of California. It was now eight years since they had been in Florida, and they had crossed virtually the entire continent.

The last stages of their journey presented an extraordinary spectacle. Indians, as cunning as credulous, had learned how to profit by the healing magic of the medicine men. Parties would take them along to the next tribe and collect a fee, which was about as good as looting. To make the business all the better, they represented the four medicine men as Children of the Sun —the same prevalent Indian legend. The Children of the Sun journeyed attended by companies of followers: three gaunt white men, one Negro, and a procession of Indians.

They moved south along the coast of the Gulf of California, and now came the final stage of the conversion of Cabeza de Vaca. As they journeyed they became aware that they were nearing their goal, the goal so long and desperately sought ever since the departure from Florida. There were signs that they were nearing the Spaniards in Mexico. They would soon meet fellow Christians. This should have brought joy akin to delirium, the summit of all happiness. To Cabeza de Vaca it brought, instead, the fullness of his moral transformation.

In his own account, written after his reunion with his countrymen, he states, as quoted by Morris Bishop:

"We passed through many territories and found them vacant: their inhabitants wandered fleeing among the mountains, without daring to have houses or till the earth for fear of Christians. The sight was one of infinite pain to us, a land very fertile and beautiful, abounding in springs and streams, the hamlets deserted and burned, the people thin and weak, all fleeing or in concealment. As they did not plant, they appeased their keen hunger by eating roots and the bark of trees.

"They related how the Christians had come through the land, destroying and burning the towns, carrying away half the men, and all the women and children, while those who had been able to escape were wandering about fugitives. We found them so alarmed they dared not remain anywhere. They would not nor could they till the earth, but preferred to die rather than live in dread of such cruel usage as they received.

"Although these showed themselves greatly delighted with us, we feared that . . . they would treat us badly, and revenge upon us the conduct of their enemies. . . . But they began to dread and respect us as the others had done, and even somewhat more, at which we no little wondered. Thence it may at once be seen that, to bring all these people to be Christians and to the obedience of the Imperial Majesty, they must be won by kindness, which is a way certain, and no other is.

"They took us to a town on the edge of a range of mountains, to which the ascent is over difficult crags. We found many people there collected out of fear of the Christians. They received us well, and presented us all they had. They gave us more than two thousand back-loads of maize, which we gave to the distressed and hungered beings who guided us to that place."

The four Children of the Sun, the three Spaniards and a Negro, proceeded to a meeting with fellow Christians. They were accompanied by a large party of Indians, who placed a trustful

[ 266 ]

faith in them. What now ensued should have been the happiest of endings, but it was the final blow for Cabeza de Vaca.

They came upon a party of Spaniards, and the reunion was tensely emotional. The captain, Diego de Alcaraz, received them with all courtesy and fervor, but the damnable truth soon became apparent. He was on a slave-hunting raid, and regarded the Indians accompanying the Children of the Sun as legitimate prey. After giving his fellow Christians a goodly welcome, he rounded up their Indians as slaves.

Cabeza de Vaca protested, but in vain. He was able to save the Indians only by an appeal to a higher Spanish official in the district who, luckily, was of merciful, decent character.

The onetime slave of the Indians now had a mission. Out of his sufferings in Texas and out of his experience since then, he had become convinced that he must dedicate himself to the welfare of the native people. This was the moral transformation of the erstwhile treasurer of the expedition of conquistadores.

The Spanish career in the Americas brought out in flaming style a contradiction noted often in the Spanish character. On one hand, there is violence and cruelty. On the other, an unworldly idealism. There is the blood sport of the bull ring and there is Don Quixote following his vision. The conquistadores, in the rapacious quest of wealth, were blood-shedders and enslavers. The Church sought to protect the Indians, and was aided by the Spanish Crown. There was a conflict in which too often Church and Crown could not control the gold-hunting soldiers and the slave-estate owners.

The great figure on the side of idealism was Las Casas, "Apostle of the Indians." This saintly cleric was, in his way, as relentless and embattled as any of the conquistadores. As a young ecclesiastic in Cuba, he was overwhelmed with pity for the Indians and with indignation at the iniquities of the Spaniards. In the West Indies, in Peru, in Mexico he preached with a flaming zeal against the enslavement of the Indians, and met with brutal hostility. He made repeated trips to Spain, pleading at court and obtaining royal edicts in behalf of the aboriginal population of the New World. Perhaps, in his *History of the Indies*, he exaggerated the atrocities perpetrated by the conquerors, but it was in the righteous wrath proper to a saint.

Cabeza de Vaca was a true disciple of Las Casas, but his mission was framed by the ideas of an hidalgo and an official. His purpose was to become governor of a province in the New World, and in that way demonstrate the truth of his conviction —that if the Indians were treated with decency they would respond in similar fashion. His ambition was to show that kindness and good government would tame the savage tribes.

He went back to Spain and pressed his mission. After disappointments, he got the assignment he sought. Spanish settlements in the South American regions of the Rio de la Plata were in bad condition and needed reform. Cabeza de Vaca was sent out as *adelantado* (governor). He was given the opportunity to put into effect in South America the principles he had come by in North America.

Sailing from Spain with a military force, his project was to begin his governorship with a great march, reminiscent of his extraordinary journey in North America. Near the mouth of the Rio de la Plata there was a wretched Spanish settlement, Buenos Aires. Northward, hundreds of miles upriver, a town had been founded, Asunción, now capital of Paraguay. That was his destination. The adelantado might have proceeded by the river route in comparative comfort, but he chose to land with his military force on the coast far to the east of Asunción, and lead an overland march of hundreds of miles through the wilderness.

The march was an exploit glorious in a way uncommon in those times. The country was desolation and jungle. The Indians were numerous and had a ferocious reputation. Cabeza de Vaca put into practice his principle of good treatment. He kept his soldiers under strict discipline and prevented any violence or looting. There was no rapacious rummaging for gold, no seizure of food or women, no arrogant insolence.

The adelantado held parley with Indian tribes in ceremonious formality, understanding their ways. He dealt with them fairly. All food was paid for with the trinkets the Indians treasured.

This good reputation spread along the route. The Indians provided abundant provisions and were friendly everywhere.

The adelantado's own soldiers didn't like it. Their lust was for gold, violence, plunder, women. Cabeza de Vaca kept them in check, and the impossible march to Asunción was made—through the blank wilderness and with no sign of Indian hostility.

On the way they came to the Iguazu River, and presently caught sight of the dazzling spectacle of falling water. This was the discovery of Iguazu Falls, an incident in a demonstration of that not too familiar quality—man's humanity to man. To-day, the waters might seem to sparkle in celebration.

But it was all too good to last. At Asunción, Cabeza de Vaca continued his policy of benevolence toward the Indians, and the Indians responded. Peace was made with neighboring hostile tribes. But, if Cabeza de Vaca's moral policy displeased the soldiers he had brought from Spain, it was far worse with the brutal crew he found at Asunción, habituated to the rapine of a lawless frontier. They could only think the idealistic adelantado a meddling fool. There was discontent and sedition.

Cabeza de Vaca led what was intended to be a monumental march across the Andes to Peru. He took an expedition deep into the frightful wilderness of the Gran Chaco, and once again his benign Indian policy was successful—with the Indians. But after a while his own soldiers balked. To them it meant merely the hardship without the fun—the fun of robbing the Indians, of swaggering and bullying and capturing Indian girls. They forced the adelantado to lead the way back to Asunción.

This was the beginning of the end. No doubt it was hastened by Cabeza de Vaca's own disqualifications. He was a poor politician, and not a skillful administrator. He had something of the obstinacy, the pride, the blindness of the zealot. He knew now how to deal with the Indians, knew the correct policy of justice, but not how to be a clever governor. After all, Don Quixote was never meant to be an adelantado.

There was a conspiracy against Cabeza de Vaca. He was seized, thrown into prison, and sent back to Spain in shackles.

That had been the fate of Columbus, too. In Spain, charges were brought against him, largely trumped up. He was put into prison and on trial. After long, dragged-out proceedings he was deprived of his title as adelantado and forbidden to return to the New World. He spent his remaining years in futile protest and in the publication of his account of his part in the expedition to Florida, the voyage to Texas, slavery among the Indians in Texas, the journey to the Pacific, and his mournful but glorious mission of justice in South America.

Some years later the ideals of Cabeza de Vaca came to an extraordinary realization in the Jesuit missions in Paraguay, in a paternal, communist form of life maintained by the Jesuits among the Indians.

South America has the highest waterfalls in the world—Angel Falls in Venezuela. The Cinerama air shots of Angel Falls are a phantasmagoria—a classic version of the "Lost World." Deep in the jungle and mountain wilderness of southern Venezuela is an immense plateau with lofty cliffs for walls, like a number of our own Western mesas put together and on top of each other. Down the sides of the "Lost World" a number of waterfalls topple, the loftiest a stream that plunges 3212 feet, twenty times as high as Niagara.

Angel Falls was discovered in 1937 by an American bush pilot, Jimmy Angel, who was flying his plane in the Caribbean area for anybody who would hire him. He found Angel Falls by accident. The quest was for something else. What? We might again be talking about the Spanish conquistadores of old. It was a gold-hunting expedition. The story is fantastic, and sounds like something out of an old romance.

In Panama City an aged, weather-beaten prospector, Bob Williamson, told of a place loaded with gold nuggets in the mountains of Venezuela. This he had discovered, and wanted to return for more treasure. So he engaged Jimmy Angel for five thousand dollars to fly him there. Jimmy would fly anywhere for five thousand dollars.

The sky voyage, which they thereupon made, led from the coast of Venezuela to blank spaces on the map, mountain wilds never charted. Williamson directed a zigzag course, until they sighted the "Lost World," like a giant fortress. As they drew near Jimmy Angel gaped at one waterfall after another. One, he reckoned, was a mile high, and he wasn't far wrong.

The spacious plateau was cut up by cliffs and canyons, and they landed at a place that Williamson pointed out. Whereupon the old prospector made his way to a stream where he gathered a load of lumps of glittering yellow. Then they took off and flew out.

Returning to civilization, Jimmy Angel gave out the news of the "Lost World" and the highest waterfalls on earth. This was received with skepticism. Back in Panama, Williamson cashed in his load of nuggets for twenty-seven thousand dollars. He died two months later, leaving most of his money behind, but taking his secret with him, the exact location of the gold. In 1930, Jimmy looked me up in New York and told me what sounded like a tall story. But Jimmy Angel was able later to locate the "Lost World" and the highest of waterfalls. That part of the story was amply verified. I never forgot that wild tale, and now, twenty-five years later, we have it in our Cinerama picture. Thomas Gilliard, of the American Museum of Natural History, led an expedition that explored the plateau and measured the height of Angel Falls. But what about the gold? No signs of the treasure-trove of nuggets have been found.

# Chapter 27

Home again, back in the U.S.A. The trip around the world had been hasty, but it was clear that the Cinerama crews, ground and air, were getting an abundance of wonders. So now back to the radio. While I was away, Charles Collingwood had been doing a smooth job of giving the nightly news—as smooth as King Saud's oil.

It was good to be back with the news. There's a fascination, day after day, as the dispatches come on the wire. For a nightly program, it's like being dealt a hand of cards every day, and you never know what spades or hearts, what aces or deuces, you'll draw. So what would I get for the first 6:45 P.M. show upon returning?

Well, January 18, 1955, was a fairly average news day. The Chinese Reds had captured a small island from the Nationalists. There were a couple of items about U.S. airmen held by the Chinese Communists. (They were subsequently released.) Congress was debating the question of building new giant aircraft carriers for atomic war, President Eisenhower's budget having provided for these. France was having symptoms of a cabinet crisis, as usual. These were examples of the serious news that day.

But was there anything light? That's always question number one for me. During my years on the air I've tried to vary the heavy news with the more amusing tidings, what the old-time editor called "human interest," and especially something funny if possible.

That first day back from the round-the-world trip, I had the following to recite:

"A dispatch from Gosport, England, tells of a naval officer who acted like a modern William Tell—using a pistol instead of a bow and arrow.

"Lieutenant Terrence Cullen was engaged in a drinking bout with his fellow officers of the submarine *Truncheon*. They all had taken a few too many when Lieutenant Nicholas Holmes dared Lieutenant Terrence Cullen to shoot his hat off with a pistol.

"Cullen accepted the challenge, reached for his gun, and fired one shot at his friend. But what with all the beers he had swallowed—his aim wasn't too good. He creased Holmes's scalp with his bullet. That sobered up the victim—who complained to the authorities and Lieutenant Cullen was court-martialed.

"Today, the decision of the Court was handed down—Lieutenant Cullen to be reprimanded, reduced to the bottom of the seniority list, and removed from his post on the submarine. The judges agreeing that it's not quite the thing for an officer in Her Majesty's Navy—to play William Tell with a pistol, especially when he has a few under his belt."

That may not have been too side-splitting, but as things go it was a relief from the solemn and weighty. I ended that broadcast with the usual "So long until tomorrow," and presently had to think—what next about the *Seven Wonders of the World?*

Bill Lipscomb put it this way: "We had taken airplanes around the world in search of wonders. The film would make one vast panorama. Very fine, no doubt, but then next recurred a feeling that something was missing. It went on recurring until someone remembered that we had nothing about America."

It wasn't quite that we were negligent. The fact is that we were involved in a contradiction. Our theme was wonders of the world, and our major purpose was to present the distant, unfamiliar, and exotic in the spectacular terms of Cinerama. There were American wonders that belonged on any list, and the chief of these were the utterly familiar. After all, how could you pass up Niagara Falls and the Grand Canyon? Then there were the technological wonders of the modern world, and we Americans live on familiar terms with miracles of applied science.

The answer was that we'd make an epilogue, a montage, a quick sequence of scenes illustrating the marvels close to home, so common in our everyday life. Thus, in the picture, the emphasis would be on the faraway exotic, with due reference to the familiar. That would be a way out of the contradiction.

The theme of technological wonders brought the reflection that nearly all the man-made structures on our list abroad were of masonry. The edifices on the list of the Seven Wonders of the Ancient World were all of stone. Today, St. Peter's, the Leaning Tower, the Taj Mahal, the temples of India, are masonry. But these are the days of structural steel, and the United States is the country, more than any other, of structural steel.

The Empire State, the tallest building in the world, is 1472 feet high. In content, 37,000,000 cubic feet. It has 6500 windows, and has a total weight of 365,000 tons. The skeleton that supports this giant edifice consists of 60,000 tons of structural steel. Adding to the amount of metal are 3500 miles of telephone and telegraph wire and 60 miles of water pipe.

In 1799 the property—the site of today's Empire State—was a farm, which John Thompson sold for $7000. But he suspected the place might someday be worth more. When he decided to dispose of his farm he published a "for sale" ad which said: "The rapid growth of the city and the villages of Greenwich and Chelsea will cause the value of this property to be greatly enhanced." John should see it now! The Thompson farm came into the possession of the Astor family, whose immense fortune was based largely on real estate. In time two Astor mansions were built on the site, which had become Fifth Avenue, between Thirty-third and Thirty-fourth streets. They were torn down toward the end of the century to make way for the Waldorf-Astoria Hotel of long legend. This in time was replaced in 1930 by a wonder of structural steel, the building that now towers above all others.

We noted to begin with that, of the Seven Wonders of the Ancient World, only one was of a utilitarian character. The other six were monumental, religious, or aesthetic. Only the Pharos, the lighthouse at Alexandria, was of practical use in the workaday world. The technological wonders of the modern world are chiefly utilitarian. Our series of glimpses shows a great steel bridge, the Hoover Dam, modern highways, jet aviation, and an oil well in a Texas front yard.

Down through history most of the great edifices have been of religious significance. To represent a typical aspect of religion in the United States we resorted to the little white church, symbol of the Protestant faith. This, in utter simplicity, is eloquent of the Puritan tradition.

Of all the wonders of nature we saw abroad, none could exceed our own Grand Canyon, which is the greatest of its kind in all the world. Two hundred and eighty miles long, four to eighteen miles wide and more than a mile deep, that vast gorge is a fantasy of cliffs, pinnacles, and chasms. But, in a way, the most astonishing wonder is not the Grand Canyon but the Colorado River. It was that rushing, turbulent stream which cut the rock and was nature's principal chisel in the prodigious work of sculpture.

One interesting thing told us by geology is that a river flowing through mountains may be older than the mountains. The river may have been there before the mountains were raised, the water stubbornly maintaining its channel, deepening its bed by wearing away the rock in a slow uplift of the land. This presupposes, of course, that the mountains were reared by imperceptible degrees over ages of time, which is indeed the common story in the creation of mountains.

The supposition is that the Grand Canyon is relatively new, as geological time goes, dating back a mere million years. Before it ever existed the river was there. The land was then a low-lying plain. An uplift began, and the plain was thrust up to form a plateau of domelike form. That is the general contour of the region today, a flattened dome some 50 miles across and 6000 feet high, through which the Grand Canyon cuts. If there had been no river, the plateau would be unbroken. As it was, the river kept cutting its bed deeper and deeper, as the land rose slowly.

It's hard to imagine mere water having any such edge and power, but the process has to be multiplied by geological numbers. If the land were to rise a tenth of an inch a year, the river wearing away a tenth of an inch of rock a year, it would take six hundred thousand years for the land to rise a mile and for the river to cut through rock a mile deep. Six hundred thousand years is not long for geology, which counts time in the millions of years. Moreover the wearing action of water is multiplied by silt, sand, and pebbles driven by a swift, swirling stream, as is the case with the Colorado.

But the river alone did not sculpture the Grand Canyon. The stream, by itself, would have cut a deep narrow chasm. Other agencies collaborated, like weather and geological forces. The rocks exposed by the cutting action of the river, the strata along cliffs at the side, had different characteristics, harder or softer for example, and there were geological faults, fractures, lines of cleavage. The underlying rocks of the region are of complex structure. The canyon sides might wear away through weather, or might fall, some parts going, other parts remaining as cliffs or pinnacles. These processes, through geological ages, completed the carving of nature's greatest masterpiece of sculpture.

The Grand Canyon of the Colorado was discovered by García López de Cárdenas, a lieutenant of Coronado's. This was in the course of that mighty journey made by Coronado and his force of Spaniards from Mexico into what is now the United States, as far as central Kansas. In northern New Mexico the Indians told them of a great river to the west, and Coronado sent Cárdenas to look for it. Cárdenas found the river—at the bottom of the Grand Canyon. There on the brink white men gazed for the first time into the greatest cleft on the surface of the earth.

Niagara Falls are new, the geologists tell us. They date back only to the end of the ice age, when much of North America was covered with immense glaciers, and the cutting of the Niagara gorge began a mere ten thousand years ago. During the glacial period the Great Lakes were gouged out by the thrusting advance of immense masses of ice. Then, when the glaciers retreated, the basins they had carved filled with water. The stupendous weight of the glaciers and then the melting of the ice, removing the weight, caused movements of the underlying ice down and up. In the final uplift the Niagara River came about, and the cliff over which the river tumbles.

But geology is secondary at Niagara, and romance is first. As all the world knows, the Falls are a favorite resort for honeymooners. For generations countless newlyweds have stood on Rainbow Bridge and made the boat voyage on the *Maid of the Mist,* gazing at the sparkling grandeur of cascading waters. Niagara is the sentimental wonder of the world, dedicated to love and wedded bliss, and reminiscence may well go back to the beginning of courtship and the first marriage.

"Now the serpent was more subtil than any beast of the field which the Lord God had made. And he said unto the woman, Yea, hath God said, Ye shall not eat of every tree of the garden?

"And the woman said unto the serpent, We may eat of the fruit of the trees of the garden:

"But of the fruit of the tree which is in the midst of the garden, God hath said, Ye shall not eat of it, neither shall ye touch it, lest ye die.

"And the serpent said unto the woman, Ye shall not surely die;

"For God doth know that in the day ye eat thereof, then your eyes shall be opened, and ye shall be as gods, knowing good and evil.

"And when the woman saw that the tree was good for food, and that it was pleasant to the eyes, and a tree to be desired to make one wise, she took of the fruit thereof, and did eat, and gave also unto her husband with her; and he did eat.

"And the eyes of them both were opened, and they knew that they were naked; and they sewed fig leaves together, and made themselves aprons.

"And they heard the voice of the Lord God walking in the garden in the cool of the day: and Adam and his wife hid themselves from the presence of the Lord God amongst the trees of the garden.

"And the Lord God called unto Adam, and said unto him, Where art thou?

"And he said, I heard thy voice in the garden, and I was afraid, because I was naked; and I hid myself.

"And he said, Who told thee that thou wast naked? Hast thou eaten of the tree, whereof I commanded thee that thou shouldest not eat?

"And the man said, The woman whom thou gavest to be with me, she gave me of the tree, and I did eat.

"And the Lord God said unto the woman, What is this that thou hast done? And the woman said, The serpent beguiled me, and I did eat.

"And the Lord God said unto the serpent, Because thou has done this, thou art cursed above all cattle, and above every beast of the field; upon thy belly shalt thou go, and dust shalt thou eat all the days of thy life:

"And I will put enmity between thee and the woman, and between thy seed and her seed; it shall bruise thy head, and thou shalt bruise his heel.

"Unto the woman he said, I will greatly multiply thy sorrow and thy conception; in sorrow thou shalt bring forth children; and thy desire shall be to thy husband, and he shall rule over thee.

"And unto Adam he said, Because thou hast hearkened unto the voice of thy wife, and hast eaten of the tree, of which I commanded thee, saying, Thou shalt not eat of it: cursed is the ground for thy sake; in sorrow shalt thou eat of it all the days of thy life;

"Thorns also and thistles shall it bring forth to thee; and thou shalt eat the herb of the field;

"In the sweat of thy face shalt thou eat bread, till thou return unto the ground; for out of it wast thou taken: for dust thou art, and unto dust shalt thou return.

"And Adam called his wife's name Eve; because she was the mother of all living."

The beginning of courtship and the first marriage, as related in Genesis, led to the fall of man, but be not discouraged by that.

Our American sequence ends with the redwoods of California. The sequoia is the largest and tallest of trees and the oldest of living things. This is indicated by the botanical name of the two species—*Sequoia gigantea* and *Sequoia sempervirens* (forever living). The *gigantea* is the larger. One, the General Sherman, is nearly 300 feet high, and at the base is more than 101 feet in circumference. Its total weight is estimated at 2150 tons, of which the foliage weighs 55 tons. The *sempervirens* is the taller, and rises up to 364 feet in height. Some of the sequoias are more than three thousand years old, and were standing when pharaohs of the line of Rameses were reigning in Egypt.

We took the three-eyed camera for a ride through the redwoods of Yosemite, which is the kind of thing to show the Cinerama technique at its best. The peripheral vision makes it seem as if trees and foliage are brushing past you. With brilliances of light and shade among the towering sequoias the effect is dazzling, and comes to a close with a gasp, as you approach a precipice and seem about to go over, but remain gazing over a glorious valley.

When our film making was done, our problems became more acute. We had enough for two pictures, and that brought up the question of length. Much would have to be left out. The necessity of dropping good material can be a headache in motion pictures of any kind, and the situation is worse in Cinerama, because of technical characteristics of the process.

The film is on large reels, each holding enough for fifty-five minutes. Two full reels make approximately a two-hour show, and there must be an intermission between reels. In ordinary movies you switch from reel to reel without a break by having two projection machines, so that when the reel on one runs out the other projector automatically goes into action with the next reel. But Cinerama has three projectors elaborately installed in a theatre, and alternate projectors for a smooth transition from reel to reel are not feasible. An intermission, as between the acts of a stage play, is needed to change reels on the three projectors.

In *This Is Cinerama* and in *Cinerama Holiday* there were two acts with an intermission between them.

The same thing in *Seven Wonders* meant the omission of a heartbreaking lot of good material, and I wanted to make it a longer show. But that was impossible unless it were a three-act show with two intermissions, which would mean a three-hour show. My Stanley-Warner colleagues said that was impossible because it would break up the theatre routine of afternoon and evening performances. You'd have to give fewer shows per day. Moreover, it was argued that it would be better, in any case, to use only the most striking of material, the high spots. I did not agree, and put up a good battle, I think, but lost. It had to be a two-act, two-hour show. So we did a remorseless cutting job which, I finally had to admit, turned out better than I expected.

The final problem was the order in which to put the wonders we had brought back from around the world. That produced plenty of debate at the Long Island studio, where we cut the picture. We'd have a round-the-world wonder-hunting trip. We wanted each of the two parts to end with a climax, which complicated the question of arrangement. Our journey should reach a climax at the end of each fifty-five-minute reel. Our Cineramic circumnavigation came out finally as follows:

Act One. A prologue of the Seven Wonders of the Ancient World. Six in paintings, shown in 35-millimeter film, with Cinerama opening on the seventh, the Pyramids. Then the wonder-seeking trip begins from New York to South America, Iguazu Falls, the battle between the sand and the jungle, Angel Falls, Rio. Then across the Pacific to Japan, Fuji Yama, and the Kamakura Buddha with sundry entertainment. Across southern Asia, Angkor Vat, and on to India, Benares, the monkey temple, the cobra dance, the Darjeeling railroad. Then Palestine, the biblical sequence, the wonder story of the world providing the first climax.

Act Two. Paul Mantz's volcano, and the other subjects in Africa, animate nature and the elephant school, the tall people, Timbuktu, Victoria Falls, and the mirror lake. Arabia, the skyscraper cities, the camel stampede, Arabian oil, King Saud. Europe, Mount Olympus, the Parthenon, Naples and Vesuvius, the Leaning Tower, Rome, the Colosseum, the Forum, St. Peter's, and the papal ceremony. This last overwhelming climax is followed by an epilogue, American technological wonders, the Grand Canyon, Niagara Falls, and the redwoods of Yosemite for a poetic end.

On my trip around the world I flew from west to east, and the whole Cinerama expedition proceeded that way. But in the *Seven Wonders of the World* on the screen it's around the world from east to west, the other way. Things are always getting turned around.

Two thousand-odd years ago the Greek sight-seer visiting the ancient wonders would have gone on a tour of the eastern Mediterranean, proceeding in short stages to Asia Minor, Rhodes, Egypt. Babylon would have meant a longer overland journey. The time required might be considerable, especially considering the way weather could delay maritime travel in those days. Mediterranean storms could be formidable, as witness St. Paul's shipwreck. But the distances were trifling in modern terms.

We had two planes: the four-engined clipper *Cinerama* and Paul Mantz's especially redesigned twin-engined bomber. They visited five continents and forty countries. Making repeated trips out of the United States, they spanned the Atlantic six times, and one crossed the Pacific as well. The two planes flew a total of some one hundred and fifty thousand miles.

This represents only part of the flying done by crew members, advance men, directors, and others, myself included. In addition to the trip around the world, I did a couple of thousand miles of flying in the cockpit with Paul Mantz, and that meant stunting, skimming over sand dunes for close-ups and skimming over water, almost touching the surface. The gross air mileage rolled up comes to more than 2,600,000, it is estimated.

Our two cameramen exposed eight hundred thousand feet of negative film, something over one hundred and fifty miles, from which an equal mileage of positive work print was made. Add to that the amount of film necessary to get the picture into theatres, and you have a length equal to a considerable part of the distance the Greek sight-seer would travel to the Seven Wonders of the Ancient World.

But we are not as presumptuous as Antipater of Sidon, who named the magic seven. We let the theatre audiences make their selection from the wonders that we photographed on our trip.

ALTHOUGH a few names are mentioned in the book, I cannot in justice end this chronicle without expressing my appreciation to the many people who participated in some or all of the journeys that made the Cinerama "Seven Wonders of the World" (and therefore this book) possible. Here they are:

John Bateman, Fred Bosch, Coleman T. Conroy, Bert Eason, Emmett Emerson, Edward R. Evans, John Farrow, Fred Fordham, Tay Garnett, Arnold Granan, Henry Hartman, Robert Herndon, Robert W. Heussler, Edward Hyland, Arthur G. W. LaShelle, Maria La Yacona, James Cortland Johnston, Ralph M. Leo, Gus Leonidas, William P. Lipscomb, Matthew Loscalzo, Michael Mahony, Paul Mantz, Andrew Marton, Eileen McCollum, Maynard Miller, James R. Morrison, George Muller, Richard J. Pietschmann, Jr., John S. Priestley, Gus Quinterio, Philip Reilly, Gayne Rescher, Edwin W. Sippel, Captain Page W. Smith, Andre Smagghe, John Sola, Harry Squire, William Terry, Gloria Tetzlaff, Ted Tetzlaff, Walter Thompson, John Wallace, Jr.